miniature orchids

miniature orchids

STEVEN A. FROWINE

Timber Press

Page 2: A petite plant and flower makes *Cadetia chionantha* a miniature that will fit in any growing space. Page 6: Once established, *Aerangis citrata* is an easy orchid to grow and produces a flurry of lemon-scented flowers. Page 8: *Rodriguezia bahiensis* has dazzling white flowers. Page 10: *Mexicoa ghiesbreghtiana* is a neatly growing dwarf plant. Page 14: The flower of *Miltoniopsis phalaenopsis* has a brightly marked lip.

Published in 2007 by
Timber Press, Inc.
The Haseltine Building
133 S.W. Second Avenue, Suite 450
Portland, Oregon 97204-3527, U.S.A.
www.timberpress.com
For contact information regarding editorial, marketing, sales, and distribution in the United Kingdom, see www.timberpress.co.uk.

Printed in China

Library of Congress Cataloging-in-Publication Data

Frowine, Steven A.
 Miniature orchids / Steven A. Frowine.
    p. cm.
 Includes bibliographical references and index.
 ISBN-13: 978-0-88192-836-5
 1. Miniature orchids. 2. Orchid culture. 3. Orchids. I. Title.
 SB409.75.F76 2007
 584'.15—dc22

                                          2006033323

A catalog record for this book is also available from the British Library.

*To my wife, Sascha,
who continues to share my
love of nature's wonders and
indulges my orchid obsession.*

To my mother and late father.

To orchid lovers everywhere.

❧ Contents

❧ Acknowledgments

A special thanks to the late Rebecca Tyson Northen for her fine orchid books, including one of her landmark works, *Miniature Orchids and How to Grow Them*. I had the privilege of meeting her a few times and was always impressed with her voluminous orchid knowledge, as well as her humility and grace. Her books set the standard in orchid literature.

I offer much gratitude to Judy Becker for the continuous and generous donation of her time in editing this book. Her knowledge of orchids is extensive, and she has a keen editing eye.

I also want to recognize Lisa Theobald, my editor at Timber Press, for trying her best to root out my errors and smooth my copy. She has made great efforts to make this book the best it could be and for this I am most thankful.

Introduction to Miniature Orchids

Welcome to the wonderful world of munchkin orchids! With the same brilliant colors, exotic shapes, and enchanting fragrances as their larger cousins, only their small stature sets them apart. Although miniature orchids have been grown and admired for some time, they occupied a small niche market until recent years. In fact, some of the most popular new orchids today are miniatures. Examples are multi-floral and miniature phalaenopsis (better suited as a pot plant than the standard white and pink hybrids); miniature and equitant (overlapping, fanlike leaves) oncidiums; small-growing primary paphiopedilum hybrids, including some of the parvisepalum and the brachypetalum species and hybrids; "mini-catts" that are in higher demand than the space-hogging full-sized cattleyas; and many different species and hybrids of dwarf dendrobiums entering the market.

Vandaceous miniatures using ascocentrums have always been popular, but newer hybrids using *Neofinetia falcata* and dwarf angraecoids are producing a range of charming and fragrant orchids. Even the more esoteric genera contain miniatures suited for growing in terrariums, including *Bulbophyllum*, *Dracula*, *Lepanthes*, *Masdevallia*, *Maxillaria*, and *Pleurothallis*, are receiving attention in popular orchid literature and at orchid shows.

The word *miniature*, when used in reference to orchids, is a relative term. The size of a miniature orchid varies dramatically depending on the genus. For instance, a miniature species of *Bulbophyllum minutissimum* grows only $^3/_8$ in. (1 cm) tall, and a magnifying glass is the only way for us to appreciate its full beauty; some species of the genus *Ornithocephalus* are also tiny.

Because miniature orchid sizes vary so greatly, I have devised my own, very unofficial, categories to indicate relative size of the orchids presented in this book:

    ⦾ Miniature: to 3 in. (7.5 cm) high and/or wide
    ⦾ Dwarf: to 8 in. (20 cm) high and/or wide
    ⦾ Compact: to 12 in. (30 cm) high and/or wide

What some of these species and hybrids lack in size they make up for with exquisite to sometimes other-worldly, bizarre flowers. As happens with many small creatures, these wonderful plants have been underappreciated and unnoticed by many orchid growers. This is changing, as indoor gardeners with limited space have graduated from more commonly available larger orchids to the fascinating world of miniatures.

This book focuses on orchids that are small and well suited for growing under lights or in greenhouses, terrariums, or windowsills. Although I will mention some of the most diminutive species and hybrids, the greatest numbers of orchids featured here do not require a magnifying glass to be seen and appreciated. I admit a bias for showy orchids—I have emphasized those that pack a great deal of flower power on a small plant.

Some genera and alliances such as *Paphiopedilum* species and hybrids, *Phalaenopsis* species and hybrids, masdevallias, the Oncidium Alliance, and the Cattleya Alliance are represented more than others because many of them display a large range of flower colors and forms on compact plants. Most that are profiled here are readily available, at least from specialty suppliers; additional plants listed in the sections at the back of the book may require more searching.

An excellent exhibit of miniatures by J & L Orchids

Some orchids are regarded in the trade as miniatures that do not qualify as miniature or compact orchids in my size definitions; for example, miniature cymbidiums are not included in this book because they are at least 18 in. (46 cm) tall, and many are much larger.

Other references on miniature orchids usually deal primarily with species, rather than hybrids. I have chosen to include both. In general, hybrids tend to be more vigorous and floriferous than their parents, so hybrids offer good options for orchid enthusiasts who have not been successful growing species. Classic examples are various *Sophronitis* species that are notorious for being difficult to grow and bloom compared to many of their more amenable hybrids.

Some orchids, such as *Ornithocephalus gladiatus*, are not much larger than a hat pin.

Sophronitis coccinea subsp. *orgaoensis* is a gorgeous miniature that is difficult to grow. A hybrid containing this species as one of its parents may be a better choice.

Miniature orchids are diminutive in size, but they offer huge rewards. Although a number of these small orchids are sometimes referred to as "botanicals," which can be a euphemistic term applied to orchids having tiny, inconspicuous flowers, many have striking blooms that emit sweet scents and are sometimes as large as the entire plant.

Fortunately for lovers of space-saving orchids, today's breeders are producing many hybrids in this size category, and some of the smaller species have gained dramatically in popularity. In earlier days, most orchids were grown for cut flowers by commercial enterprises, so the size of the plants was of no real concern. Most of today's orchids are produced to be sold as potted plants. Many amateur orchid growers do not own large greenhouses and instead are growing their prized beauties in small hobby greenhouses, windowsills, terrariums (and orchidariums), and under lights. A small home greenhouse can accommodate an entire botanical garden of specimens.

In this book, I have profiled and pictured more than 300 orchids and have listed more that 200 others. This is merely a sampling of available plants, but I hope it offers a sufficient selection to entice you to explore this fascinating group of small but revered orchids.

ONE

୧ Basics of Miniature Orchid Cultivation

Miniature orchids are no more difficult to grow than standard sized orchids. Like all plants, to perform their best they require that certain needs be met. In this chapter, I detail their fundamental requirements and the simplest, most effective ways to provide them, based on my 40 years of experience growing them in windowsills, under lights, and in a greenhouse. Your efforts in modifying your growing environment to make your orchids feel at home will pay off in healthy plants that provide plenty of flowers.

Light

Light is essential for all green plants, including orchids. Along with water and carbon dioxide, light is a necessity for plants to produce food. Providing sufficient light can be a challenging cultural requirement for most indoor gardeners, especially those who live in areas that experience short days and low light during the winter—such as the northeastern and midwestern United States, Canada, England, and northern Europe. Orchid growers blessed with naturally high light in such locales as Hawaii, California, and Florida face the challenge of reducing the light intensities and lowering temperatures.

Orchids are traditionally categorized by their light requirements—high, medium, and low. Most fall in the medium light category. Those requiring low to medium intensities of light can be grown under artificial lights or in bright windowsills. From a practical point of view, orchids with high light requirements are most successfully grown in bright greenhouses, the most efficient collectors of natural light. The amount of light penetrating the greenhouse is determined by the glazing material used, the geographical location, how the structure is sited, and whether it is impacted by shade from surrounding trees or a commercial shading compound or fabric.

Small hobby greenhouses can be ideal orchid growing environments.

Of course, a greenhouse is also the most expensive option, and owning one is not necessary for growing most of the orchids discussed in this book. In fact, most orchid species and hybrids profiled do not require super high light intensities and are adaptable to indoor cultivation in most temperate climates.

Windowsills are the most readily available and cost effective sources of light. Most compact orchids and miniatures do well on a windowsill.

The amount of light that windowsills can provide is determined by several factors: the size of the windows, the direction the windows face, how far back the windows are recessed, whether an overhanging roof affects the available light, how far the plants are placed from the windows, and the age and condition of the glass. The time of year can also be a factor in the amount of light available on the windowsill. During the winter, the sun is lower in the sky and the day length is shorter. The opposite is true during the summer, of course. As a result, a particularly sunny window may be fine for certain orchids during the winter, but you may have to move them to a less sunny window during the summer.

The extent of the roof overhang also affects the amount of light the orchids will receive, and bay windows increase the size of the growing area and the amount of light available to the plants because light can penetrate from multiple angles. Keep your windows clean, especially during the winter when the light intensity is low, to allow your orchids to receive as much light as possible. Tinted and reflective glass can dramatically reduce light intensity.

Orchids bloom in my windowsill during the winter.

Window orientation and light levels

A window's orientation to the sun has a lot to do with the amount of light and the time of day that sunlight will be provided to your orchids.

A window that receives direct sunlight for most of the day offers the most possibilities and is ideal for orchids that demand the strongest light, including many of the vandaceous plants, Cattleya species and hybrids, and oncidiums. Orchids that demand less light, such as phalaenopsis and paphiopedilums, can be placed a few feet back from the window, or the light from the window can be diffused with a sheer curtain. Most orchids with medium to high light requirements will perform best in a windowsill that receives direct sun for most of the day, especially during the winter in cold climates with lower light levels. This exposure can be too hot during the summer, so some orchids may prefer to summer in a window that receives only morning light during this time.

A windowsill that receives morning sunlight is bright, but not too hot. This exposure usually does not provide enough light for orchids that require extremely high light (such as vandas). During the spring, summer, and fall, morning sunlight is ideal exposure for orchids that require low to medium light. During the short, dark days of winter, however, many of these orchids could be moved to a windowsill that receives direct sun for most of the day.

A windowsill that receives afternoon light is much hotter, so this location is not as desirable as a location with morning sunlight. If orchids are placed in a spot

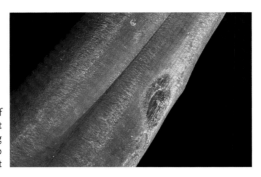

Paphiopedilum leaf showing an oval spot or "sunburn" resulting from exposure to too much light

that receives direct afternoon sunlight, make sure the plants do not become too dry because of the increased heat.

A window that receives no direct exposure to sunlight simply does not provide enough light to sustain healthy, strong growth of most orchids. Use this spot for low light plants such as ferns.

Deciphering orchid light requirements

Orchids hail from a wide range of habitats—some thrive in full sun on exposed rocks, while others are at home in dense jungle shade. The leaves of a plant give you some clue as to their light requirements. Those with tough, thick, stout, and sometimes tubular leaves frequently are adapted to high light intensity. Leaves that are soft, succulent, and wide usually appreciate a lower light environment.

Orchid plants are good indicators of light. They will tell you by their growth habits and leaf color if they are receiving adequate, too little, or too much light. When orchids receive sufficient light, the mature leaves are usually a medium to light green; the new leaves are the same size or larger and the same shape as the mature ones; the foliage is stiff and compact, not floppy; and the plants are flowering on schedule.

One of the most frequent results of inadequate light is succulent, dark green foliage with no flowering. Other symptoms include "stretching," where the distance between the new leaves on the stems of orchids such as paphiopedilums, phalaenopsis, or vandas are farther apart than that of older, mature leaves. New leaves and leads also tend to be longer and thinner.

When orchids receive too much light, the leaves turn yellow-green or take on a reddish cast and may appear stunted. In extreme cases, the leaves show large circular or oval, brown sunburn spots. The "sunburn" discoloration is caused by the leaf overheating. Although this leaf damage may not cause extreme harm to the plant if it is isolated to a small area, it does look unsightly. If the sunburn occurs at the growing point, it can kill that lead or the entire plant. Higher light intensities than recommended are acceptable by some orchids if ventilation is increased to lower the elevated leaf temperatures.

Viable alternatives to natural light

Artificial light sources allow orchid growers without greenhouses or bright windowsills to enjoy cultivating the plants in their homes. These light sources provide a practical method of growing orchids with low to medium light requirements, and

How to compare and calculate light

The Canadian Orchid Congress published a handy chart to demonstrate which light sources are the most appropriate for the needs of orchids. The calculation of watts per square meter (1 square meter equals about 10 square feet) with fluorescent lights is a way to measure recommended light levels. The greenhouse figures compare windowsill and fluorescent light levels with the equivalent percent of light of a greenhouse in full sun. To produce the amount of shading needed for each light level for a greenhouse, you would deduct the percent of summer light from 100 percent. For example, to determine the density of the shade cloth needed to produce light levels for orchids requiring very high light, the last category in the chart, you would subtract 45 percent from 100 percent, with the result being a shading material with 55 percent shade density.

COMPARISON OF LIGHT SOURCES

LIGHT	WINDOWSILL	GREENHOUSE	FLUORESCENT LIGHTS
low	bright morning or diffused sunlight, 1–2 hours	15 percent of summer light	100–200 watts/meter^2
medium	morning or afternoon sunlight, 2–3 hours	25 percent of summer light	200 watts/meter^2
high	sunny, direct or afternoon sunlight, 4 hours	35 percent of summer light	400 watts/meter^2
very high	direct sunlight, 5–6 hours	45 percent of summer light	not recommended

possibilities are limited only by equipment and electricity costs. It can be daunting for a beginner to wade through the many lighting options available today.

Fluorescent light gardening is simple and economical. The best artificial light sources for orchids are fluorescent and high-intensity discharge lamps, abbreviated as HID. Individual fixtures from 2 to 8 feet long (0.6 to 2.4 meters) are readily available from hardware stores or home centers. These units can be suspended from ceilings or installed in banks. The 4 foot long fixtures are the North American standard and are usually the best buy, and lamps or bulbs for these units are most readily available.

Commercially made, multiple-tiered light carts are highly versatile and practical. Most are about 2 feet wide by 4 feet long (0.6 by 1.2 meters) with three shelves, providing 24 square feet of growing area. This provides enough space to include at least one or more compact orchids in bloom year-round. For miniatures, a cart provides a growing space that is adequate for an entire collection. You can place it in a heated garage, in a basement, or in a spare bedroom.

The best choice of bulbs or lamps is a highly debated topic. Years ago, the only real choices were "cool white" and "warm white" tubes. Some growers mixed the two. Then companies began manufacturing tubes designed to provide light that more closely replicated the spectrum of light that plants use in photosynthesis. This started a new race to produce the "best" plant bulb. The evolution of lamps has gone from wide-spectrum to full-spectrum types. Reputedly, the light cast by the full-spectrum lamp most closely resembles sunlight. For those who want flowers to appear most naturally colored and do not mind paying a premium for the lamps, full-spectrum types are the best choice. The most economical and still satisfactory choice is a 50/50 split of warm white to cool white lamps. A compromise would be a blend of half warm white and cool white tubes and half wide-spectrum or full-spectrum lamps.

With energy costs soaring, it pays to invest in the most efficient light sources. High efficiency 34 watt, T8 fluorescent lamps are replacing the standard 40 watt, T12 fluorescent lamps in the United States and Europe. These newer lamps are more energy efficient, produce more light per watt, contain less harmful mercury, produce less heat, and are usually powered by silent, instant-start, flicker-free electronic ballasts. Unlike the older lamps, these newer models burn longer at their full light output. If you are shopping for a light setup, look for one that uses T8 lamps. If you have older fixtures with T12 tubes, their ballasts will not properly power the T8s. Although T8s will burn in such units, since the wattage of the ballast is higher than these tubes require, the lamps will age prematurely—evident from the black rings that form at the tubes' ends.

Older light units that use T12 lamps can be converted to T8 lamps by replacing the ballasts with those designed for T8s. An electrician can do this, or, if you are handy and can read simple wiring diagrams, you can do it yourself. The lamp holders in the older units will still work with the T8s, so they don't have to be replaced. However, the newer lamp holders are better designed and have a mechanism that locks the bulbs into place.

T5 tubes are the next generation of fluorescent technology. They are another step up in energy efficiency and higher light output. I use a unit that contains four, 54 watt high-output tubes and am amazed at the light output—5000 foot candles 6 in. (15 cm) from the tubes. T5 tube units have a modest heat output and no ballast buzz and they are relatively expensive. They are not easily retrofitted into T12 or T8 units since they require different ballasts and the tubes are slightly shorter. They are a great choice if you want to grow a few orchids that demand very high light intensities.

A three-tier light cart provides ample growing space with a small floor footprint.

I have grown ascocendas and other compact vandaceous plants under them with excellent flowering results.

Another lighting option is high-intensity discharge lights (HIDs). These are efficient in their production of light and especially useful if you want to grow orchids requiring higher light intensities than standard fluorescent lamps can provide and/or where greater working distance between the lights and plants are necessary. Using them allows more room for tall flower spikes on such orchids as phalaenopsis and oncidiums.

Both the ballasts and lamp of the HID can produce quite a bit of heat, so the plants should not be placed too close to the bulbs. Take precautions to ensure that the lamp or bulb is protected by a glass lens; otherwise an accidental splash from your hose or sprinkling can on the searing hot bulb could cause it to shatter. Also, the higher wattage bulbs, such as those of 400 or 1000 watts, emit such an intense light that it is advisable not to look directly at the bulb after it is fully lit.

In some setups, the light fixture is mounted on a rail with a moving chain, so the unit moves back and forth over the growing area. This results in a larger growing area, lights the orchids more uniformly, and reduces the chance of the orchids getting burned from too much light or heat from the bulb.

The two most frequently used lamps for these HID systems are metal halide and high pressure sodium. High pressure sodium is more energy efficient (produces more light per watt) than metal halide, but the light it emits is orange-yellow and distorts the color of the flowers and foliage. Metal halide produces blue light that is more pleasing to the eye. Either will grow orchids satisfactorily. Some manufacturers now produce lamps the combine the advantages of both.

Another alternative is the high-intensity compact fluorescent lights. The fixtures for these

HID units provide intense light that allows plants to be placed farther away from them and still receive adequate illumination. This makes them especially useful for orchids with long flower spikes.

look much like HID units. They do not produce quite as much light as HID, but they produce little heat, so orchids are less likely to burn.

If you are a beginner light gardener, I recommend that you start with practical fluorescent light setups. You can give the high intensity discharge lamps a try if you need them.

Humidity

You cannot see humidity, but you can feel it on a muggy, summer day or in a steamy greenhouse. The vast majority of orchids come from the tropics, where high rainfall and humidity prevail. When orchids receive ample humidity, they grow lushly and their leaves have a healthy shine. Insufficient humidity can cause stunting of the growth and, in severe cases, brown tips on leaves. It can also contribute to buds falling off (called *bud blast*), wrinkling leaves, drying of the sheaths, and pouch-like structures that surround developing flower buds, resulting in twisted or mal-formed flowers.

During the winter, most homes have a relative humidity of about 15 percent, especially those in cold climates with forced-air heating systems. Since this is the average humidity found in most desert areas, something must be done to raise the humidity to the 50-percent-plus level that better suits orchids. For greenhouses, this is a relatively simple matter. Either the walkways can be regularly hosed down or fog-gers and commercial humidifiers can be attached to a humidistat so that the entire operation is automatic.

Home growers require a different approach, however. High humidity levels that would be no problem in a greenhouse will cause paint, plaster, and wallpaper to peel off the walls inside a home. You can take several steps to reach the desirable humidity range without damaging results, however. First, locate your orchid growing area in a naturally damp part of the house, such as a basement. Even in a damp location, a room humidifier will be needed. The best types are evaporative cooler units, which use a fan to draw air across a pad dampened by water in a reservoir and expel cool, humid air. A superior approach for the in-home grower, these units, unlike the mist types, do not result in white film from the minerals in the water being deposited on leaves or furniture.

To increase the humidity level directly around the plants, start with a waterproof tray filled with pebbles. Add water to a level just below the surface of the pebbles, and then place the plants on top of this damp gravel bed. If you try this system, be sure to place inverted saucers under the pots to keep them above the water level—without the saucers, pots can sink into the pebbles, resulting in the media getting soggy. After repeated waterings, the pebbles can become clogged with algae and are a

Humidity trays help provide an environment appreciated by all orchids.

repository for insects and various disease organisms.

A better approach is to add sections of eggcrate louvers, sold in home supply stores for diffusing fluorescent lights, to the trays. This material can be cut with a hack saw to whatever size you need, it is rigid enough to support the plants above the water, and it will expose more water to the air, resulting in more humidity. The grating can be cleaned by removing and spraying it with warm water. To prevent algae or disease buildup, you can add a disinfectant to the water in the trays. You can also purchase premade humidity trays from garden centers.

Misting can also increase humidity, but you need to mist plants several times a day, since the water quickly evaporates. In addition, if your water source is mineral laden, your orchid's leaves may become encrusted in white residue, which is unsightly and hinders light penetration to the leaves. A side benefit of misting is that it can clean the dust from the leaves.

Air Circulation

In most tropical lands where orchids reside, they luxuriate in incessant, but gentle, trade winds. Air movement in a growing environment ensures a uniform air temperature and dramatically reduces disease problems by preventing the leaves from staying wet too long. It also evenly distributes the carbon dioxide that is produced by the plants in the dark and used by the plants to produce food during daylight hours. The intention is not to create gale force winds in your growing area, but to produce enough airflow to cause the leaves of the orchids to sway slightly in the breeze.

Ceiling and oscillating fans are effective methods of providing airflow in both a hobby greenhouse and an indoor setting. Ceiling fans move a huge volume of air at a low velocity in a circular pattern, preventing severe temperature stratification. They are inexpensive to operate (most use about the same electricity as a 100 watt bulb) and quiet, offer variable speeds, and are easy to install. They stand up well to moist conditions, especially if you purchase the outdoor types. In addition, the air circulation pattern on most models can be adjusted to pull cool air up (in summer) or push hot air down (in winter).

Oscillating fans effectively cover large areas with a constantly changing airflow pattern that does not excessively dry the plants. Splurge for the better grade fans because the inexpensive models frequently use plastic gears that strip easily, so the oscillating feature will not last long. In small hot or cold spots in the greenhouse, windowsill, or light cart, where just a touch of airflow is needed, small muffin fans are perfect for the job. They are efficient, quiet, and inexpensive to operate.

Temperature

Orchids are frequently placed by professional orchid growers into three different categories, based on their nighttime temperature preferences: cool, 45° to 55°F (7° to 10°C); intermediate, 55° to 60°F (10° to 16°C); and warm, 60° to 65°F (16° to 18°C). The assumption is that the daytime temperatures will be 10° to 15°F (5° to 8°C) warmer than the nighttime temperatures. Some overlap exists in these temperature ranges, indicating that these numbers are not absolutes, but rather guidelines. Most orchids are quite adaptable and tolerant of varying temperatures, short of freezing, but for optimum growth these ranges are good targets.

If orchids are exposed to temperatures cooler than the recommended ranges, their growth will be slowed and in extreme cases buds will fall off before they open. Also, cooler temperatures can reduce the plant's disease resistance. A short bout of higher than desired temperatures will not prove harmful so long as the humidity stays high. If daytime temperatures routinely run much above those recommended, the plant will be stressed and growth will be retarded or will stop altogether. Flower buds will wilt before they open, leaves and stems will shrivel, and in extreme cases plants will die.

One critically important factor with orchids is their temperature differential requirement of at least 10° to 15°F (5° to 8°C) between the warmer day temperatures and the cooler evening temperatures. If this differential is not met, the orchids will not grow vigorously, and most importantly, they will usually not set flower buds. Failure to meet this requirement is one of the most common reasons that home-grown orchids do not bloom. A maximum/minimum thermometer is a great help in recording day and evening temperatures to insure that your orchids are experiencing the required temperature differential.

A maximum/minimum thermometer is essential for orchid growers.

Maintaining balance

Orchid growers should keep in mind some important factors for maintaining balance in growing areas.

- ✿ If the air temperature is cool, orchids grow slower and need less water and light.
- ✿ If the humidity is high, orchids need more air circulation.
- ✿ If the light is very bright and/or the temperature is high, high humidity is necessary.
- ✿ When orchids are not actively growing, reduce or stop fertilizing.
- ✿ If the temperatures are high, light and humidity need to be high and the orchid will require more frequent watering.

Summering Orchids Outdoors

Some orchid growers continue growing their plants indoors under lights, in windowsills, or in their greenhouse throughout the summer. The challenge during this time is to reduce the light intensity and control the high heat, both of which can damage plants. For these reasons, summering orchids outdoors is an attractive option. For the light gardener, this means a welcome relief from high electric bills; for the greenhouse and windowsill grower, it provides an opportunity to clean up the growing area. As most orchids are not in bloom during the summer, they are not at their best visually and respond favorably to a summer vacation outdoors. I summer my orchids in a lath house of simple construction using pressure-treated wood supports and lath.

Shading, usually about 50 to 60 percent or more, depending on the location of the shade house and the types of orchids grown, is necessary and can be provided by lath or shading fabrics. In my shade house, I installed a watering system using multiple small sprayers and misters controlled by a timer with a manual override. I grow the plants on stepped wire frame benches that ensure even lighting and easy watering.

I covered the roof of the lath house with 6 mil clear plastic, stretched over a peaked wooden frame. Before adding the plastic, I left the roof open to receive natural rainfall, but I found that it sometimes rained when I did not want it to (at night, when it was too cool, or when it was already wet). The covered roof gives me the control to water only when it is needed.

I have also summered orchids in a portable greenhouse on the deck. If you use such a structure, be sure to locate it in a place that receives shade during the heat of the day, or use a commercial shading fabric to diminish the light intensity. Also, be mindful of the daytime temperatures inside such a structure. These units require good ventilation systems; otherwise, temperatures inside can skyrocket during sunny

Summering orchids in the shade of a lath house

Summering orchids in my patio greenhouse

Cold frames can be useful for summering orchids if adequate shading and ventilation are provided.

periods. I use a fan on the lowest shelf with the airflow directed upward to assist the natural flow of air.

Cold frames can also be handy for summering orchids. Some shading must be provided, ventilation must be adequate, and the pots should not be placed directly on the ground, to inhibit snail or slug damage.

Orchids with higher light requirements, such as vandas and ascocendas, grow wonderfully dangling from pot hangers clipped to the pot and then hung from a pole or other support. Just make sure the light intensity of this growing area matches the needs of the particular orchids.

In addition to providing an opportunity to clean up your indoor growing area, summering your orchids outdoors allows you to apply heavy-duty pest controls, if necessary—something you cannot do inside your house. Another plus is the natural temperature differential between day and night, especially in the early fall, which is effective in setting flower buds for the upcoming late fall and winter indoor blooming.

Insect and Disease Control

Although orchids are relatively pest-free plants, an invasion of some bug or disease will inevitably occur. Insect and disease problems can be reduced by good sanitation.

Fortunately, orchids contend with few pests, and they are not difficult to identify. You can prevent pest problems from getting out of hand by taking a few steps.

- Make a practice of regularly inspecting the tips of new growth and the undersides of the leaves. This is where most bugs hang out.
- Provide the best growing conditions possible. When orchids are stressed, they are more susceptible to disease and insect infestations.
- When repotting, always use new or cleaned and sterilized pots.
- Buy plants that are clean and healthy. Beware of bargain or leftover plants; many have serious problems. Unless they are in excellent condition, stay away from them.
- Do not allow weeds to infest your pots of orchids; they can harbor insects.
- Keep the floor or ground in your growing area free of weeds, dead leaves, and flowers.
- Always isolate new orchids from other plants for four to six weeks. During this time, inspect them for signs of insects.

To prevent spread of disease, sterilize your cutting tools. I use two methods to do this: chemical and heat. For chemical sterilization, I use household bleach: one part bleach to nine parts water. I soak my tools in this solution for a few minutes before using them. Because most chemicals used to sterilize tools—including bleach—are highly corrosive, I rinse them thoroughly with clean water after use to prevent rust.

Heat is a fast and clean way to sterilize tools. I use a compact butane hand torch—a kitchen model used to make the sugary crust on crème brûlée. I flame the tool along its cutting edges until they turn red. I let the tool cool and it is ready to use.

If you have tried every preventative and curative measure and your orchid does not seem to be recovering, it is sometimes best to discard it. Once a plant becomes too weakened by infection or a serious insect infestation, it is not likely to recover, and in the process of your hoping for this to happen, the plant can serve as a carrier of its problem to your healthy orchids.

A most important aspect of pest control is vigilance. Even though most insects do reproduce faster than rabbits, infestations do not occur overnight; still, insect populations can get out of hand quickly if you do not closely and regularly inspect your orchids. If you can detect the pests when they are small in number, it is

I use a handheld butane torch to sterilize my cutting tools.

easy to eradicate them. Many pests, such as mites and thrips, are tiny and difficult to see with the naked eye. Buy a 10× hand lens at a camera or stamp shop to make the task easier.

Common pests

Respond quickly to signs of insect problems. Miniature plants have small leaf areas and can quickly become infested and seriously damaged.

Aphids are probably the most ubiquitous insect pests of them all. They come in many colors—green, red, pink, black, and yellow—and are usually clustered on new, succulent growth, including flower buds. They feed with sucking mouth parts and are particularly damaging to buds, causing them to be deformed when they open. Aphids are also effective carriers of disease, especially viruses. If you see clear sticky droplets anywhere on your plant, look for aphids. This sticky substance, euphemistically called honey dew, is actually aphid excrement. This material is also excreted by other piercing-sucking insects such as scale.

The name of the next creature, mealy bug, pretty much describes the insect's appearance—mealy or cottony masses. They frequently hide in the crevices of leaves, stems, and bud sheaths. One type is also found on roots. This bothersome pest has a waxy body that makes controls less effective. As a result, multiple insecticide treatments are usually necessary to get rid of it.

Mealy bugs seek out hiding places in crevices of leaves, buds, and flowers (see the flower at left).

Thrips can be destructive, especially to flower buds, maturing flowers, and young leaves. These miniscule creatures look similar to long gnats but are difficult to see with the naked eye; they are best viewed with a magnifying glass. Their damage is easier to detect—light streaks on the flowers or stippling on the leaves. Flower buds are often deformed.

Snails and slugs attack at night and leave evidence of their damage on young, tender new leaves, roots, and flower buds.

Scale comes in various forms, but most of these insects have a shell that serves as armor for the soft insect body protected by it. You must penetrate the shell with a chemical or by rubbing it off before you can kill the insect. Scale are frequently found on the undersides of leaves, near the middle vein or on the edges of a leaf, and on the flower stems. Scale are difficult to eradicate, but with persistence, they can be effectively controlled.

Spider mites are not insects, but spiders, often found in hot and dry growing conditions. They can be green or red, but in any color they are difficult to see because of their diminutive size. In extreme infestations, fine webbing will appear on the leaves. Before the infestation gets this bad, the foliage will take on a stippling effect, which is a result of their feeding.

Snails and slugs top most people's lists as some of the most revolting of all orchid pests. They can do extensive damage to young orchid roots and stems and developing and maturing flowers. These culprits usually come out at night, so if you suspect they are lurking around your plants, use a flashlight in the evening to search for them. Also, look on the bottom of the flowerpots—a favorite hiding place. They love cool, damp spots. If they travel across dry surfaces, they leave a telltale slime trail.

Other unpopular beasts, cockroaches, also feed at night and enjoy munching on flowers and flower buds.

More than once, to my great consternation, upon inspecting my plants in the morning, I have discovered that mice had nibbled off the flower buds of some of my prized beauties, right before they opened. Luckily, these creatures can be easy controlled.

Bees and pollinating insects are not harmful creatures, in the sense that they do not cause physical damage to orchids, but if they land on the flowers and pollinate them, the flowers will soon collapse. To make flowers last as long as possible, keep pollinating insects out of your growing area.

Safe pest control measures

Some of the least toxic solutions must be applied frequently, since they kill on contact and are not residual. Most do not smell bad, an important feature if you are using them in the house. Some also serve as pest repellents. I sometimes use more heavy-duty materials when an infestation is severe or when less toxic controls have not done the job. These are reasonably priced, readily available, systemic materials, which means they are absorbed into the plant sap and are somewhat residual. These features make pesticides highly effective, but they are more toxic than some other solutions and many of them smell horrible, so never apply them indoors.

The controls discussed here are readily available and listed in their approximate order of safety—try the first suggestion, and if that does not work, try the second. Although many products are available, I have limited my suggestions to those that have worked well for me.

To find more technical information on orchid pests and their controls, I recommend an excellent booklet published by the American Orchid Society, *Orchid Pest and Diseases.*

Aphids
- Wash them off with warm water.
- Use insecticidal soap, an orange oil product, horticultural oil, or isopropyl alcohol.
- If aphids are on an orchid's flower buds, try repeatedly washing them off with warm water. Using any pesticide may damage the delicate developing buds or flowers.

Mealy bugs
- Use a cotton swab drenched with isopropyl alcohol.
- Use insecticidal soap, horticultural oil, neem oil, or Imidacloprid (an active ingredient in many pesticides, such as Merit—do not apply these inside the house).
- For orchids with mealy bugs on their roots, remove the orchid from the pot, soak the roots in a solution of insecticidal soap for a few hours, and then repot in a clean new pot with new potting material.

Thrips
- Use neem oil, horticultural oil, or insecticidal soap.
- Use Imidacloprid (such as Merit).

Scale
- Soak a cotton swab with isopropyl alcohol and wipe it across the insect's armored shell, making sure that you penetrate the shell.
- Use an orange oil product, insecticidal soap, neem oil, horticultural oils, or Imidacloprid.
- This pest is difficult to eradicate, so you will need to apply controls repeatedly to get rid of it. Before spraying, try to rub off the armored shells of the scale with your fingers. Then wash the leaf with mild soapy water before spraying with a control.

Spider mites
- Wash them off with a strong stream of warm water.
- Use insecticidal soap, horticultural oils, or Acephate (such as Orthene).
- To prevent mite infestations, keep your orchids properly watered and in a growing area that is not too hot. If you decide to use Acephate, look for the wettable powder (WP) form.

Snails and slugs

⚬ Try some beer. The yeast in beer is a strong attractant to snails and slugs. Place a shallow platter of beer, about ¹/₂ in. (1 cm) deep, and wait for the creatures to belly up to the bar at nightfall. The next day, you will find them drowned in the brew. You can also put out pieces of lettuce in the evening, which will attract slugs and snails. The next morning, simply discard the lettuce, with feeding slugs attached.

⚬ If you use a commercial product, use one that is harmless to pets and other animals, such as a bait that includes iron phosphate as the active ingredient (such as Sluggo); this chemical occurs naturally in the soil.

Mice

⚬ Live traps and old-fashioned snap traps baited with peanut butter can be effective.

⚬ I do not recommend using poison baits. They can harm your pets, and the mice that eat this poison can end up in your pets' bellies, or in the walls of your house, where they decompose.

Roaches

⚬ Use an orange oil product, which both repels and kills roaches—and it smells good.

⚬ Use roach aerosol sprays on the floor, not on plants.

Pests in the potting media

⚬ Fungus gnats come to mind. A simple, safe, and effective control is to drown them by submerging the pot and media for an hour or so in water. Before dunking the pot, wrap the top of it with a cloth to prevent the bark or other potting media from floating out of the container when submerged.

Pesticide particulars

When you find pests, try to identify them promptly and properly so you can apply the most effective control. In many cases, especially if many pests are present, repeated sprays will be necessary to gain control of the pest—usually, once every seven to ten days for a total of three to four sprayings. Many insect eggs are resistant to the sprays.

A teat sprayer is ideal for applying sprays to the undersides of leaves, where most bugs hide. Photo by Marc Herzog.

By repeating the control, you will kill the next generation of pests after they emerge from their eggs.

Apply the chemical where the bugs are—usually under the leaves and on new growth. I use a teat sprayer, an upward-spraying bottle designed to disinfect cow teats and available at feed stores, to apply chemicals to the undersides of leaves.

If misused, many chemical insect and disease controls can damage the plants to which they are applied. To be on the safe side, always read the pesticide label to see if orchids are listed as a plant unsuitable for treatment with the chemical. When applying the pesticide, never use more than the recommended dosage. Apply it in the cool of the early morning and make sure that the potting media is damp. Pesticides can easily damage a moisture-stressed orchid.

Most plant damage from pesticides, such as leaf burn, is caused not by the active ingredient, but by its chemical carrier. To reduce the likelihood of chemical damage, try to obtain the materials in the wettable powder (WP) forms rather than as emulsifiable concentrates (EC). The wettable powders will not suffer degradation if they freeze, and, most importantly, they are much less phytotoxic (plant damaging).

Always use the least poisonous solution. The label on the pesticide container will tell you its relative toxicity. Key words to look for on the label, in order from the least to most toxic, are *Caution*, *Warning*, and *Danger*. Most of the pesticides you use should fall in the first two categories. Use extreme care with any in the Danger group.

Do not spray household aerosol insect controls, such as those designed for killing ants, roaches, and wasps, on orchid plants. These are intended for use outdoors or in the kitchen, and they contain petroleum distillates that if sprayed directly on your orchid plants can cause serious tissue damage.

All horticultural oils are not the same. Use "superior" oils; do not use dormant oils. Superior oils are much thinner and more refined, and they are meant to be used when the plants are actively growing.

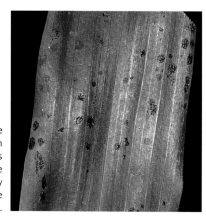

Leaf spots are commonly found on soft-leaved orchids and can usually be prevented by providing adequate air circulation.

Common diseases and controls

Orchids are tough plants, and if you grow them in appropriate cultural conditions using appropriate preventative measures, they will rarely suffer from fatal diseases. Still, it is best to be aware of what can happen when things go wrong. Diseases are not as easy to detect as insect infestations. Damage, such as rotten plant centers or spots on the leaves, provides the evidence of their presence.

The damage caused by most fungal and

bacterial problems appears as small circular or oblong spots of dead tissue on the foliage and/or flowers. Sometimes diseases also cause the center growing point, or crown, to turn black or rot and may lead to the death of the plant. The pattern of spots or rots is one way of identifying a particular disease. Fortunately, most of the controls mentioned here will be effective against a broad range of diseases, so an exact diagnosis is seldom necessary to remedy the problem.

To reduce the likelihood of crown rot or basal rot from striking your orchids, water plants during the day so that their foliage is dry by evening.

Orchid growers dread viruses because no practical cures for them exist. The most obvious symptom of a virus infection is streaking or color breaks in the flower. However, orchid viruses are rare, and if they do occur, they can be difficult to detect. In fact, in my 40 years of growing orchids, I have rarely seen (or, more accurately, positively identified) a virus on my orchids. If you buy high quality plants from reputable growers or suppliers and follow appropriate prevention methods, your plants should not suffer from viruses.

A few prophylactic measures can go a long way toward keeping your orchids healthy.

- Buy only healthy, disease-free plants from a reliable grower or seller of orchids.
- Water your orchids during the day when the moisture will evaporate from the leaves before nightfall. Cool, damp leaves and water left in the crowns of the plants in the evening are an invitation to disease.
- Provide sufficient airflow to reduce the time moisture stays on the leaves and remove stagnant air.
- Sterilize your cutting tools each time before you use them on another plant.
- Remove diseased leaves with a sharp, sterile knife or scissors.
- When you find a disease problem, treat it immediately; procrastinating could cost your orchid its life. This is especially true with miniatures, since disease can overcome a small plant in days.

Treating disease

Nearly all chemical pesticides are poisons with some toxicity to humans. Read the precautions on the pesticide label and follow them carefully. Wear rubber gloves (disposable gloves work great) when mixing and spraying these materials.

If the plant is badly diseased, discard it. It is unlikely you will save it, and it could infect other healthy plants. If dark brown spots appear that look like disease and they are close to the end of a leaf, remove (cut off) this section of the leaf.

Literally cutting out the infection is a simple and effective way to stop the spread of a disease. A single-edge razor blade is ideal for the job, because it is extremely sharp and sterile, and it can be disposed of after the operation. The sharpness is important so that as little as possible of the healthy tissue is damaged in the process.

Remove all of the damaged or diseased bits by cutting the leaf about $1/2$ to 1 inch (1 to 2.5 cm) into healthy leaf tissue that shows no signs of disease. Be careful not to cut into the diseased tissue and then into healthy tissue, or you will spread the disease. Some people dress the edge of the cut with a simple fungicide such as sulfur or cinnamon, but this is not usually necessary.

As a general sanitation practice, after you have performed surgery or if your orchid has a disease spot that cannot be removed surgically, spray the leaves with a mild fungicide or bactericide and hope for the best. Reevaluate the area in which you are growing the orchid to ensure that air circulation is adequate, and follow the recommended disease preventative measures.

Potting Orchids

The process of choosing containers and potting materials, potting, and then repotting orchids can seem daunting. Orchids do have special requirements, but after you repot a few orchids, you will realize that doing so is a fun and rewarding part of orchid growing.

Potting materials

Orchid potting materials must drain rapidly yet retain moisture. Since a year or more can pass before repotting is necessary, the potting medium must be slow to decompose.

No single potting material works best for every orchid or orchid grower. The accompanying table shows the most common materials used, with some of their advantages and disadvantages.

To choose the potting material combinations that work best for your plants, consider various factors: How often do you water? If you tend to be heavy handed with the sprinkling can or hose, use materials that drain well and decompose slowly. What type of orchid are you growing? Orchids that naturally grow on or in the ground usually prefer to be kept slightly damp, while those that live in trees or grow on rocks must dry out thoroughly between waterings. How mature is the plant? Large plants usually do best in coarse potting materials. How big are the roots of the plant? In

COMPARISON OF POTTING MATERIALS

POTTING MATERIAL	ADVANTAGES	DISADVANTAGES
aliflor (expanded clay)	Never decomposes. Provides good aeration.	Heavy.
coco husk chunks	Retains moisture while also providing sufficient air. Slower to decompose than bark.	Must be rinsed thoroughly to remove any salt residue. Smaller grades may retain too much moisture.
coco husk fiber	Retains water well. Decomposes slowly.	Does not drain as well as bark or coco husk chunks.
diatomite	Retains moisture and air. Does not decompose.	Somewhat expensive.
fir bark	Easy to obtain and inexpensive. Available in many grades (sizes).	Can be difficult to wet. Decomposes quickly.
gravel	Inexpensive. Drains well.	Heavy. Holds no nutrients.
hardwood charcoal	Slow to decompose. Absorbs contaminants.	Holds little moisture. Can be dusty to handle.
lava rock	Never decomposes. Drains well.	Heavy.
osmunda fiber	Retains moisture. Slow to break down.	Expensive. Difficult to find.
perlite (sponge rock)	Inexpensive and lightweight. Provides good aeration and water retention.	Retains too much water if used alone. Can be dusty.
redwood bark	Lasts longer than fir bark.	Difficult to find.
Spanish moss	Used for decorative purposes on top of potting material.	Can contain chiggers. Inspect before using.
sphagnum moss	Readily available. Retains water and air.	Can retain too much water if packed tightly in the pot or after it starts to decompose.
Styrofoam peanuts	Inexpensive and readily available. Does not decompose. Rapid draining.	Should not be used alone because it does not retain water or nutrients. Best used as drainage in bottom of pots. Can be too light for top-heavy plants.
tree fern fiber	Rapidly draining. Slow to decompose.	Expensive. Low water retention.

Orchid potting materials, clockwise from upper left: coco chunks, Spanish moss, diatomite, aliflor (expanded clay), sphagnum moss, and charcoal

general, smaller roots grow better in fine, water-retentive materials, while larger roots perform best in coarse materials.

Potting recipes

Seldom are individual potting materials used alone. They are usually formulated into mixtures, so the final product will retain water, drain well, and last a reasonable amount of time.

Every orchid grower has his or her own favorite potting formulations—like a favorite apple pie recipe. Some orchid specialists have developed complicated formulations for each type of orchid they grow, but for miniature and compact growers, the two mixtures outlined here fit the bill. They are based on the texture or particle sizes of the mix, which correlates to the size of the orchid roots and their need for water retention. Always keep your watering habits in mind. If your orchids tend to dry out too often, use plastic pots rather than clay and use the fine mix. If you tend to be a heavy waterer, consider using clay pots with a coarser potting material.

Fine mix
4 parts fine grade fir bark or fine grade coco husk chips or redwood bark
1 part fine charcoal
1 part horticultural grade perlite or small grade aliflor
This mix will work well for smaller orchids, slipper orchids, most oncidiums,

A wide range of containers is suitable for growing orchids. Good drainage is a necessity.

miltonias, and any other orchids with small roots that like to stay on the damp side. I use this mix most frequently for miniature and dwarf orchids.

Medium mix
4 parts medium fir bark or medium coco husk chunks
1 part medium charcoal
1 part horticultural grade perlite or medium grade alifor
This mix is good is for cattleyas, phalaenopsis, and most mature size orchids. I use this mix most often for compact orchids in larger pots and with coarser roots.

Ready-made mixes, similar to those you can make yourself, are available from most orchid sellers, including home improvement stores. Most contain fir bark, perlite, charcoal, and sometimes peat moss and are suitable for most orchids. Whatever potting material or mix you choose, be sure to wet it before you use it; otherwise, it will take too long to retain water properly and will dry out too quickly.

Potting containers

Of the many containers on the market—including ornamental varieties and those with functional designs—the most common container for orchids is the basic pot, plastic or clay. The big differences between standard garden pots and those used for orchids are the number and size of drainage holes in the container and its depth. Orchid pots have larger and more drainage holes, both in the bottom and sides of the pot, to ensure better drainage. Most orchid pots are shallow and short, especially those of 4 in. (10 cm) or larger in diameter. These are referred to in the trade as "azalea pots," because azaleas, like orchids, often prefer a container with good drainage. Another advantage of this short, squat pot is a larger base that makes it more stable, especially for top-heavy orchids.

Repotting Orchids

When the orchid roots overflow the pot, when the plant itself is growing over the edge of the pot, or when the potting material is getting soggy and drains poorly, it is time to repot the orchid. The plant usually tells you when it is time to repot. With most orchids, when a plant starts new growth, usually just after it flowers, it is time to repot. At this point, the plant is putting out new roots. Some orchids, such as the cattleyas, will swell at their base; this is the beginning of a new lead or shoot that will form the next stem, leaf, and flowers. If the orchid is not repotted at this stage, these new roots and growths are easily exposed to breakage, and new roots will lack potting material into which to grow and will therefore be more likely to dry out. If the orchid plant becomes too large for the pot, it will be difficult to transplant it later without damaging it.

A step-by-step method works well for repotting orchids.

1. Remove the orchid from the pot. You may need to use a knife to circle the inside of the pot to loosen the roots.
2. Remove the old, loose, rotted potting material and damaged or dead roots.
3. Choose a pot one size larger than the one from which it was removed.
4. Place the older growth toward the back so the new lead or growth has plenty of room in front. Some orchidists like to add a coarse material such as broken clay pots or Styrofoam in the bottom of the pot to improve drainage. This is not necessary if you are using a shallow pot with good drainage.
5. Place the plant in the pot so its crown rests at the same depth as it was in the original pot. The new shoot should be level with the pot rim.
6. Firm the fresh potting material into the pot and around the orchid roots with your thumbs and forefinger. It is important that the orchid be secure in the pot so it does not wiggle; otherwise, new roots will not form properly.
7. Place a wooden or bamboo stake in the center of the pot, and attach the new and old leads to the stake with soft string or twist ties.

For monopodial orchids—those with one growing point that always grow vertically, such as phalaenopsis, angraecums, and vandas—the potting process is similar to that of the cattleya, except the plant should be placed in the center of the container, rather than toward the back.

Mounting Orchids

Many miniature orchids found growing in trees in nature can be mounted on cork, tree fern slabs, or pieces of hard wood such as sassafras rather than being placed in pots. This provides perfect drainage, simulates their natural habitat, and can be an easy way to maintain them.

Place the plant on a small handful of moistened, squeeze-dried sphagnum moss. Spread the roots around the sphagnum moss. When the orchid is centered properly, wrap either stainless steel wire or clear fishing line (monofilament) around the top and bottom of the moss to hold it in place. In several months, after the new roots have taken hold, the wire or line can be removed. Fashion a wire hook on the top of the slab for hanging, and the mounted orchid can be hung in a bright place in a home greenhouse or windowsill. Because mounts drain so rapidly, the plants need to be watered frequently—sometime more than once a day during hot summer months.

You can also place such orchids in baskets constructed of teak or some other rot-resistant wood.

The Art of Watering Orchids

For standard-sized orchids growing in 6 in. (15 cm) or larger pots, over-watering is probably the most common cause of death. For miniatures, the opposite is frequently true—they perish from lack of water—because they are kept in small containers or mounted and dry out quickly. Discovering how and when to water orchids can be the most challenging aspect of growing these plants. Several factors determine how often and how much you should water.

Potting material, such as bark, dries more slowly in plastic pots than in clay pots. In plastic, the potting material dries out from the top down, so even though it may feel dry on top, the material may be damp 1 in. (2.5 cm) or so below the surface. With clay pots, the potting material dries out more uniformly (clay is porous, so it "breathes" and allows water to evaporate through the pot's walls). If you are using plastic pots, you can water less often than you would with clay pots.

Clay or plastic pots can be used to grow orchids, but the best pot depends on the needs of the plant. I use plastic pots for orchids that do best in constantly damp material, such as miltonias, slippers, and moth orchids. I use clay pots for orchids that need to dry out more between waterings, such as cattleyas and most of the dendrobiums.

Potting materials also vary dramatically in terms of the amount of water they retain. For instance, sphagnum moss, a highly water-absorbent plant harvested from bogs and frequently used as a potting material, usually stays wet much longer than

These miltoniopsis leaves are pleated because the plant did not receive a constant supply of moisture.

bark, which is not as water retentive. Fresh potting material requires much more frequent watering for the first few weeks, until it gets properly wetted or moistened. As it gets older, the material retains water longer.

An overgrown or potbound orchid will dry out much more quickly than a plant with plenty of room in the pot. When pot space is limited, less potting material is available to hold onto the water, so the overgrown plant quickly uses it up.

Orchids and potting materials in low humidity dry out more quickly, because the drier air quickly absorbs the moisture from both the plant and the potting material. Warmer temperatures increase water evaporation because warmer air absorbs more moisture and because the plants are growing quicker in warmer temperatures and require more water. If orchids are growing in a cooler temperature, they do not need water as often.

The more ventilation an orchid receives, the quicker the water in the potting material evaporates—especially if air is vented to the outside or if air is hot and dry, as found in most centrally heated homes. Gentle air movement is ideal and will keep the air fresh without excessively drying out the plants or potting material.

When species of certain orchids, such as some of the dendrobiums, are in their winter dormancy period, they need and should be given little water. When they start active growth in the spring and summer, they require copious amounts of water.

Some orchids, such as cattleyas, like to dry out between waterings; others, such as paphiopedilums, phalaenopsis, and miltonias, prefer to stay damp. This preference has a lot to do with where the particular type of orchid is found in nature. If the orchid naturally grows in an area that does not receive rainfall on a regular basis, it will not need watering as often as an orchid that grows naturally in areas of frequent rainfall.

A proven watering technique

After you have considered the potting material, environment, and type of orchid you will grow, you must decide when and how much to water. The "pot-weighing" method of determining when to water is one of the easiest for me, because it lets me rely on feel instead of precise weights.

First, I thoroughly water the orchid in its pot. Then I "weigh" the pot by picking it up. This lets me know how heavy it is when saturated with water. After a day or so, I "weigh" it again. As the potting material becomes drier, I can feel the weight difference. I "weigh" the plant every day until I judge, by looking at the surface and sticking my finger into the top 1 in. (2.5 cm) or so of the potting material to check for dampness, that it is time to water.

When watering an orchid, always keep in mind whether the plant prefers to be on the damp or dry side. If you make a mental note of its dry "weight," you will know when the plant is ready to be watered.

Watering tips

Place orchids of the same type, media, pot type, and size in one area. This strategy will make proper watering easier, because all the plants have similar moisture requirements.

Water with warm water. If water is too cold, root and bud shock can result, which sets back the plant and slows its growth.

Always use a water breaker (a diffuser attached to the front of a hose that softens the flow of water). For a few orchids, a sprinkling can with a long spout and rose (water diffuser on the spout) with many small holes works well. These devices allow thorough watering without washing out the potting material. A huge selection of watering wands is available. I like those with multiple settings on the head that allow you to drench or mist without changing attachments. Regulating the flow of water is much easier with wands equipped with finger triggers rather than on-and-off valves.

Keep the water breaker or end of the hose off the ground or floor. This commandment was spoken by my first horticulture professor, D. C. Kiplinger, who preached that floors and soil are where the diseases and insects hang out, and a hose can be an all-too-effective way of spreading them.

Water thoroughly. The water should pour out from the bottom of the pot. This ensures that the potting material is saturated and flushes out excess fertilizer salts.

Never let pots of orchids sit in water. If you place saucers under the pots, make sure they are also free of water. Standing water will rot the media and roots and will be a source of accumulating fertilizer salts and pathogens (bacteria, fungi, and viruses).

Water the orchids early in the day or afternoon. This gives the foliage time to dry before nightfall. Wet foliage in the evening is an invitation for disease.

Evaluating watering problems

Over- and under-watering show many of the same symptoms on the plant, because the net effect of both practices is the same—damaged or destroyed roots, which results in the orchid becoming dehydrated. Signs of dehydration include pleated leaves on orchids such as miltonia and miltoniopsis; excessively shriveled pseudobulbs (thickened, swollen stems) of orchids such as cattleyas; droopy, soft, and puckered leaves on cattleyas; yellow and wilted bottom leaves on phalaenopsis; and bud blast (buds fall off instead of opening) on all orchids.

To evaluate whether over- or under-watering has caused a problem, you must remove the orchid from its pot. Many beginner growers are reluctant to do this, but if you are careful, removing it from its pot will not disturb most orchids, and this is absolutely necessary to view the plant's root system. Turn the orchid plant, and its pot, upside down. Gently rap a hard object (such as the handle of a gardening tool) against the pot to loosen the potting material. Cup your hand over the surface of the pot to hold the loosened potting material as it falls out. You can do this over a workbench or a table covered with clean newspaper to make cleanup easier. If necessary, use a thin knife to circle the inside of the pot to loosen the material from the wall of the pot.

After you remove the orchid from the pot, check out the potting material. Is it soggy? Does it have a bad (rotting) smell? Are the roots dark and mushy? These are all signs of over-watering. If the roots are dry and shriveled, not stiff and plump, and have no or few growing root tips, the orchid probably has received insufficient water. The potting material may also be too coarse, making poor contact with the roots.

If the roots look healthy or only slightly damaged, repot the orchid in fresh potting material. If you see badly damaged roots, take immediate action. The approach you take to remedy root damage depends on the degree of damage. If the orchid has some healthy, firm roots, you can cut off all the soft, mushy roots with a sterile tool, such as a single-edged razor blade, and repot the orchid in new material. Go light on the watering for a few weeks to encourage root development. Use a spray bottle to mist the orchid a few times a day to prevent the leaves from drying out.

If the roots are almost gone, you need to employ emergency measures, and recovery is not guaranteed. First, cut off all the dead or damaged roots. Drench the roots with a liquid rooting hormone. Let the liquid hormone dry on the roots for about an hour, and then repot the orchid in fresh pre-moistened potting material. Do not water for a day, water once the second day, and then put the potted orchid in an enclosed terrarium (such as a high-top propagator, a clear plastic box with vents at the top and a tray below to hold potting material, or an empty aquarium) with damp sphagnum moss or pebbles on the bottom to add humidity. Close the top of the terrarium and place it in a location with diffused light. In a greenhouse, place the plant in a shady spot. Under fluorescent lights, place the terrarium near the ends of the tubes, where there is less illumination. If the terrarium is in the cool part of the greenhouse or growing area, put the entire terrarium on water-resistant seedling heating mats, available at most garden centers. A mat with a built-in thermostat set for about 70°F (21°C) provides bottom heat to stimulate root growth.

If you are concerned about disease, spray the orchid leaves with a disinfectant solution. You can find appropriate disinfectants from mail-order orchid supply companies or at garden centers.

In this environment of 100 percent humidity, the leaves will not dehydrate, so the orchid will not suffer stress while it reestablishes roots. Water the potting material only when it gets dry, keep the gravel or moss in the bottom of the terrarium damp, and keep the orchid enclosed until new root growth is apparent. This may take a few months.

Although this method comes with no guarantees, it has saved orchids for me that were in the "hopeless" category.

Fertilizers: Not Magic Potions

Fertilizers will not save dying orchids. In fact, if the roots are damaged and the plant is suffering, applying fertilizer will worsen the problem. Damaged roots cannot absorb fertilizer, and if the orchid does not use the fertilizer, it can accumulate in the potting material, causing a buildup of salts that can further dehydrate and damage the remaining roots.

Many people mistakenly think of fertilizer as food—which it is not. Plants produce their own food from sunlight, carbon dioxide, and water via photosynthesis. Fertilizers merely provide minerals that orchids can use to make photosynthesis more efficient. Fertilizers are most useful as a boost to help an already healthy orchid grow better.

The number and types of fertilizers on the market can make your head spin. Although you are likely to hear a lot of mumbo-jumbo about why one fertilizer is better than another, the choice is not as complicated as some manufacturers seem to make it.

The correct application rates or dosages of all fertilizers vary. The safest procedure is to check the fertilizer container carefully for the recommended application rates. Never apply more than the amount recommended or plant damage can result.

What to look for in fertilizers

From experience, and after listening to other veteran orchid growers, I have come to some conclusions about fertilizers. These apply to most orchid growing situations.

Fertilizer burn

Fertilizer "burn" can result when too much fertilizer of any type has been applied, when it has been applied on dry media, or if the orchid's roots are hypersensitive to fertilizer salts. Orchid roots can become dehydrated by these moisture-robbing salts, resulting in brown or black root tips and/or leaf tips. The damaged root tips or leaves appear to have been burned—thus the term.

To prevent fertilizer burn, do not apply more fertilizer than is recommended, and fertilize only when the media is damp. It is also a good practice to "leach" your orchids every few weeks. Water them thoroughly one or twice in succession with clear water that is fertilizer free to flush out any accumulated fertilizer salts.

Before using any fertilizer, study the list of chemicals posted on the container. All fertilizers are required by law to include a list of chemicals and their sources.

Nitrogen sources are available in several different chemical forms. Although plants can use all forms, research has showed that the nitrate and ammoniacal forms, not urea, are usually the most beneficial and readily available to orchids. This is especially true when growing temperatures are lower and the organisms that convert urea to a soluble form of fertilizer are not very active. High amounts of nitrogen—more than 20 percent—are not necessary to grow the best orchids, no matter what media is used. Too much of any nutrient cannot be used by the orchid plant and, as a result, merely ends up as a pollutant.

In the past, orchid growers believed that a high phosphorus fertilizer was necessary for better orchid bloom. This has been found not to be the case. Like nitrogen, excess phosphorous ends up not being used by the plant.

In most cases, a fertilizer with supplementary calcium (up to 15 percent) and magnesium (up to 8 percent) is a real plus. However, before applying these nutrients, have your water tested at a local dealer of water softening units to determine whether your water already has sufficient quantities of these. If it does, you do not need to add calcium and magnesium to your plants.

Trace elements, chemicals in very small amounts, including sodium, manganese, copper, zinc, boron, iron, and molybdenum, have been found to be beneficial to orchid growth. Again, check for these on the fertilizer label.

COMPARISON OF FERTILIZER FORMS

FORM	ADVANTAGES AND DISADVANTAGES
granule applied in dry form on top or incorporated into media	Readily available. Easy to Use. Inexpensive. Short term—lasts a few to several weeks. Can easily burn orchid roots. Frequently does not include valuable trace elements.
slow release in dry form applied on top or incorporated into media	Easy to use. Lasts three to nine months, depending on formulation. Can burn sensitive orchid roots. In coarse media, can be washed out when watered. Relatively expensive.
water-soluble form diluted in water and applied by watering can or through a proportioning device	Readily available in a wide range of formulations. Easy to apply. Nutrients are instantly available for plants. Must be applied every few weeks when plants are actively growing.

Do not use water on your orchids that has passed through water softening units. Such water may contain high amounts of sodium that can harm the plants.

Fertilizer forms

Fertilizers come in three forms: granule, slow-release, and water-soluble. Most granule fertilizers (which look like small pieces of gravel) are best suited for agricultural or lawn applications. Slow-release fertilizers contain chemicals encapsulated in a resinous perforated shell that slowly releases nutrients. Although some orchid growers use this type, I have found, especially with the porous potting materials frequently used with orchids, that the fertilizer can wash out of the media and not be effective. Also, some orchid roots are sensitive to fertilizer salts, and these fertilizer capsules can damage or burn their roots.

The most common fertilizer used for orchids is the water-soluble type that is packaged as a concentrated liquid or in dry form. Water-soluble fertilizers offer several advantages: They are readily available in a wide range of formulations. They are soluble in water and are easily and quickly absorbed by roots and leaves of various orchids. They are simple to use. They are dissolved in water and can be applied with a sprayer or sprinkling can. If the orchids are mounted on slabs or in baskets, they can be dunked in the fertilizer solution.

Water-soluble fertilizers have disadvantages as well: The nutrients do not last long in the media, so the fertilizer needs to be applied once every two to three weeks (or constantly if you are using a very low dosage). In addition, these fertilizers, in their original containers, are concentrated and can damage the orchids if they are not diluted correctly.

Tips for using fertilizers

- ☙ When in doubt apply less, not more, fertilizer.
- ☙ Never apply more fertilizer than is recommended by the manufacturer.
- ☙ It is better to fertilize frequently at a more dilute rate than less often at a higher concentration. Some orchid growers, including me, find that fertilizing your orchids every time you water with a dilute amount of fertilizer works well and is the most natural way to supply nutrients, rather than the "feast or famine" routine of fertilizing at a higher concentration every two or three weeks.
- ☙ Remember that fertilizers are a form of salt, and salts will damage orchids at high concentrations.
- ☙ Dark green leaves that are succulent and floppy can be a sign of over-fertilizing.
- ☙ When orchids are actively growing, fertilize them. When they are not actively growing, do not fertilize.
- ☙ If an orchid is diseased and in poor condition, stop fertilizing it.
- ☙ If an orchid is over-fertilized, it produces poor quality flowers.
- ☙ As water evaporates from the potting material in a pot, it leaves behind solid minerals, or salts, that were dissolved in the water, including fertilizer salts. These can accumulate on the edges of the pots. When you notice salt crusting, remove it with a damp cloth; otherwise, these deposits can burn any orchid leaves that touch them.
- ☙ Because clay pots are porous, they tend to accumulate more salt deposits on their edges than plastic pots do. To avoid this, dip the top of the clay pot into about 1/2 in. (1 cm) melted paraffin before potting the orchid.

TWO

❧ Selecting and Buying Miniature Orchids

Fortunately for those of us who love diminutive orchids, nature has produced an ample supply of miniature to compact species. Today's orchid breeders continue to develop new hybrids that are perfect for small spaces.

Narrowing Your Choices

Although it may come as a surprise, judging by the number of large orchids that dominate flower shows, the available species and hybrids of small orchids outnumber those of larger ones. In fact, choosing only a few for a collection can be quite a daunting task. Deciding which of these miniature delights will be appropriate for the growing area you can provide requires some homework. Your first considerations should be plant size, light requirements, and temperature requirements.

Plant size

I have placed all of the orchids in the book into size categories—miniature, dwarf, and compact—as outlined earlier on in the book's introduction and mentioned again with the orchid profiles in chapter 3. This makes it simple for you to select those that best fit your space restrictions. Remember that the heights provided are usually for the vegetative parts of the plants. Many of their flower spikes are twice or more the height of the plant. In some cases, I include this information as well.

Light requirements

All the orchids in this book can be grown in windowsills, under lights, or in a greenhouse. Because the plants are small, it is easier to provide the plants sufficient light, especially with artificial sources, since the distance between the top and bottom of the plant is short.

For windowsill gardeners, the amount of light available for growing orchids depends on the direction your windows face and their exposure to the sun, plus the size of the windows. If you can provide a spacious window with no obstructions that receives at least five to six hours of sunlight per day, those orchids requiring high light are a possibility. For most other window exposures, the orchids preferring medium to low light intensities will be the better choice.

Temperature requirements

Greenhouse owners will find that choosing orchids that are mostly in the intermediate temperature range—55° to 60°F (13° to 16°C) for night temperatures, and 10° to 15°F (5° to 8°C) warmer during the day—will be the most logical choice. Fortunately, most orchids in cultivation fall in the intermediate temperature category. All greenhouses have microclimates that are warmer or cooler than average. In these spots, you can grow some of the orchids with warmer or cooler temperature requirements. Growers in hot climates such as southern Texas, southern Florida, and Arizona will find it challenging to grow orchids requiring cooler night temperatures. Without heroic efforts on the grower's part, these orchids usually suffer a slow death in such climates.

Most home growers will find the orchids that prefer intermediate temperatures easiest for them to manage. If your air temperature is on the cool side, and you want to grow the warm-loving orchids such as phalaenopsis, try placing their pots on waterproof heating pads used for starting seed; I have found that this increases the media and root zone temperature by 10° to 15°F, and this costs much less than heating the entire growing area.

To provide lower temperatures, windowsill growers can place the plants closer to the windows, where heat is lost during the evening. For light growers using tiered carts, remember that heat rises, so place cooler loving orchids on the bottom shelf (which is also closer to the cool floor) and warm loving plants on the top so that they will benefit from the warm air rising from the bulbs and ballasts. If you are using HID lights, the warmest area is closest to the bulb.

Purchasing Orchids

After you have determined which orchids fit your requirements, you are ready to shop. To find the closest orchid supplier, check out the American Orchid Society web site (www.orchidweb.org/aos/) and search for vendors in your state or country. *Orchids*, the monthly publication of the American Orchid Society, also includes advertisements from various orchid growers.

After arriving at the greenhouse or nursery, examine the plants around you to make sure they look healthy. If you notice that they are covered with bugs or disease, chances are the plant that you choose will be similarly challenged—even if this is not apparent. If the plants in the greenhouse or nursery look good overall, closely examine the specific plants that interest you. Make sure they are clearly labeled. Gently lift up each plant to see how firmly it is rooted in the pot. If it wobbles around, indicating few roots, pass it up. Look for weeds in the pot. A few weeds may be acceptable, but too many weeds is a sign of careless culture. The only way you can get rid of these weeds totally is to remove them roots and all; to do this, you have to repot the orchid. Check out the leaves. They should be free of spots from disease and should be a healthy green color.

If you are new to orchids, you are better off purchasing a plant that is as mature as possible. If you can buy it in bloom, so much the better. You will pay more for a mature, blooming orchid, but you will see what the flower looks like, how it smells, and how large the plant gets when mature; it will not take long for it to bloom again.

If you decide to buy immature plants, beware that the designations used by many growers to indicate the size or maturity of their plants—BS (blooming size) and NFS (near flowering size)—can vary quite a bit regarding how long it will take until they flower. The rule of thumb is that NFS plants should bloom within 12 months, and BS plants should bloom within six months. Ask the supplier for an estimate of how long you will wait before the plants bloom.

Selecting compact orchids and keeping them that way

Some orchids are naturally compact. Many of the hybrids or grexes of orchids that have not been cloned can be quite variable in their growth habit. Hand-select the plants that are most compact. For sympodial type of orchids (such as cattleyas), look for varieties with a "tight" growing habit with short rhizomes. For monopodial types (such as phalaenopsis and vandas), choose varieties with a short stem distance between leaves (a short internodal length).

Even naturally small growing orchids can eventually grow too large and unruly for their allotted growing space. Although genetics has much to do with the growth habit of an orchid, environmental factors and cultural practices can also play important roles. To keep your orchids compact, keep a few points in mind.

- Provide your orchids ample light. If new growth does not receive adequate light, new leads will stretch and become elongated. This weaker growth will cause the plants to be spindly and taller than they would be if grown in better light.
- Do not grow your plants in environments warmer than recommended, especially when the light intensity is also lower than ideal. This combination will lead to longer, taller, weaker growth.

꙰ Do not over-pot your plants. Big pots take up more growing space and frequently lead to over-watering problems, because the excess growing media takes too long to dry out and becomes waterlogged. Plant your orchids in pots just large enough to accommodate one or two years' new growth.

꙰ Divide larger plants to share with friends or as they outgrow their growing space, but do not be too eager to do so. Larger plants perform better, generally produce more flowers, and bloom more frequently. If a plant has outgrown its container, it is usually better to repot it in a larger pot than divide it.

꙰ If the orchids are of the monopodial type (vandas and phalaenopsis) and they start to get too tall for the growing space, cut off the top section with adequate roots and repot them.

Buying orchid plants by mail

Buying smaller growing orchids by mail may be your only viable alternative if you cannot find a local supplier. Specialty growers that sell by mail typically offer a much larger selection of species and hybrids of miniature orchids. Fortunately, plenty of highly reputable orchid dealers have excellent quality plants and the expertise to ship them across the country so they will arrive at your home in top condition. If you are searching for miniature orchids, your best bet is to deal with a grower who has knowledge about and interest in these types of orchids. Some of these dealers are included at the end of this book.

THREE

ꙮ Profiles of Miniature Orchids

In this chapter, I describe a sampling of the many miniature, dwarf, and compact orchids available. I have tried to provide the most salient facts about these horticultural gems so you can be successful in growing and flowering them. These profiles include information according to several categories.

- ꙮ A guide to pronunciation.
- ꙮ Synonyms for the orchid name. In some cases, these names are used interchangeably among orchid growers, sellers, and collectors. If you cannot locate a source for an orchid by one name, you might have luck finding it under a synonym.
- ꙮ The origin of the orchid—that is, where in the world it has been found growing.
- ꙮ A description and qualities of the orchid. This tells you why a plant is unique or why it is similar to another. It also offers tidbits of information about pollinators, foliage, and desirable traits.
- ꙮ The orchid's flower size, shape, and fragrance (if any).
- ꙮ The season of bloom.
- ꙮ The mature size and habit of the plant: miniature, to 3 in. (7.5 cm) high and/or wide; dwarf, to 8 in. (20 cm) high and/or wide; and compact, to 12 in. (30 cm) high and/or wide.
- ꙮ Its cultural requirements: easy, intermediate, and difficult. For example, if you are a beginning orchid grower, you might try some of the orchids in the easy category first. As you gain more confidence and experience, you can try growing others.
- ꙮ Its light and temperature requirements.

❦ Its potting mix preference and tips on watering.
❦ A little history of the plant, when available.
❦ Related species and hybrids that you might also seek out.

I have also provided information about more than 200 additional orchids in the various lists at the end of the book. There are so many more! Please consult the book's bibliography to explore on your own and discover other "little pretties."

Ada aurantiaca

PRONUNCIATION: AY-dah ore-an-TIE-ah-kah
SYNONYM: *Ada lehmannii*
ORIGIN: Venezuela, Colombia, Ecuador
DESCRIPTION AND QUALITIES: Attracted by its brilliant flowers, hummingbirds pollinate this orchid.
FLOWER: Flaming orange to red, bell-shaped, 1 in. (2.5 cm), borne in groups of five to seven on 12 in. (30 cm) or longer spike
SEASON OF BLOOM: Winter to spring
MATURE SIZE, HABIT: Compact, 10–12 in. (25–30 cm)
CULTURE: Easy
LIGHT: Medium
TEMPERATURE: Cool to intermediate
POTTING MEDIUM: Fine to medium mix
CULTURAL TIPS: Keep on the dry side during its winter rest period.
HISTORY: First arrived as a living plant in England in 1853 and described by John Lindley the following year.
RELATED SPECIES, HYBRIDS: *Ada elegantua*

Ada aurantiaca 'Cata' has flowers as bright as flames.

Aerangis articulata

PRONUNCIATION: ay-er-AN-giss ar-tick-you-LAH-tah
ORIGIN: Madagascar
DESCRIPTION AND QUALITIES: This species is considered one of the finest in the genus and is highly recommended.
FLOWER: Waxy, white, long-lasting, jasmine-scented, 1½ in. (4 cm), with a 4 in. (10 cm) spur, arranged on a pendulous inflorescence
SEASON OF BLOOM: Fall
MATURE SIZE, HABIT: Dwarf, 6 in. (15 cm)
CULTURE: Intermediate
LIGHT: Medium
TEMPERATURE: Intermediate to warm
POTTING MEDIUM: Fine, well-draining mix, or mounted
HISTORY: Named by Rudolf Schlechter in 1914.
RELATED SPECIES, HYBRIDS: Similar to *Aerangis modesta* but larger and showier.

Aerangis biloba

PRONUNCIATION: ay-er-AN-giss
by-LOW-bah

ORIGIN: Africa

DESCRIPTION AND QUALITIES: This
choice dwarf angraecoid blooms pro-
lifically.

FLOWER: Fragrant, up to 10 waxy,
white or flushed-pink, 1 in. (2.5 cm)
across with a 4 in. (10 cm) spur on
12 in. (30 cm) inflorescence

SEASON OF BLOOM: Winter to spring

MATURE SIZE, HABIT: Dwarf, 6 in. (15
cm) spread and slow vertical growth

CULTURE: Easy

LIGHT: Medium

TEMPERATURE: Intermediate to warm

POTTING MEDIUM: Frequently grown
on slab but also grown in pots in
fine, well-draining media

HISTORY: First described by John
Lindley in 1840 as *Angraecum
bilobum*.

Aerangis citrata

PRONUNCIATION: ay-er-AN-giss
si-TRAH-tah

SYNONYM: *Angraecum citratum*

ORIGIN: Africa

DESCRIPTION AND QUALITIES: This
easy, choice, and adaptable plant
thrives in moderate light conditions.
It blooms several times a year.

FLOWER: To 15 or more lemon-
scented, small, white, long spurs on
6–10 in. (15–25 cm) spikes

SEASON OF BLOOM: Spring

MATURE SIZE, HABIT: Dwarf, $3^1/2$ in.
(9 cm), with 5 in. (12.5 cm) leaf
spread

CULTURE: Easy

LIGHT: Medium

TEMPERATURE: Intermediate to warm

POTTING MEDIUM: Fine, well-
draining

Elegant, star-shaped
flowers borne in
abundance make
Aerangis articulata
one of the most
popular in the genus.
Grown by Parkside
Orchid Nursery.

Aerangis biloba is
another fragrant
white orchid.

Once established, *Aerangis citrata* is an easy orchid to grow and produces a flurry of lemon-scented flowers.

The red "eye" (column) of *Aerangis luteo-alba* var. *rhodosticta* stands out prominently against its pristine white flower. Grown by J & L Orchids.

CULTURAL TIPS: Keep in small pots, 3 in. (7.5 cm) on average, 4 in. (10 cm) maximum. Does best with good air circulation.
HISTORY: Placed in the genus *Aerangis* in 1916 by Rudolph Schlechter.

Aerangis luteo-alba var. rhodosticta

PRONUNCIATION: ay-er-AN-giss LOO-tee-oh AL-bah var. roe-doe-STICK-tah
SYNONYMS: *Aerangis rhodosticta, Angraecum rhodostichum*
ORIGIN: Africa
DESCRIPTION AND QUALITIES: Glistening white flowers make this gem a highly desirable miniature.
FLOWER: To 25, creamy white, $^1/_2$ in. (1 cm), with contrasting red column, borne in two rows
SEASON OF BLOOM: Fall
MATURE SIZE, HABIT: Miniature, to 6 in. (15 cm); slow growing and takes years to reach this size
CULTURE: Intermediate
LIGHT: Medium
TEMPERATURE: Cool to intermediate
POTTING MEDIUM: Fine mix, or mounted
HISTORY: Originally described by F. Kraenzlin as *Angraecum rhodostichum* in 1896.
RELATED SPECIES, HYBRIDS: Closely related to *Aerangis luteo-alba*, which has all white flowers with a white column. A desirable hybrid that is more vigorous than the species is *Aerangis* Somasticta.

Aerides fieldingii

PRONUNCIATION: ay-AIR-ih-deez FEEL-ding-ee-eye
SYNONYMS: *Aerides rosea, Aerides williamsii*
ORIGIN: India
DESCRIPTION AND QUALITIES: A pendulous inflorescence of many luminous pink flowers makes this a welcome addition to any orchid collection.
FLOWER: Up to 30, $^3/_4$ in. (2 cm), lily-of-the-

valley–scented, pink, sometimes spotted, on long racemes

SEASON OF BLOOM: Summer to fall

MATURE SIZE, HABIT: Compact, leaves reach 8 in. (20 cm) long. Slow vertical growth.

CULTURE: Intermediate

LIGHT: Medium

TEMPERATURE: Intermediate to warm

POTTING MEDIUM: Medium mix, well-draining

CULTURAL TIPS: Frequently grown in wood or plastic baskets. Grow on the cooler side during winter.

HISTORY: First described by in 1845 and named after an Indian army officer named Colonel Fielding.

RELATED SPECIES, HYBRIDS: *Aerides crassifolia, Aer. flabellata*

Agasepalum Blue Butterfly

PRONUNCIATION: ah-gah-SEP-ah-lum

ORIGIN: *Zygosepalum labiosum* × *Aganisia cyanea*

DESCRIPTION AND QUALITIES: A combination of uncommon species results in a striking blue-flowered orchid.

FLOWER: 3 in. (7.5 cm), lavender blue with a darker blue lip

SEASON OF BLOOM: Fall to winter

MATURE SIZE, HABIT: Dwarf, 6 in. (15 cm)

CULTURE: Intermediate

LIGHT: Medium

TEMPERATURE: Cool to intermediate

POTTING MEDIUM: Fine, well-draining

CULTURAL TIPS: Always keep media damp.

Angraecum leonis

PRONUNCIATION: an-GRY-kum lee-OH-niss

SYNONYM: *Angraecum humblotti*

ORIGIN: Madagascar, Comoro Islands

DESCRIPTION AND QUALITIES: The Madagascan form is smaller vegetatively than the Comoro Islands form. Both have impressively large, jasmine-scented flowers and handsome succulent foliage.

The fragrant, pendulous flowers of *Aerides fieldingii* are a delight.

Agasepalum Blue Butterfly's spectacular color makes it worth searching out.

FLOWER: 1¹/₂ in. (4 cm), three to five per spike

SEASON OF BLOOM: Winter to spring

MATURE SIZE, HABIT: Compact, 6–10 in. (15–25 cm)

CULTURE: Easy

LIGHT: Medium

TEMPERATURE: Intermediate to warm

For those who adore the jasmine scent of most angraecums but have limited space, *Angraecum leonis* is the answer.

Angraecum mauritianum is one of the smaller growing angraecums.

POTTING MEDIUM: Place on slab or loose epiphytic mix

CULTURAL TIPS: This species is popular because of its compact habit and relatively large flower.

HISTORY: Named by James Veitch in 1894.

Angraecum mauritianum

PRONUNCIATION: an-GRY-kum more-it-ee-AY-num

SYNONYM: *Aeranthes gladiifolia*

ORIGIN: Mascarene Islands, eastern and central Madagascar

DESCRIPTION AND QUALITIES: A petite angraecum with branching pendant growth.

FLOWER: Bright white, $1^1/_2$ in. (4 cm), jasmine-scented, slightly curved back and borne singly

SEASON OF BLOOM: Summer to fall

MATURE SIZE, HABIT: Dwarf, slow to grow vertically. Stems tend to be pendulous. Leaves are $2^1/_2$ in. (6 cm) long.

CULTURE: Intermediate

LIGHT: Medium

TEMPERATURE: Intermediate

POTTING MEDIUM: Medium mix, well-draining, or mounted

Angranthes Grandalena

PRONUNCIATION: an-GRAN-theez

ORIGIN: *Angraecum magdalenae* × *Aeranthes grandiflora*. Registered by Fred Hillerman in 1979.

DESCRIPTION AND QUALITIES: Definitely one of my favorites, it is a fitting tribute to its hybridizer, Fred Hillerman, the Angraecoid King. My mature plant is rarely out of flower. Dark green, glossy leaves are handsome.

FLOWER: 3 in. (7.5 cm), green-white spurred, waxy, jasmine-scented, borne singly

SEASON OF BLOOM: Variable

MATURE SIZE, HABIT: Compact, 8–10 in. (20–25 cm). Forms additional plants at base.

CULTURE: Easy

Because of its ease of culture and frequency of blooming, *Angranthes* Grandalena has become one of my favorites of the angraecoids.

LIGHT: Medium
TEMPERATURE: Intermediate
POTTING MEDIUM: Medium orchid bark or coco chips
CULTURAL TIPS: Like most angraecoids, this plant resents repotting; do so as infrequently as possible.

Ascocenda Dong Tarn 'Robert' AM/AOS

PRONUNCIATION: ass-koh-SEN-dah
ORIGIN: *Ascocenda* Medasand × *Ascocenda* Eileen Beauty. Registered by C. Sakuldejtana in 1973.
DESCRIPTION AND QUALITIES: This hybrid is not too large for windowsills or under lights.
FLOWER: $1^{1}/_{4}$ in. (3.5 cm), glowing, dark red with yellow and red lip. Twelve or more per inflorescence.
SEASON OF BLOOM: Variable
MATURE SIZE, HABIT: Compact, will take years to reach 10 in. (25 cm)

Brilliant red flowers on compact plants are the hallmarks of *Ascocenda* Dong Tarn 'Robert' AM/AOS.

CULTURE: Easy
LIGHT: Medium to high
TEMPERATURE: Intermediate to warm
POTTING MEDIUM: Medium mix, well-draining
CULTURAL TIPS: Frequently grown in baskets to accommodate sprawling roots and to provide excellent drainage
RELATED SPECIES, HYBRIDS: *Ascocentrum*

Ascocenda Motes Mandarin 'Mary Motes' HCC/AOS produces luscious apricot-colored flowers.

An older *Ascocenda* Peggy Foo '#1' is still a knockout.

curvifolium in its background gives this hybrid its compact growth habit.

Ascocenda Motes Mandarin 'Mary Motes' HCC/AOS

PRONUNCIATION: ass-koh-SEN-dah
ORIGIN: *Vanda* Satta × *Ascocenda* Yip Sum Wah. Cross made by Sakri Sari and registered by M. Motes in 1991.
DESCRIPTION AND QUALITIES: M. Motes has produced and introduced many new compact and cold-tolerant (compared to other vandaceous plants) vandas and ascocendas. Many of his hybrids also require less light than others to bloom well.
FLOWER: $1^1/_2$ in. (4 cm), apricot-orange
SEASON OF BLOOM: Variable
MATURE SIZE, HABIT: Compact. Like all vandaceous plants, it will keep growing taller, but its growth is so slow it will take years to reach 12 in. (30 cm).
CULTURE: Easy
LIGHT: Medium to high
TEMPERATURE: Intermediate to warm
POTTING MEDIUM: Medium to coarse, well-draining
CULTURAL TIPS: Can be grown in pots or baskets. Excellent drainage is a must.

Ascocenda Peggy Foo '#1'

PRONUNCIATION: ass-koh-SEN-dah
ORIGIN: *Vanda* Bonnie Blue Fukumura × *Ascocentrum curvifolium*. Cross made by R. Fukumura and registered by Foo Hock Lee in 1970.
DESCRIPTION AND QUALITIES: Though this cross was made decades ago, it still ranks as one of the greats. Its abundant blossoms are luminous, and several color forms of the grex are available. It inherits its growth habit from *Ascocentrum curvifolium*. The hybrid has been used extensively as a parent to produce larger flowering ascocendas.
FLOWER: $1^1/_2$ in. (4 cm), to 15 or more flowers on each inflorescence

Ascocentrum ampullaceum 'Crownfox' is a brilliantly colored selection from R. F. Orchids.

SEASON OF BLOOM: Variable
MATURE SIZE, HABIT: Compact, takes years to reach 12 in. (30 cm). Leaves 10 in. (25 cm).
CULTURE: Easy
LIGHT: Medium to high
TEMPERATURE: Intermediate to warm
POTTING MEDIUM: Medium to coarse, well-draining
CULTURAL TIPS: Can be grown in pots, but wooden or plastic baskets are preferred, as plants require excellent drainage. In warm, humid climates they are frequently grown in wooden baskets with no media.

Ascocentrum ampullaceum var. *aurantiacum* offers an orange alternative.

Ascocentrum ampullaceum

PRONUNCIATION: ass-koh-SEN-trum am-pew-LAY-see-um
SYNONYM: *Saccolabium ampullaceum*
ORIGIN: India to Thailand
DESCRIPTION AND QUALITIES: This species is available in various color forms, from purple to shades of orange and white. It is a perfect size to fit under lights or on a windowsill. The cloned selection 'Crownfox' is superior. Orange-flowered *Ascocentrum ampullaceum* var. *aurantiacum* is also gorgeous.
FLOWER: To 40 or more, borne on an erect inflorescence, magenta, $1/2–3/4$ in. (1–2 cm)
SEASON OF BLOOM: Variable
MATURE SIZE, HABIT: Dwarf, 8 in. (20 cm), with leaves 5–6 in. (12.5–15.0 cm). Many shoots from its base produce a bushy plant.
CULTURE: Easy
LIGHT: Medium

Ascocentrum garayi is a small grower that fits nicely in any bright windowsill.

TEMPERATURE: Intermediate to warm

POTTING MEDIUM: Medium mix, well-draining

CULTURAL TIPS: Can be grown in pots or baskets. Foliage is spotted with red if plant is exposed to bright light.

HISTORY: Discovered by Smith in Bangladesh.

RELATED SPECIES, HYBRIDS: *Ascofinetia* Cherry Blossom

Ascocentrum garayi

PRONUNCIATION: ass-koh-SEN-trum gah-RAY-eye

SYNONYMS: *Ascocentrum miniatum, Saccolabium miniatum*

ORIGIN: Indochina

DESCRIPTION AND QUALITIES: One of the smaller ascocentrums, it has a reputation for being quite adaptable. When grown well it is covered with flowers. This species has been used frequently in breeding to

The tiniest species in this genus, *Ascocentrum pumilum* is a true miniature.

impart its bright flowers and dwarf growth to its vandaceous offspring. It is commonly known by its earlier name, *Ascocentrum miniatum*.

FLOWER: $1/2$ in. (1 cm), yellow to bright orange, on erect spike 4–6 in. (10–15 cm) tall

SEASON OF BLOOM: Variable

MATURE SIZE, HABIT: Dwarf, usually 2–4 in. (5–10 cm) tall with stiff leaves 5–6 in. (12.5–15.0 cm) long

CULTURE: Easy

LIGHT: Medium

TEMPERATURE: Intermediate to warm

POTTING MEDIUM: Medium mix, well-draining

CULTURAL TIPS: Can be grown in pots or baskets.

HISTORY: Introduced in England by Veitch in 1846.

Ascocentrum pumilum

PRONUNCIATION: ass-koh-SEN-trum PEW-mi-lum

ORIGIN: Taiwan

DESCRIPTION AND QUALITIES: One of the smallest ascocentrums, this charming species frequently blooms more than once a year. The leaves are tubular or semi-terete.

FLOWER: Five to ten, rose-pink, $1/4$ in. (6 mm)

SEASON OF BLOOM: Variable

MATURE SIZE, HABIT: Miniature, to 3 in. (7.5 cm)

CULTURE: Easy

LIGHT: Low to medium

TEMPERATURE: Intermediate

POTTING MEDIUM: Fine, well-draining

CULTURAL TIPS: Generally prefers less light and cooler conditions compared to other *Ascocentrum* species.

RELATED SPECIES, HYBRIDS: *Ascocentrum pusillum* is another small grower with pink flowers, from Vietnam.

A perfect plant for small spaces, *Ascofinetia* Cherry Blossom is a popular hybrid.

Ascofinetia Cherry Blossom

PRONUNCIATION: ass-koh-fin-AY-tee-ah

ORIGIN: *Neofinetia falcata* × *Ascocentrum ampullaceum*. Registered by E. Iwanaga in 1961.

DESCRIPTION AND QUALITIES: Extremely compact, multi-growth plants. It inherited its fragrance from *Neofinetia falcata* and its pink color from *Ascocentrum ampullaceum*. We have Japanese orchid breeders to thank for most of the *Neofinetia* hybrids.

FLOWER: Many $1/2$ in. (1 cm), pastel rose-lavender, with spurs. Lightly fragrant.

SEASON OF BLOOM: Variable

MATURE SIZE, HABIT: Dwarf, 4–6 in. (10–15 cm), will take years to reach this height

CULTURE: Easy

LIGHT: Medium

TEMPERATURE: Intermediate to warm

POTTING MEDIUM: Fine, well-draining. Sometimes grown in plastic or wooden baskets.

Ascofinetia Cherry Blossom 'Apricot'

PRONUNCIATION: ass-koh-fin-AY-tee-ah

ORIGIN: *Neofinetia falcata* × *Ascocentrum ampullaceum* var. *aurantiacum*. Registered by E. Iwanaga in 1961.

DESCRIPTION AND QUALITIES: An unusual apricot-orange color form of this popular hybrid.
FLOWER: Many $^1/_2$ in. (1 cm), orange sherbet–colored, with spurs. Lightly scented.
SEASON OF BLOOM: Variable
MATURE SIZE, HABIT: Dwarf, 6 in. (15 cm)
CULTURE: Easy

Ascofinetia Cherry Blossom 'Apricot' displays a rare flower color for this hybrid.

Baptistonia echinata buds are just starting to open.

LIGHT: Medium
TEMPERATURE: Intermediate to warm
POTTING MEDIUM: Fine, well-draining. Sometimes grown in plastic or wooden baskets.

Baptistonia echinata

PRONUNCIATION: bap-tis-TOE-nee-ah eck-i-NAH-tah
SYNONYM: *Oncidium brunleesianum*
ORIGIN: Brazil
DESCRIPTION AND QUALITIES: This brightly colored, small growing plant vegetatively looks much like any oncidium. It used to be rare but is now more commonly offered.
FLOWER: $^3/_4$–1 in. (2.0–2.5 cm) wide, yellow with maroon markings, displayed on arching inflorescence of 10 in. (25 cm)
SEASON OF BLOOM: Variable
MATURE SIZE, HABIT: Dwarf, 6 in. (15 cm) tall with leaves 1 in. (2.5 cm) wide
CULTURE: Intermediate
LIGHT: Medium
TEMPERATURE: Intermediate
POTTING MEDIUM: Fine, well-draining
CULTURAL TIPS: Does well mounted on tree fern plaques.
HISTORY: First described by João Barbosa Rodrigues in 1882. It was named for Brazilian ethnologist Baptista Caetano d'Almeida Nogueira.

Barbosella cucullata

PRONUNCIATION: bar-boh-SELL-ah kew-kew-LAH-tah
ORIGIN: Brazil
DESCRIPTION AND QUALITIES: Similar in looks and cultural needs to pleurothallis.
FLOWER: Tall, narrow, $1^1/_2$ in. (4 cm) long flowers tower above its leaves. Colors from bronzy yellow, to yellow-green, to yellow.
SEASON OF BLOOM: Winter
MATURE SIZE, HABIT: Miniature, 3 in. (7.5 cm)
CULTURE: Intermediate

A fine specimen of *Barbosella cucullata.* Grown by J & L Orchids.

Barkeria lindleyana presents an attractive spray of flowers.

LIGHT: Low to medium
TEMPERATURE: Cool to intermediate
POTTING MEDIUM: Fine, well-draining
CULTURAL TIPS: Likes a cool spot with high humidity and modest light.
RELATED SPECIES, HYBRIDS: *Barbosella australis, Bar. caespitifica, Bar. handori, Bar. miersii, Bar. prorepens*

Barkeria lindleyana

PRONUNCIATION: bar-KARE-ee-ah lind-lee-AH-nah
ORIGIN: Mexico
DESCRIPTION AND QUALITIES: One of the taller species in this genus. Like other barkerias it is deciduous in the winter.
FLOWER: Graceful, brightly colored, dark lavender with white and darker purple lips, 2½ in. (6 cm) across. Borne in clusters at the end of the spike.
SEASON OF BLOOM: Fall

MATURE SIZE, HABIT: Compact, to 12 in. (30 cm) but usually smaller
CULTURE: Intermediate
LIGHT: Medium to high
TEMPERATURE: Intermediate
POTTING MEDIUM: Medium mix, well-draining
CULTURAL TIPS: Like all barkerias, should be kept on the dry side when dormant (with no leaves) with regular watering resumed when new growth begins.
RELATED SPECIES, HYBRIDS: *Barkeria dorotheae, Bark. halbingeri, Bark. naevosa, Bark. palmeri, Bark. shoemakeri, Bark. spectabilis*

Beardara Henry Wallbrunn

PRONUNCIATION: bare-DAR-ah
ORIGIN: *Asconopsis* Irene Dobkin × *Doritis pulcherrima.* Registered by Henry Wallbrunn of Fort Caroline's (nursery) in 1978.
DESCRIPTION AND QUALITIES: Usually a

The apricot-colored flowers of this selection of *Beardara* Henry Wallbrunn are mouthwatering.

Bifrenaria harrisoniae features waxy white flowers with a sweet scent.

TEMPERATURE: Intermediate to warm
POTTING MEDIUM: Medium epiphytic mix

Bifrenaria harrisoniae

PRONUNCIATION: bye-fren-AIR-ee-ah har-i-SO-nee-ee
SYNONYMS: *Colax harrisoniae, Dendrobium harrisoniae, Maxillaria harrisoniae*
ORIGIN: Brazil
DESCRIPTION AND QUALITIES: A rarer pure white form is highly sought after.
FLOWER: 2–3 in. (5.0–7.5 cm) waxy, fleshy, usually white, last to six weeks. Strong, fruity scent.
SEASON OF BLOOM: Spring
MATURE SIZE, HABIT: Compact, pseudo-bulbs 2–3 in. (5.0–7.5 cm) long, leaves 8–10 in. (20–25 cm) long
CULTURE: Easy
LIGHT: Medium
TEMPERATURE: Cool to intermediate
POTTING MEDIUM: Medium epiphytic mix
CULTURAL TIPS: Does not require a total rest period, but reduced watering during the winter will improve bud set. Divide sparingly.
HISTORY: Sent to England from Rio de Janeiro by William Harrison in the 1820s.

Brassavola Little Stars

PRONUNCIATION: bra-SAH-voh-lah
ORIGIN: *Brassavola nodosa* × *Brassavola subulifolia* (now *Brassavola cordata*). Registered by Stewart, Inc., in 1983.
DESCRIPTION AND QUALITIES: A commonly offered orchid that is fast and easy to grow and bloom. Thick, fleshy leaves.
FLOWER: Cream/green petals and sepals with white, heart-shaped lips, 3¹/₂ in. (9 cm) wide. Soapy sweet scent in the evening.
SEASON OF BLOOM: Winter
MATURE SIZE, HABIT: Compact, leaves to 12 in. (30 cm)
CULTURE: Easy

slow grower, which partially accounts for the high price it fetches
FLOWER: Found in a range of colors, from apricot to cerise and dark pink, 1¹/₂ in. (4 cm), round
SEASON OF BLOOM: Winter to spring
MATURE SIZE, HABIT: Compact, 8 in. (20 cm) leaf spread. Very slow vertical growth.
CULTURE: Easy
LIGHT: Medium

LIGHT: High

TEMPERATURE: Intermediate to warm

POTTING MEDIUM: Grow in clay pot or wooden basket supplemented with cork chunks

CULTURAL TIPS: Needs as much light as possible to bloom. Full, direct sun is best, except during summer, when bright, diffused light is best.

Brassavola Little Stars is easy to grow and bloom.

Brassavola nodosa

PRONUNCIATION: bra-SAH-voh-lah no-DOH-sah

SYNONYMS: *Brassavola venosa, Epidendrum nodosum*

ORIGIN: Mexico, Central America, Colombia, Venezuela

DESCRIPTION AND QUALITIES: Heavy evening fragrance of freesia or lily-of-the-valley. It frequently passes on its ease of blooming, habit, and fragrance to its offspring. Stems and leaves are subterete.

FLOWER: One to six per 8 in. (20 cm) erect inflorescence. Each pale green to creamy white and 3 to 6 in. (7.5–15.0 cm) across. The lip is sometimes marked with purple.

SEASON OF BLOOM: Variable

MATURE SIZE, HABIT: Dwarf, clump-forming. Reaches 18 in. (46 cm), but is usually much shorter.

CULTURE: Easy

LIGHT: Medium to high

TEMPERATURE: Intermediate to warm

POTTING MEDIUM: Plastic pots are sometimes preferred because they maintain moisture.

CULTURAL TIPS: Flowers look best on a large specimen plant, so do not divide unnecessarily.

HISTORY: One of the early orchids in cultivation, it was first described in 1735 as an *Epidendrum* and was transferred the genus *Brassavola* in 1831.

A night delight, *Brassavola nodosa* fills up the evening air with its enchanting scent.

Brassocattleya Binosa 'Kirk' AM/AOS combines a sweet scent with striking colors.

Brassocattleya Binosa

PRONUNCIATION: brass-oh-KAT-lee-ah

ORIGIN: *Brassavola nodosa* × *Cattleya bicolor*. Registered by R. Tanaka in 1950.

DESCRIPTION AND QUALITIES: This popular grex usually results in compact, colorful plants.

FLOWER: Fragrant, 3 in. (7.5 cm), with bright green sepals and petals and a flared white lip sprinkled with purple spots
SEASON OF BLOOM: Variable
MATURE SIZE, HABIT: Compact, 8–10 in. (20–25 cm)
CULTURE: Easy
LIGHT: Medium to high
TEMPERATURE: Intermediate to warm
POTTING MEDIUM: Medium mix, well-draining

Brassocattleya Cynthia

PRONUNCIATION: brass-oh-KAT-lee-ah
ORIGIN: *Brassavola digbyana* (now *Rhyncholaelia digbyana*) × *Cattleya walkeriana*. Reg-

Brassocattleya Cynthia 'Pink Lady' is a pleasant and strongly scented hybrid with impressively sized flowers on a windowsill-sized plant.

The dramatic contrast between the sepals, petals, and lip make *Brassolaeliocattleya* Haw Yuan Beauty 'Orchis' a stunner.

istered by St. Quintin in 1917.
DESCRIPTION AND QUALITIES: One of my favorite mini-catts.
FLOWER: 3 in. (7.5 cm) or more across, deep pink with yellow throats and a heavenly fragrance, a trait passed on by both scented parents.
SEASON OF BLOOM: Summer to fall
MATURE SIZE, HABIT: Compact, 8–10 in. (20–25 cm)
CULTURE: Easy
LIGHT: Medium to high
TEMPERATURE: Intermediate
POTTING MEDIUM: Medium mix, well-draining

Brassolaeliocattleya Haw Yuan Beauty

PRONUNCIATION: brass-oh-lay-lee-oh-KAT-lee-ah
ORIGIN: *Brassolaeliocattleya* Haw Yuan Moon × *Laeliocattleya* Mari's Song. Bred by Haw Yuan and registered by C. H. Hsieh in 1997.
DESCRIPTION AND QUALITIES: Few hybrids in the Cattleya Alliance sport this striking flower color pattern, which draws attention at orchid shows.
FLOWER: $2^{1}/_{2}$–3 in. (6.0–7.5 cm), white sepals and purple-red petals and lip. Vanilla fragrance.
SEASON OF BLOOM: Winter
MATURE SIZE, HABIT: Compact, 12 in. (30 cm)
CULTURE: Intermediate
LIGHT: Medium to high
TEMPERATURE: Intermediate
POTTING MEDIUM: Medium mix, well-draining

Brassolaeliocattleya Orange Treat

PRONUNCIATION: brass-oh-lay-lee-oh-KAT-lee-ah
ORIGIN: *Brassolaeliocattleya* Orange Nugget × *Laeliocattleya* Trick or Treat. Bred by W.

Cousineau and registered by H. Rohrl in 1995.

DESCRIPTION AND QUALITIES: During the dull days of winter, this cheerful orange-flowering orchid is especially appreciated.

FLOWER: 3 in. (7.5 cm), pure clear orange, frequently in groups of three or more

SEASON OF BLOOM: Winter to spring

MATURE SIZE, HABIT: Dwarf, 8 in. (20 cm)

CULTURE: Easy

LIGHT: Medium

TEMPERATURE: Intermediate

POTTING MEDIUM: Medium mix, well-draining

Brassolaeliocattleya Yellow Imp

PRONUNCIATION: brass-oh-lay-lee-oh-KAT-lee-ah

ORIGIN: *Brassocattleya* Daffodil × *Laeliocattleya* Neon. Registered by Clarelen's in 1958.

DESCRIPTION AND QUALITIES: Sometimes simple flower colors make the strongest statement, and this is true with this hybrid. It has been around for almost 50 years and still holds its own with clear yellow flowers.

FLOWER: 3 in. (7.5 cm), bright yellow

SEASON OF BLOOM: Winter to spring

MATURE SIZE, HABIT: Compact, 10 in. (25 cm)

CULTURE: Easy

LIGHT: Medium

TEMPERATURE: Intermediate

POTTING MEDIUM: Medium mix, well-draining

Broughtonia sanguinea

PRONUNCIATION: brow-TOE-nee-ah san-GWIN-ee-ah

SYNONYM: *Epidendrum sanguineum*

ORIGIN: Cuba, Jamaica

DESCRIPTION AND QUALITIES: This genus includes only two species—this and *Broughtonia negrilensis*. Because *Bro. san-*

guinea is considered by most as horticulturally superior, it is most commonly found for sale and has been used to produce multi-flowering hybrids. *Cattleytonia* hybrids are probably some of the most successful introductions.

FLOWER: 1¹/₂ in. (4 cm), usually in shades

Nothing is subtle about the flower color of *Brassolaeliocattleya* Orange Treat.

Flowers of *Brassolaeliocattleya* Yellow Imp light up a room like sunshine

Broughtonia sanguinea produces a cluster of bright, rounded flowers.

Bulbophyllum annandalei in bloom commands attention.

of red-pink with darker veins, borne in a panicle (cluster) of 5 to 15. Rarer forms in white and yellow.

SEASON OF BLOOM: Fall to winter
MATURE SIZE, HABIT: Dwarf, 5–6 in. (12.5–15.0 cm)
CULTURE: Easy
LIGHT: Medium to high
TEMPERATURE: Intermediate

POTTING MEDIUM: Fine, well-draining, or mounted
HISTORY: First named *Viscum radice bulbosa minimus* in 1696.

Bulbophyllum annandalei

PRONUNCIATION: bulb-oh-FILL-um an-un-DALE-ee-eye
ORIGIN: Thailand, Malaysia
DESCRIPTION AND QUALITIES: A striking and handsome bulbophyllum.
FLOWER: 2 in. (5 cm) long, burnt-orange, with dark red speckles, presented in a whirl
SEASON OF BLOOM: Spring to summer
MATURE SIZE, HABIT: Dwarf, 5 in. (12.5 cm)
CULTURE: Intermediate
LIGHT: Medium
TEMPERATURE: Intermediate
POTTING MEDIUM: Fine, well-draining
RELATED SPECIES, HYBRIDS: Those bulbophyllums that appear in this book represent only a small portion of the species and

The cultivar name of *Bulbophyllum falcatum* 'Standing Tall' AM/AOS says it all.

hybrids of this fascinating group. For more information, consult Emly Siegerist's excellent book, *Bulbophyllums and Their Allies: A Grower's Guide.*

Bulbophyllum falcatum

PRONUNCIATION: bulb-oh-FILL-um fal-KAH-tum

SYNONYMS: *Bulbophyllum dahlemense, Megaclinum falcatum*

ORIGIN: Africa

DESCRIPTION AND QUALITIES: *Bulbophyllum* species and hybrids are regaining growers' interest; this unusual species is one of the most popular.

FLOWER: $^{1}/_{2}$ in. (1 cm) yellow and red, with interesting articulating (moving) lips, "sprout" from a dark red rachis (part of the inflorescence)

SEASON OF BLOOM: Spring to summer

MATURE SIZE, HABIT: Dwarf, 6 in. (15 cm)

CULTURE: Easy

LIGHT: Medium

TEMPERATURE: Intermediate

POTTING MEDIUM: Fine, well-draining

CULTURAL TIPS: Grows well in pots.

HISTORY: Originally described by John Lindley in 1826 as *Megaclinum falcatum*.

Bulbophyllum flammula petals resemble colorful streamers.

Bulbophyllum flammula

PRONUNCIATION: bulb-oh-FILL-um FLAM-you-lah

DESCRIPTION AND QUALITIES: An unusual, and until recently, rarely seen species.

Bulbophyllum Jersey is richly colored with large flowers.

FLOWER: 3 in. (7.5 cm) long petals
SEASON OF BLOOM: Spring to summer
MATURE SIZE, HABIT: Dwarf, 4 in. (10 cm)
CULTURE: Intermediate
LIGHT: Medium
TEMPERATURE: Intermediate
POTTING MEDIUM: Fine, well-draining

Bulbophyllum Jersey

PRONUNCIATION: bulb-oh-FILL-um
ORIGIN: *Bulbophyllum lobbii* × *Bulbophyllum echinolabium*. Registered by Eric Young Orchid Foundation in 1996.
DESCRIPTION AND QUALITIES: One of the real stunners of the bulbophyllum hybrids. Parent *Bulbophyllum echinolabium* contributes the large flower size to this hybrid.
FLOWER: 4 in. (10 cm) high and $2^{1}/_{2}$ in. (6 cm) wide, triangular shaped, in shades of orange and red
SEASON OF BLOOM: Summer to fall
MATURE SIZE, HABIT: Compact, 12 in. (30 cm)
CULTURE: Intermediate
LIGHT: Medium
TEMPERATURE: Intermediate
POTTING MEDIUM: Fine, well-draining

Bulbophyllum rothschildianum

PRONUNCIATION: bulb-oh-FILL-um roths-child-ee-AH-num
SYNONYM: *Cirrhopetalum rothschildianum*
ORIGIN: India
DESCRIPTION AND QUALITIES:. One of the most spectacular species of all the bulbophyllums.
FLOWER: Fragrant, each 1 in. (2.5 cm) wide and to 7 in. (18 cm) long, five or six per umbel
SEASON OF BLOOM: Summer to fall
MATURE SIZE, HABIT: Compact, 12 in. (30 cm)
CULTURE: Easy
LIGHT: Medium
TEMPERATURE: Intermediate to warm

Bulbophyllum rothschildianum is a showstopper.

POTTING MEDIUM: Well-draining
CULTURAL TIPS: Best when grown on
tree fern slab or in shallow container
HISTORY: First described as a *Cirrhopetalum* by J. O'Brien in 1895.

Bulbophyllum tingabarinum
PRONUNCIATION: bulb-oh-FILL-um
ting-ah-bar-EYE-num
SYNONYMS: *Cirrhopetalum tinga-
barinum, Bulbophyllum flaviflorum*
ORIGIN: Laos, Vietnam, Cambodia
DESCRIPTION AND QUALITIES: This
petite plant puts on a brilliant show.
FLOWER: Eight per inflorescence,
each slender, bright burnt-orange
to cinnamon-red, and 3–4 in. (7.5–
10.0 cm) long
SEASON OF BLOOM: Fall to winter
MATURE SIZE, HABIT: Miniature,
3 in. (7.5 cm)
CULTURE: Easy
LIGHT: Medium to high
TEMPERATURE: Warm
POTTING MEDIUM: Fine, well-
draining, or mounted on tree fern
slabs
CULTURAL TIPS: Likes high humidity

Cadetia chionantha
PRONUNCIATION: ka-DET-ee-ah
kye-oh-NAN-thah
SYNONYM: *Dendrobium chionanthum*
ORIGIN: New Guinea
DESCRIPTION AND QUALITIES: This
floriferous diminutive orchid quickly
grows into a clump. Leaves are dark
glossy green.
FLOWER: Vanilla scented, $1/4$ in. (0.75
cm), crystalline white, held well
above the foliage
SEASON OF BLOOM: Variable
MATURE SIZE, HABIT: Miniature,
3–4 in. (7.5–10.0 cm)
CULTURE: Intermediate

*Bulbophyllum
tingabarinum* flowers
look like a miniature
fireworks display.

A petite plant and
flower makes *Cadetia
chionantha* a minia-
ture that will fit in any
growing space.

This gaily colored orchid has quite a name to live up to, *Catcylaelia* John Davison of Bryn Ingli.

LIGHT: Medium
TEMPERATURE: Cool to intermediate
POTTING MEDIUM: Fine to medium, well-draining mix, or mounted
CULTURAL TIPS: Plants must be kept damp and in high humidity with good air circulation. They are suited for slabs or pots. Sensitive to transplanting.
RELATED SPECIES, HYBRIDS: *Cadetia chamaephyton, Cad. dischorensis, Cad. taylori*

Catcylaelia John Davison of Bryn Ingli

PRONUNCIATION: kat-klee-LAY-lee-ah
ORIGIN: *Encyclia incumbens × Laeliocattleya* Trick or Treat. Registered by the Royal Horticultural Society in 2004.
DESCRIPTION AND QUALITIES: An uncommonly found combination of genera produced this bright, cheery hybrid.
FLOWER: Cinnamon-orange, 2¹/₂ in. (6 cm) across with ruffled lips, borne in a cluster

SEASON OF BLOOM: Winter to spring
MATURE SIZE, HABIT: Compact, 12 in. (30 cm)
CULTURE: Easy
LIGHT: Medium
TEMPERATURE: Intermediate
POTTING MEDIUM: Medium grade epiphytic mix

Cattleya aurantiaca

PRONUNCIATION: KAT-lee-ah or-an-TYE-ah-kah
SYNONYM: *Epidendrum aurantiacum*
ORIGIN: Mexico, Central and South America
DESCRIPTION AND QUALITIES: This easy-to-grow species is quite adaptable to a wide range of growing conditions. The flower color varies from shades of yellow to orange and red. Its vigorous growth habit makes it a popular parent.
FLOWER: Clusters of 10 to 15, 2 in. (5 cm), somewhat cup-shaped

SEASON OF BLOOM: Winter to spring
MATURE SIZE, HABIT: Compact, 12 in.
(30 cm)
CULTURE: Easy
LIGHT: Medium
TEMPERATURE: Intermediate
POTTING MEDIUM: Medium grade epi-
phytic mix
HISTORY: Introduced into England in 1835
from Guatemala by George Ure-Skinner.

Cattleya Baby Kay

PRONUNCIATION: KAT-lee-ah
ORIGIN: *Cattleya bicolor* × *Cattleya luteola*.
Registered by Keller in 1963.
DESCRIPTION AND QUALITIES: Parent *Catt-
leya luteola* gave this hybrid its petite stat-
ure while *C. bicolor* lent its bright colors.
The result is delightful.
FLOWER: 3 in. (7.5 cm), chartreuse with
rose-purple lip
SEASON OF BLOOM: Winter to spring

A compact growing species, *Cattleya aurantiaca* has glossy green leaves with clusters of bright orange flowers.

Cattleya Baby Kay displays a refreshing color combination of chartreuse petals and sepals punctuated with a rose-purple lip.

MATURE SIZE, HABIT: Compact, 10 in. (25 cm)
CULTURE: Intermediate
LIGHT: Medium
TEMPERATURE: Intermediate
POTTING MEDIUM: Medium grade epiphytic mix

Cattleya forbesii
PRONUNCIATION: KAT-lee-ah FORBS-ee-eye
SYNONYM: *Epidendrum pauper*
ORIGIN: Brazil
DESCRIPTION AND QUALITIES: A good starter orchid because of its ease of culture and dependable flowering.
FLOWER: Clusters of two to five, 2$^{1}/_{2}$–4 in. (6–10 cm), soft green tinged in bronze, with a bubble gum fragrance

Cattleya forbesii deserves to be in more collections.

The flower of *Cattleya intermedia* displays a wide range of color forms in various shades of pink and white.

SEASON OF BLOOM: Spring to summer
MATURE SIZE, HABIT: Dwarf, 6 in. (15 cm)
CULTURE: Intermediate
LIGHT: High
TEMPERATURE: Intermediate to warm
POTTING MEDIUM: Fine grade epiphytic mix
HISTORY: Introduced by the Horticultural Society of London in 1823.

Cattleya intermedia
PRONUNCIATION: KAT-lee-ah in-ter-MEE-dee-ah
SYNONYM: *Cattleya ovata*
ORIGIN: Brazil
DESCRIPTION AND QUALITIES: An intermediate-sized cattleya—not dwarf or full sized. The splash-petalled (petals and lip have the same color pattern) hybrids of today have mostly come from a special flower form of this species that was dubbed *Cattleya acquinii.*
FLOWER: Deliciously fragrant, to 6 in. (15 cm) across, pinks to whites
SEASON OF BLOOM: Variable
MATURE SIZE, HABIT: Compact, stems to 15 in. (38 cm), leaves 6 in. (15 cm) long
CULTURE: Intermediate
LIGHT: Medium to high
TEMPERATURE: Intermediate
POTTING MEDIUM: Medium grade orchid mix
HISTORY: Introduced in 1824 by Captain Graham and first grown at the Royal Botanical Garden in Glasgow, Scotland.

Cattleya luteola
PRONUNCIATION: KAT-lee-ah loo-tee-OH-lah
SYNONYM: *Cattleya flavida*
ORIGIN: Brazil, Peru, Ecuador
DESCRIPTION AND QUALITIES: This cute little *Cattleya* species has been used frequently by hybridizers to impart its diminutive growth habit to its offspring. The early morning fragrance of this orchid is appar-

ently synchronized with its pollinator, a type of bee.

FLOWER: Fragrant, 2 in. (5 cm), borne in sprays of two to five, pale yellow with a darker yellow gold in the lip

SEASON OF BLOOM: Spring

MATURE SIZE, HABIT: Dwarf, 5–7 in. (12.5–18.0 cm)

CULTURE: Easy

LIGHT: Medium to high

TEMPERATURE: Intermediate to warm

POTTING MEDIUM: Medium grade epiphytic mix

HISTORY: This species was first cited in the *Gardeners' Chronicle* in 1853.

Cattleya Peckhaviensis

PRONUNCIATION: KAT-lee-ah

ORIGIN: *Cattleya aclandiae* × *Cattleya schilleriana*. Registered by Marriott in 1910.

DESCRIPTION AND QUALITIES: Combines the best of both species in a hybrid with crisp dark markings. Easier to grow than either of its parents.

FLOWER: Fragrant, 3 in. (7.5 cm), brown-orange, spotted with maroon, with contrasting dark pink lip

SEASON OF BLOOM: Spring to summer

MATURE SIZE, HABIT: Dwarf, 6 in. (15 cm)

CULTURE: Intermediate

LIGHT: Medium

TEMPERATURE: Intermediate

POTTING MEDIUM: Medium grade epiphytic mix

Cattleya schilleriana

PRONUNCIATION: KAT-lee-ah shill-er-ee-AH-nah

SYNONYM: *Epidendrum schillerianum*

ORIGIN: Brazil

DESCRIPTION AND QUALITIES: With markings similar to *Cattleya aclandiae*, this species is a delightful, honey-scented dwarf, but it is difficult to grow. Look for some of its hybrids for easier culture. Leaves are frequently red spotted, especially if grown in strong light.

FLOWER: Borne singly or in pairs, 3–4 in. (7.5–10.0 cm) across and multicolored

An underappreciated mini, *Cattleya luteola* deserves to be in more home orchid collections.

A primary hybrid with *Cattleya aclandiae* and *C. schilleriana* as parents, *C.* Peckhaviensis emits its strongest scent on a sunny, warm afternoon.

Cattleya schilleriana displays an unlikely, but arresting, color combination.

The lavender flowers of *Cattleya walkeriana* 'Pinkie' glisten in bright light.

Cattleytonia Why Not is a popular hybrid because of its tight growth habit and dependable flowering.

HISTORY: The first plant of this species was recorded in 1857 as part of Consul Schiller's collection in Hamburg, Germany, imported from Brazil.

Cattleya walkeriana

PRONUNCIATION: KAT-lee-ah walk-er-ee-AH-nah

ORIGIN: Brazil

DESCRIPTION AND QUALITIES: A favorite parent for breeding mini-catts because of its small stature, ease of growth, and vanilla-citrus fragrance that is frequently passed on to its offspring.

FLOWER: Red-purple, borne singly or in pairs, 4 in. (10 cm) across

SEASON OF BLOOM: Variable

MATURE SIZE, HABIT: Dwarf, to 6 in. (15 cm)

CULTURE: Easy

LIGHT: Medium

TEMPERATURE: Intermediate

POTTING MEDIUM: Medium grade, well-draining epiphytic mix

CULTURAL TIPS: An easy to grow and popular species.

HISTORY: This species was discovered by George Gardner in Brazil in 1839.

Cattleytonia Why Not

PRONUNCIATION: kat-lee-TOE-nee-ah

ORIGIN: *Cattleya aurantiaca* × *Broughtonia sanguinea*. Registered in 1979 by Stewart, Inc.

DESCRIPTION AND QUALITIES: This hybrid brings out the best of both of its parents. It has a tight growth habit and a multitude of bright red flowers of heavy substance that frequently appear more than once a year. Highly recommended for beginners.

FLOWER: Clusters of 1–1½ in. (2.5–4.0 cm), round, deep red, with yellow throat

SEASON OF BLOOM: Spring to summer

MATURE SIZE, HABIT: Dwarf, 8 in. (20 cm)

CULTURE: Easy

LIGHT: Medium to high

SEASON OF BLOOM: Spring to summer

MATURE SIZE, HABIT: Dwarf, 6 in. (15 cm). Various races of the species can be slightly shorter or taller.

CULTURE: Intermediate

LIGHT: Medium to high

TEMPERATURE: Intermediate

POTTING MEDIUM: Medium grade epiphytic mix

Centroglossa macroceras 'Stoney Point' cloaks itself in cream-colored flowers. Grown by J & L Orchids.

TEMPERATURE: Intermediate
POTTING MEDIUM: Medium mix, well-draining

Centroglossa macroceras

PRONUNCIATION: sen-troh-GLOSS-ah mack-roh-SEER-us
ORIGIN: Brazil
DESCRIPTION AND QUALITIES: Related to the genus *Ornithocephalus*, this miniature produces many flowers in a small space.
FLOWER: $^1/_2$ in. (1 cm) across, cream-colored, borne on a $1^1/_2$ in. (4 cm) spike
SEASON OF BLOOM: Winter to spring
MATURE SIZE, HABIT: Miniature, 2 in. (5 cm)
CULTURE: Intermediate
LIGHT: Medium
TEMPERATURE: Intermediate
POTTING MEDIUM: Best grown mounted with sphagnum moss.
CULTURAL TIPS: Must always be kept damp and humid.
RELATED SPECIES, HYBRIDS: *Centroglossa tripollinica*

The pinwheel of multiple flowers of *Cirrhopetalum* Daisy Chain 'Monkey' piques everyone's curiosity.

Cirrhopetalum Daisy Chain

PRONUNCIATION: seer-oh-PET-ah-lum
ORIGIN: *Cirrhopetalum makoyanum* × *Cirrhopetalum amesianum*. Registered by Stewart, Inc., in 1969.
DESCRIPTION AND QUALITIES: These easy to grow hybrids always elicit admiration for their unique cream and red circular flower arrangement.
FLOWER: Individual, narrow, $1^1/_2$ in. (4 cm)

Cirrhopetalum Sunshine Queen 'Orange' is an apricot-colored beauty. Grown by Parkside Orchid Nursery.

Flowers of *Cirrhopetalum yasnae* 'Aussie' are as bright as small flames.

long and creamy orange, with a suffusion of red on the top of the lip and on the short petals and sepals
SEASON OF BLOOM: Spring to summer
MATURE SIZE, HABIT: Dwarf, 5 in. (12.5 cm)
CULTURE: Easy
LIGHT: Medium
TEMPERATURE: Intermediate
POTTING MEDIUM: Fine, well-draining mix, or in pot of tree fern
CULTURAL TIPS: Enjoys high humidity

Cirrhopetalum Sunshine Queen

PRONUNCIATION: seer-oh-PET-ah-lum
ORIGIN: *Cirrhopetalum mastersianum* × *Cirrhopetalum curtisii*. Registered by Suphachadiwong in 1995.
DESCRIPTION AND QUALITIES: Full, wide petals stand well above the foliage, characteristics popular with breeders. This hybrid also comes in a yellow form.
FLOWER: Apricot-orange, (mostly lip) is $2^{1}/_{2}$ in. (6 cm) long and half as wide, with darker, much smaller, petals.
SEASON OF BLOOM: Spring to summer
MATURE SIZE, HABIT: Dwarf, 6 in. (15 cm)
CULTURE: Intermediate
LIGHT: Medium
TEMPERATURE: Intermediate
POTTING MEDIUM: Fine, well-draining

Cirrhopetalum yasnae

PRONUNCIATION: seer-oh-PET-ah-lum YAZ-nay
SYNONYMS: *Bulbophyllum papillosum*, *Bulbophyllum thaiorum*
ORIGIN: Vietnam, Thailand
DESCRIPTION AND QUALITIES: An attractive species with long, narrow flowers on tiny plants.
FLOWER: 1 in. (2.5 cm), dark orange or lighter in color
SEASON OF BLOOM: Spring to summer
MATURE SIZE, HABIT: Miniature, 2 in. (5 cm)
CULTURE: Intermediate
LIGHT: Medium
TEMPERATURE: Intermediate to warm
POTTING MEDIUM: Usually grown mounted or in pot of tree fern
CULTURAL TIPS: Should always be kept damp and in high humidity.

Cischweinfia popowiana

PRONUNCIATION: see-SHWINE-fee-ah pop-oh-WE-ah-nah
DESCRIPTION AND QUALITIES: The flower of this species and others in this genus resemble its cousin *Oncidium*.
FLOWER: Soft yellow with orange markings, 1 in. (2.5 cm) across, borne in short sprays
SEASON OF BLOOM: Spring to summer
MATURE SIZE, HABIT: Dwarf, 8 in. (20 cm)

The flowers of *Cischweinfia popowiana* are similar to those of oncidiums.

Brilliant red flowers of *Cochlioda rosea* make it a standout.

CULTURE: Easy
LIGHT: Medium
TEMPERATURE: Intermediate
POTTING MEDIUM: Fine, well-draining
HISTORY: Named in honor of Charles Schweinfurth, who worked for years at Oakes Ames Orchid Herbarium at Harvard University.
RELATED SPECIES, HYBRIDS: *Cischweinfia colombiana, Cisch. dasyandra, Cisch. platychila, Cisch. pusilla, Cisch. rostrata*

Cochlioda rosea

PRONUNCIATION: kok-lee-OH-dah ROH-zee-ah
SYNONYM: *Odontoglossum rosea*

ORIGIN: Ecuador, Colombia
DESCRIPTION AND QUALITIES: This genus is related to *Miltonia, Oncidium,* and *Odontoglossum* and is crossed with them to produce hybrids in the Oncidium Alliance.
FLOWER: To 20, rose-red, 1 in. (2.5 cm) wide, and borne on a vertical inflorescence 12 in. (30 cm) tall
SEASON OF BLOOM: Winter to spring
MATURE SIZE, HABIT: Dwarf, 6–8 in. (15–20 cm)
CULTURE: Intermediate
LIGHT: Medium
TEMPERATURE: Cool to intermediate
POTTING MEDIUM: Fine, well-draining
HISTORY: Discovered by Theodor Hartweg

in Ecuador. Described by John Lindley as *Odontoglossum rosea* in 1844.

RELATED SPECIES, HYBRIDS: *Cochlioda roezliana*

Cochlioda vulcanica

PRONUNCIATION: kok-lee-OH-dah vul-KAN-i-kah

SYNONYM: *Cochlioda vulcanica* var. *splendida*

ORIGIN: Peru, Ecuador, Colombia

DESCRIPTION AND QUALITIES: Pollinated by hummingbirds.

FLOWER: 1³/₄ in. (4.5 cm), on 10 in. (25 cm) inflorescence

SEASON OF BLOOM: Summer to fall

MATURE SIZE, HABIT: Compact, 12 in. (30 cm)

CULTURE: Intermediate

LIGHT: Medium

TEMPERATURE: Intermediate

POTTING MEDIUM: Fine, well-draining

Coelogyne cristata

PRONUNCIATION: see-LODGE-i-nee kris-TAH-tah

ORIGIN: Himalayas

DESCRIPTION AND QUALITIES: Because these are fast growing orchids, it is in not unusual to see a large mounted specimen at botanical gardens or orchid shows—a real showstopper.

FLOWER: 3 in. (7.5 cm) wide, white, with a white lip with yellow markings. Sweet banana or candy fragrance.

SEASON OF BLOOM: Winter to spring

MATURE SIZE, HABIT: Compact, 8–10 in. (20–25 cm)

CULTURE: Intermediate

LIGHT: Medium to high

TEMPERATURE: Intermediate to warm

POTTING MEDIUM: Medium mix

CULTURAL TIPS: Best if mounted or grown in basket because of its rambling habit.

Cochlioda vulcanica is one of the larger flowering species in this genus.

HISTORY: First described by John Lindley in 1822.

RELATED SPECIES, HYBRIDS: *Coelogyne confusa, Coel. corymbosa, Coel. fimbriata, Coel. fuliginosa, Coel. merrillii, Coel. odoratissima*

Coelogyne lawrenceana

PRONUNCIATION: see-LODGE-i-nee lore-en-see-AH-nah

SYNONYM: *Coelogyne fleuryi*

ORIGIN: Vietnam

DESCRIPTION AND QUALITIES: Tolerates a wide range of growing temperatures. Soft, pleated foliage.

FLOWER: To 4 in. (10 cm), waxy, tan with a white lip. Fragrant and long-lasting, open in succession.

SEASON OF BLOOM: Winter to spring

MATURE SIZE, HABIT: Compact, 12 in. (30 cm)

CULTURE: Intermediate

LIGHT: Medium

TEMPERATURE: Warm

POTTING MEDIUM: Medium mix

CULTURAL TIPS: Repot before new growth begins.

Coelogyne lawrenceana is an uncommon and desirable species from Vietnam.

Coelogyne cristata flowers are as white and bright as snow.

Coelogyne ochracea

PRONUNCIATION: see-LODGE-i-nee aw-KRAY-see-ah
SYNONYM: *Coelogyne nitida*
ORIGIN: India to China
DESCRIPTION AND QUALITIES: An easy to

The white flowers of *Coelogyne ochracea* glisten in the sunlight.

grow, stunning orchid, especially as a large plant.
FLOWER: 1^1/$_2$ in. (4 cm) pure white, fragrant, with striking yellow and orange markings on the lip
SEASON OF BLOOM: Spring
MATURE SIZE, HABIT: Dwarf, 8 in. (20 cm)
CULTURE: Easy
LIGHT: Medium
TEMPERATURE: Cool
POTTING MEDIUM: Medium mix
CULTURAL TIPS: This species does not lose its leaves during the winter.

Comparettia speciosa

PRONUNCIATION: kom-pah-RET-ee-ah spee-see-OH-sah
ORIGIN: Colombia
DESCRIPTION AND QUALITIES: In full bloom, this plant demands attention.
FLOWER: Intense orange, 2 in. (5 cm) tall and 1 in. (2.5 cm) wide, marked with darker veins
SEASON OF BLOOM: Summer to fall
MATURE SIZE, HABIT: Dwarf, to 8 in. (20 cm)
CULTURE: Intermediate
LIGHT: Medium
TEMPERATURE: Intermediate
POTTING MEDIUM: Fine, well-draining, or mounted
RELATED SPECIES, HYBRIDS: *Comparettia coccinea, Comp. falcata, Comp. macroplectron*

Comparettia speciosa displays a spray of sizzling orange flowers.

Crepidium mieczyskawi

PRONUNCIATION: kreh-PEE-dee-um myeh-chiss-KOV-eye
SYNONYM: *Malaxis species*
ORIGIN: Southeast Asia
DESCRIPTION AND QUALITIES: Foliage is as handsome as its flower, lime green and heavily speckled and blotched with purple. The genus comprises more than 250 species. This species is rare in cultivation but is worth seeking out.
FLOWER: About 25, ^{3}/$_8$ in. (1 cm), triangu-

lar, with yellow throats, borne on a 6 in.
(15 cm) vertical inflorescence
SEASON OF BLOOM: Spring to summer
MATURE SIZE, HABIT: Dwarf, 6 in. (15 cm)
CULTURE: Intermediate
LIGHT: Low
TEMPERATURE: Intermediate to warm
POTTING MEDIUM: Fine, well-draining
CULTURAL TIPS: Should be kept damp dur-
ing the growing season but a bit drier
during the winter.

Cycnoches Rocky Clough

PRONUNCIATION: SICK-noh-keez
ORIGIN: *Cycnoches pentadactylon × Cyc-
noches egertonianum.* Registered by G. Carr
of H & R Nurseries in 1995.
DESCRIPTION AND QUALITIES: This unusual
orchid is a perfect choice for those looking
for eclectic green flowers. Because they are
borne below the leaves, the presentation resembles a designed floral arrangement.
FLOWER: Green, 4 in. (10 cm) across with a
white lip
SEASON OF BLOOM: Winter to spring
MATURE SIZE, HABIT: Compact, 12 in.
(30 cm)
CULTURE: Intermediate
LIGHT: Medium
TEMPERATURE: Intermediate
POTTING MEDIUM: Medium mix, well-
draining

Darwinara Charm

PRONUNCIATION: dar-win-ARE-ah
ORIGIN: *Neofinetia falcata × Vascostylis*
Tham Yuen Hae. Registered by Takaki's in
1987.
DESCRIPTION AND QUALITIES: Glowing blue
flowers make this a winner.
FLOWER: Fragrant, 1 in. (2.5 cm) across,
borne on an upright inflorescence. Most in
this grex display various shades of purple-
blue, but some have a wine-purple color.
SEASON OF BLOOM: Spring to summer

A rare species,
*Crepidium
mieczyskawi* has both
an interesting flower
and gorgeous foliage.

The "upside down"
green orchid,
Cycnoches Rocky
Clough, is a curiosity.
Grown by Parkside
Orchid Nursery.

Darwinara Charm 'Blue Star' offers both a desirable blue flower color and fragrance.

Dendrobium aberrans is a cute, uncommon orchid. Grown by J & L Orchids.

MATURE SIZE, HABIT: Dwarf, 6 in. (15 cm) leaf spread. Slow vertical growth.
CULTURE: Easy
LIGHT: Medium
TEMPERATURE: Intermediate
POTTING MEDIUM: Medium mix, well-draining
CULTURAL TIPS: Grow in shallow pots with ample drainage holes or in wooden baskets.

Dendrobium aberrans
PRONUNCIATION: den-DROH-bee-um AB-er-anz
ORIGIN: New Guinea
DESCRIPTION AND QUALITIES: Grows in forest with high humidity and almost constant moisture.
FLOWER: White and a bit more than ¹/₂ in. (1 cm) across
SEASON OF BLOOM: Winter to spring
MATURE SIZE, HABIT: Dwarf, 4–5 in. (10.0–12.5 cm)
CULTURE: Intermediate
LIGHT: Medium
TEMPERATURE: Cool to intermediate
POTTING MEDIUM: Fine, well-draining. Can be grown in pots or mounted.
CULTURAL TIPS: Always keep media damp.

Dendrobium aggregatum
PRONUNCIATION: den-DROH-bee-um ag-ri-GAH-tum
SYNONYM: *Dendrobium lindleyi*
ORIGIN: Indochina, India
DESCRIPTION AND QUALITIES: This long-time favorite is readily available. Flowers are borne in great profusion.
FLOWER: Golden yellow-orange, fragrant, 1¹/₄ in. (3 cm) across, and borne in sprays of 15 or more
SEASON OF BLOOM: Winter to spring
MATURE SIZE, HABIT: Dwarf, 3–4 in. (7.5–10.0 cm)
CULTURE: Intermediate
LIGHT: Medium
TEMPERATURE: Intermediate
POTTING MEDIUM: Frequently grown on slabs of tree fern, but can be grown in pots with excellent drainage
CULTURAL TIPS: A dry, cool period is required during the winter to induce early spring blooming.
HISTORY: The earliest known cultivated specimen of this orchid was located at the Royal Botanic Garden Edinburgh in 1836.

Dendrobium Andrée Millar

PRONUNCIATION: den-DROH-bee-um

ORIGIN: *Dendrobium atroviolaceum* × *Dendrobium convolutum*. Registered by P. Spence in 1987.

DESCRIPTION AND QUALITIES: The height of this hybrid varies greatly. Some will qualify as miniatures while others grow larger. Hand-select plants to get the size you want.

FLOWER: Chartreuse petals and sepals, 2 in. (5 cm) across, with a large, conspicuous green lip veined in burgundy

SEASON OF BLOOM: Winter to spring

MATURE SIZE, HABIT: Compact, but highly variable. Smaller forms 8–10 in. (20–25 cm).

CULTURE: Easy

LIGHT: Medium

TEMPERATURE: Intermediate

POTTING MEDIUM: Fine, well-draining

Dendrobium Bonnie Riley

PRONUNCIATION: den-DROH-bee-um

ORIGIN: *Dendrobium farmeri* × *Dendrobium chrysotoxum*. Registered by R. F. Fuchs in 2003.

DESCRIPTION AND QUALITIES: Another example of two excellent parents with resulting offspring being more vigorous and easier to grow and flower.

FLOWER: 2 in. (6 cm), bright yellow-orange, borne in groups of 15 or more on a pendulous inflorescence

SEASON OF BLOOM: Spring

MATURE SIZE, HABIT: Compact, 12 in. (30 cm)

CULTURE: Intermediate

Dendrobium aggregatum produces a shower of sunny yellow flowers.

Exotic and flamboyant markings are trademarks of *Dendrobium* Andrée Millar.

LIGHT: Medium to high
TEMPERATURE: Cool to intermediate
POTTING MEDIUM: Fine, well-draining

Dendrobium Charming

PRONUNCIATION: den-DROH-bee-um
ORIGIN: *Dendrobium* Jacquelyn Thomas ×
Dendrobium dicuphum. Registered by
Richella in 1981.
DESCRIPTION AND QUALITIES: This hybrid
is not a shy bloomer. A well-grown plant
will be covered with pink blossoms.
FLOWER: 1^1/$_2$ in. (4 cm), soft pink
SEASON OF BLOOM: Winter to spring
MATURE SIZE, HABIT: Compact, 12 in.
(30 cm)
CULTURE: Intermediate
LIGHT: Medium
TEMPERATURE: Intermediate
POTTING MEDIUM: Fine, well-draining

Dendrobium Chinsai

PRONUNCIATION: den-DROH-bee-um
ORIGIN: *Dendrobium moniliforme* × *Dendrobium unicum*. Registered by S. Takagi in
1981.
DESCRIPTION AND QUALITIES: This bright
and cheery hybrid is the result of combining two dwarf species. Most plants in this
grex have yellow or orange flowers, being
strongly influenced by parent *Dendrobium
unicum*. Some, however, are on the pink
side, the coloration frequently found in the
other parent, *Den. moniliforme*. Some
members of this grex have a mild orange
fragrance.
FLOWER: 2 in. (5 cm), light pink, yellow, or
orange, with a single, prominent dark burgundy spot on the lip
SEASON OF BLOOM: Winter to spring
MATURE SIZE, HABIT: Dwarf, 6 in. (15 cm)

Dendrobium Chinsai presents imposing flowers on a dwarf plant.

CULTURE: Intermediate
LIGHT: Medium
TEMPERATURE: Intermediate
POTTING MEDIUM: Fine, well-draining

Dendrobium cruentum

PRONUNCIATION: den-DROH-bee-um kroo-EN-tum
DESCRIPTION AND QUALITIES: This attractive, neat, easy to grow dendrobium has fragrant flowers that last more than a month.
FLOWER: $1^{1}/_{2}$ to $1^{3}/_{4}$ in. (4.0 to 4.5 cm), scented, waxy, creamy white with red markings in the throat, borne singly along the cane
SEASON OF BLOOM: Winter to spring
MATURE SIZE, HABIT: Compact, 10–12 in. (25–30 cm)
CULTURE: Easy
LIGHT: Medium
TEMPERATURE: Intermediate to warm
POTTING MEDIUM: Medium mix, well-draining
CULTURAL TIPS: Keep damp except for several weeks of drier conditions in the winter to induce early spring flowering.

Dendrobium cuthbertsonii

PRONUNCIATION: den-DROH-bee-um kuth-burt-SOH-nee-eye
ORIGIN: New Guinea
DESCRIPTION AND QUALITIES: $1^{1}/_{4}$–2 in. (3–5 cm) wide, various color forms
SEASON OF BLOOM: Fall, winter, spring
MATURE SIZE, HABIT: Miniature, to 3 in. (7.5 cm)
CULTURE: Challenging
LIGHT: Medium
TEMPERATURE: Cool to intermediate
POTTING MEDIUM: Fine, well-draining. Does well in pots of tree fern. Requires excellent air movement, high humidity, and constant moisture.

The creamy white, green-veined flowers of *Dendrobium cruentum* offer a sweet scent.

A sparkling orange form of *Dendrobium cuthbertsonii*

The variable flower colors of *Dendrobium cuthbertsonii* includes a two-toned pink and white form.

Rich pink flower forms are also found in *Dendrobium cuthbertsonii*.

A yellow-flowered form of *Dendrobium cuthbertsonii*

Dendrobium dichaeoides

PRONUNCIATION: den-DROH-bee-um dye-kay-OY-deez
ORIGIN: Northern Papua New Guinea
DESCRIPTION AND QUALITIES: Another form has green leaves with white edges.
FLOWER: $1/4$ in. (6 mm), bright purple-pink, borne in clusters of up to 10 on a short inflorescence
SEASON OF BLOOM: Fall to winter
MATURE SIZE, HABIT: Dwarf, 1–2 in. (2.5–5.0 cm), with tiny $1/2$ in. (1 cm) leaves
CULTURE: Intermediate
LIGHT: Medium

The tubular, down-facing flowers of *Dendrobium dichaeoides* are clustered on pendulous canes.

One of my favorites, *Dendrobium* Iki will bloom more than once a year.

TEMPERATURE: Cool to intermediate
POTTING MEDIUM: Fine, well-draining mix, or mounted
CULTURAL TIPS: Reduce water somewhat and fertilize only lightly during the winter. Does best with high humidity year-round.
HISTORY: Described by Schlechter in 1912.

Dendrobium Iki

PRONUNCIATION: den-DROH-bee-um
ORIGIN: *Dendrobium bellatulum* × *Dendrobium cruentum*. Registered by W. A. Chang in 1985.
DESCRIPTION AND QUALITIES: Easy to grow and bloom. It flowers on new and old canes.
FLOWER: 1 in. (2.5 cm) across, white with red and yellow markings. Sweetly fragrant.
SEASON OF BLOOM: Winter to spring
MATURE SIZE, HABIT: Dwarf, 4 in. (10 cm)
CULTURE: Easy
LIGHT: Medium

TEMPERATURE: Intermediate
POTTING MEDIUM: Fine, well-draining

Dendrobium jenkinsii

PRONUNCIATION: den-DROH-bee-um jen-KINZ-ee-eye
SYNONYM: *Dendrobium aggregatum* var. *jenkinsii*
ORIGIN: India
DESCRIPTION AND QUALITIES: Similar to *Dendrobium aggregatum* but smaller in habit. Develops into a superb specimen plant.
FLOWER: Last seven to ten days, fragrant golden yellow, 1 in. (2.5 cm) across, borne in groups of two or three. The lips are wide and almost heart shaped.
SEASON OF BLOOM: Winter to spring
MATURE SIZE, HABIT: Miniature; pseudobulbs slightly larger than 1 in. (2.5 cm)
CULTURE: Intermediate
LIGHT: Medium to high
TEMPERATURE: Intermediate

Dendrobium jenkinsii is a bright, fragrant, and welcome addition to any orchid collection.

POTTING MEDIUM: Best on a slab of tree fern or cork, but can be grown in pot with well-draining media.

CULTURAL TIPS: Transplant infrequently so as not to disturb roots.

HISTORY: Discovered in 1836 in India by a military man named Jenkins.

Dendrobium kingianum

PRONUNCIATION: den-DROH-bee-um king-ee-AH-num

ORIGIN: Australia

DESCRIPTION AND QUALITIES: One of the easiest of the Australian orchid to grow, it adapts well to a variety of growing situations. Some clones or selections have more fragrant flowers than others. The foliage is attractive and dark green.

FLOWER: Huge color range includes purple, red, white, and striped, averaging 1–1$^{1}/_{2}$ in. (2.5–4.0 cm), and borne on an inflorescence up to 8 in. (20 cm) long; 'Baby Blue'

A red selection of *Dendrobium kingianum* (*Den. kingianum* 'Red Devil' × *Den. kingianum* 'Red Ink')

is 1 in. across, purplish rather than true blue. Fragrance varies by clone or selection and flowers can last two weeks.

SEASON OF BLOOM: Spring

MATURE SIZE, HABIT: Variable growth habit, from less than 6 in. (15 cm) to 20 in. (50 cm); 'Baby Blue' is dwarf, 4 in. (10 cm).

Dendrobium kingianum var. *alba*, like other plants of this species, can grow rapidly into showy clumps.

CULTURE: Easy to intermediate

LIGHT: Medium to high

TEMPERATURE: Cool to intermediate; tolerates temperatures of 35°F (2°C) and lower

POTTING MEDIUM: Mount on a slab or grow in shallow pot in well-draining media

CULTURAL TIPS: Must be kept cool in the fall and winter to set buds. Reduce watering in the winter until buds are showing. During the growing season water and fertilize heavily with a low-nitrogen fertilizer.

HISTORY: Discovered in mountainous areas of Australia in 1844.

Dendrobium kingianum var. alba

PRONUNCIATION: den-DROH-bee-um king-ee-AH-num var. AL-bah

FLOWER: 1 in. (2.5 cm) across, white and fragrant

SEASON OF BLOOM: Winter to spring

MATURE SIZE, HABIT: Dwarf, 4 in. (10 cm)

CULTURE: Intermediate

LIGHT: Medium

TEMPERATURE: Intermediate

POTTING MEDIUM: Mount on slab or grow in shallow pot in well-draining media

Flowers of *Dendrobium kingianum* 'Baby Blue' are purplish in color, but the species is found in a broad range of flower colors and sizes.

Dendrobium laevifolium

PRONUNCIATION: den-DROH-bee-um lay-vi-FOH-lee-um
SYNONYM: *Dendrobium occulatum*
ORIGIN: Island off New Guinea
DESCRIPTION AND QUALITIES: A lot of flower power is packed in this small plant. Electric cerise flowers that are long-lasting (to a month) make it a standout despite its diminutive size.
FLOWER: To four, $1^1/_2$ in. (4 cm), cerise with contrasting orange columns, borne on a short inflorescence
SEASON OF BLOOM: Winter to spring
MATURE SIZE, HABIT: Miniature, 3 in. (7.5 cm)
CULTURE: Intermediate
LIGHT: Medium
TEMPERATURE: Cool to intermediate
POTTING MEDIUM: Small textured, well-draining. Frequently mounted on tree fern.
CULTURAL TIPS: Performs best when kept

Dendrobium laevifolium is a colorful miniature. Grown by Parkside Orchid Nursery.

constantly damp, cool, and in high humidity.

Dendrobium masarangense

PRONUNCIATION: den-DROH-bee-um mass-ah-ran-GEN-see
SYNONYM: *Dendrobium pumilio*
ORIGIN: New Guinea to Fiji Islands
DESCRIPTION AND QUALITIES: *Dendrobium*

Creamy flowers cloak a well-grown specimen of *Dendrobium masarangense.*

Dendrobium Nalene Bui displays large flowers on a small plant.

LIGHT: Medium
TEMPERATURE: Intermediate
POTTING MEDIUM: Usually mounted
CULTURAL TIPS: Must be kept damp and in high humidity.
RELATED SPECIES, HYBRIDS: This species is part of a section of dendrobiums called *Oxyglossum,* most of which are miniature to dwarf species with large, attractive flowers on small plants. *Dendrobium violaceum* is in this section.

masarangense subsp. *theionanthum* has larger yellow flowers but similar growth habit and cultural requirements.
FLOWER: Fragrant, light creamy white, $^1/_2$ in. (1 cm)
SEASON OF BLOOM: Winter to spring
MATURE SIZE, HABIT: Miniature, $1^1/_2$ in.(4 cm), with narrow, tubular leaves
CULTURE: Challenging

Dendrobium Nalene Bui
PRONUNCIATION: den-DROH-bee-um
ORIGIN: *Dendrobium* Ise × *Dendrobium* Princess. Registered by J. K. Lau of H & R Nurseries in 2004.
DESCRIPTION AND QUALITIES: A floriferous, tiny orchid

FLOWER: $1^{1}/_{4}$ in. (3 cm) across, mauve-pink with a white lip
SEASON OF BLOOM: Winter to spring
MATURE SIZE, HABIT: Dwarf, 5 in. (12.5 cm)
CULTURE: Easy
LIGHT: Medium
TEMPERATURE: Intermediate
POTTING MEDIUM: Fine, well-draining

Dendrobium petiolatum

PRONUNCIATION: den-DROH-bee-um pet-ee-oh-LAH-tum
ORIGIN: New Guinea
DESCRIPTION AND QUALITIES: A brilliantly colored, eye-catching orchid. Semi-deciduous.
FLOWER: Clusters of $^{3}/_{4}$ in. (2 cm), bright purple, somewhat cupped with contrasting orange lips, on a short inflorescence
SEASON OF BLOOM: Spring to summer
MATURE SIZE, HABIT: Dwarf, 5–6 in. (10–15 cm)
CULTURE: Intermediate
LIGHT: Medium to high
TEMPERATURE: Cool to intermediate
POTTING MEDIUM: Fine, well-draining
CULTURAL TIPS: Reduce water and fertilizer during the winter when plant naturally slows its growth. Return to normal watering schedule in the spring when new growth starts.

Dendrobium rhodostictum

PRONUNCIATION: den-DROH-bee-um roh-doh-STICK-tum
SYNONYM: *Dendrobium madonnae*
ORIGIN: Papua New Guinea
DESCRIPTION AND QUALITIES: The

Dendrobium petiolatum packs a pot with color.

Dendrobium rhodostictum flowers resemble a bird in flight or a nun's hat. Grown by J & L Orchids.

flower of this orchid reminds me of the hat worn by Sally Field in the 1960s television show "The Flying Nun."
FLOWER: Fragrant, white, sometimes with pink-edged lips, last at least a month and are borne in groups of two to six on a short inflorescence, spreading $2^{1}/_{2}$–$3^{1}/_{2}$ in. (6–9 cm)
SEASON OF BLOOM: Winter to spring
MATURE SIZE, HABIT: Compact, 10 in. (25 cm)
CULTURE: Intermediate
LIGHT: Medium
TEMPERATURE: Intermediate
POTTING MEDIUM: Well-draining in pots. Frequently mounted.
CULTURAL TIPS: Should always be kept damp.

The uniquely shaped and marked flowers of *Dendrobium unicum* distinguish this species.

Dendrobium violaceum subsp. *violaceum*, the upright form, is quite variable in its flower color from pink to shades of purple and blue. Grown by J & L Orchids.

Dendrobium unicum

PRONUNCIATION: den-DROH-bee-um YOU-ni-kum
ORIGIN: Thailand, Laos, Vietnam
DESCRIPTION AND QUALITIES: This tiny orchid with strangely beautiful, brightly colored flowers is easy to grow and flower as long as the plant is given a dry period for one to two months during the winter.
FLOWER: Tangerine-scented, 2 in. (5 cm), reflexed, orange-red with a cream-colored, tubular lip veined in orange-red
SEASON OF BLOOM: Winter to spring

MATURE SIZE, HABIT: Dwarf, to 3^1/$_2$ in. (9 cm)
CULTURE: Easy
LIGHT: Medium
TEMPERATURE: Intermediate
POTTING MEDIUM: Fine, well-draining mix in pots, or mounted on slabs
CULTURAL TIPS: Allow to dry out gradually from winter to early spring.

Dendrobium violaceum

PRONUNCIATION: den-DROH-bee-um vye-oh-LAY-see-um
SYNONYM: *Dendrobium tenuicalcar*
ORIGIN: New Guinea
DESCRIPTION AND QUALITIES: A variable with at least two subspecies: the upright form, *Dendrobium violaceum* subsp. *violaceum*, and a more pendulous growth form, *Den. violaceum* subsp. *cyperifolium*
FLOWER: 1^1/$_2$ in. (4 cm), violet-pink, in tight clusters
SEASON OF BLOOM: Winter to spring

MATURE SIZE, HABIT: Dwarf, to 6 in.
(15 cm)
CULTURE: Intermediate
LIGHT: Medium
TEMPERATURE: Cool to intermediate
POTTING MEDIUM: Fine, well-draining mix
in pots, or mounted on slabs
CULTURAL TIPS: Should always be kept
damp.

Dendrochilum cootesii

PRONUNCIATION: den-droh-KYE-lum
KOOTS-ee-eye
ORIGIN: Philippines
DESCRIPTION AND QUALITIES: The fleshy
pendulous flowers of this species make it
unique to the genus.
FLOWER: Buff to pink, almost 1 in. (2.5 cm)
wide and tall, borne on pendulous spikes
SEASON OF BLOOM: Spring to summer
MATURE SIZE, HABIT: Dwarf, to 5 in.
(12.5 cm)
CULTURE: Intermediate
LIGHT: Medium
TEMPERATURE: Intermediate
POTTING MEDIUM: Fine, well-draining
HISTORY: First named by Henrik Pederson
in 1997.

Dendrochilum filiforme

PRONUNCIATION: den-droh-KYE-lum fill-i-
FORM-ee
ORIGIN: Philippines
DESCRIPTION AND QUALITIES: Brighter and
more floriferous than most others in the
genus.
FLOWER: Nearly round, ¹/₄ in. (6 mm) in
diameter, bright green-yellow
SEASON OF BLOOM: Spring
MATURE SIZE, HABIT: Dwarf, to 6 in.
(15 cm)
CULTURE: Intermediate
LIGHT: Medium
TEMPERATURE: Intermediate
POTTING MEDIUM: Fine, well-draining

Fleshy flowers of *Dendrobium cootesii* are borne on graceful, arching inflorescences.

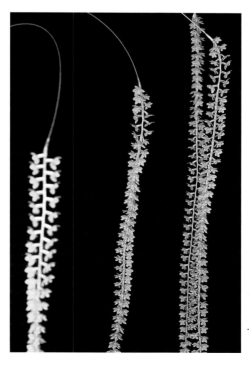

The plentitude of *Dendrochilum filiforme* flowers makes up for their diminutive size.

Dark red is the most desirable color form of *Dendrochilum wenzelii.*

Dipteranthus duchii is frequently mounted on tree fern or cork.

Dendrochilum wenzelii

PRONUNCIATION: den-droh-KYE-lum wen-ZELL-ee-eye
ORIGIN: Philippines
DESCRIPTION AND QUALITIES: One of the most commonly found species in this genus makes a handsome specimen plant.
FLOWER: Up to 30, ¼ in. (6 mm), on a semi-arching inflorescence. Color variable from shades of red to orange or green.
SEASON OF BLOOM: Spring to summer
MATURE SIZE, HABIT: Compact, to 10 in. (25 cm)
CULTURE: Intermediate
LIGHT: Medium
TEMPERATURE: Intermediate
POTTING MEDIUM: Fine, well-draining

Dipteranthus duchii

PRONUNCIATION: dip-ter-AN-thus DOOK-ee-eye
ORIGIN: Brazil

DESCRIPTION AND QUALITIES: This delicate species is closely related to *Ornithocephalus*.
FLOWER: $1/8$ in. (4 mm), on 3 in. (7.5 cm) inflorescence
SEASON OF BLOOM: Winter to spring
MATURE SIZE, HABIT: Miniature, $2^1/2$ in. (6 cm), 2 in. (5 cm) leaves
CULTURE: Intermediate
LIGHT: Medium
TEMPERATURE: Intermediate to warm
POTTING MEDIUM: Best mounted
CULTURAL TIPS: Needs high humidity with good air circulation

Doritaenopsis Musick Lipstick

PRONUNCIATION: dor-rye-tye-NOP-siss
ORIGIN: *Phalaenopsis* Kuntrarti Rarashati × *Doritaenopsis* Abed-nego. Registered by F & M Kaufmann in 2004.
DESCRIPTION AND QUALITIES: Modern breeding produced this colorful, smaller flowering, compact doritaenopsis.
FLOWER: $1^1/2$ in. (4 cm), rose-red, round
SEASON OF BLOOM: Winter to spring
MATURE SIZE, HABIT: Compact, leaves spread 10 in. (25 cm). Slow vertical grower.
CULTURE: Easy
LIGHT: Low to medium
TEMPERATURE: Warm
POTTING MEDIUM: Fine to medium, well-draining mix, or sphagnum moss

Doritaenopsis Musick Surprise

PRONUNCIATION: dor-rye-tye-NOP-siss
ORIGIN: *Doritis pulcherrima* × *Phalaenopsis chibae*. Registered by F & M Kaufmann in 2003.
DESCRIPTION AND QUALITIES: This charming plant owes its size to *Phalaenopsis chibae* and its colorful flowers to *Doritis pulcherrima*.
FLOWER: $1/2$ in. (1 cm) across, usually reflexed, red-purple, borne on an erect, 10 in. (25 cm) spike
SEASON OF BLOOM: Spring to summer

MATURE SIZE, HABIT: Dwarf, leaves spread to 8 in. (20 cm). Slow vertical grower.
CULTURE: Easy
LIGHT: Low to medium
TEMPERATURE: Warm
POTTING MEDIUM: Fine to medium, well-draining mix, or sphagnum moss

Doritaenopsis Purple Gem

PRONUNCIATION: dor-rye-tye-NOP-siss
ORIGIN: *Doritis pulcherrima* × *Phalaenopsis*

The small red flowers of *Doritaenopsis* Musick Lipstick are a delight.

Doritaenopsis Musick Surprise displays many small flowers on an upright inflorescence.

Doritaenopsis Purple Gem is an easy-to-grow hybrid that makes a perfect windowsill plant.

Doritis pulcherrima var. *alba* shows the typical flower shape found in this species, but flowers are white instead of purple.

equestris. Registered by E. Iwanaga in 1963.

DESCRIPTION AND QUALITIES: A popular and commonly offered hybrid because of its easy culture and flowering.

FLOWER: 1 in. (2.5 cm) across, usually light to dark purple but a white form is known. Better forms do not have much reflexing of petals.

SEASON OF BLOOM: Spring to summer

MATURE SIZE, HABIT: Dwarf, leaves spread 6 in. (15 cm). Slow vertical grower.

CULTURE: Easy

LIGHT: Low to medium

TEMPERATURE: Warm

POTTING MEDIUM: Fine to medium, well-draining mix, or sphagnum moss

Doritis pulcherrima var. *alba*

PRONUNCIATION: dor-RYE-tiss pull-KAIR-i-mah var. AL-bah

ORIGIN: Southeast Asia

DESCRIPTION AND QUALITIES: The species is usually purple rather than white and is frequently crossed with *Phalaenopsis* species and hybrids to add its bright color, upright inflorescence, and dwarf growing habit to its offspring.

FLOWER: 1 in. (2.5 cm), clear white, on 12 in. (30 cm) inflorescence

SEASON OF BLOOM: Spring to summer

MATURE SIZE, HABIT: Dwarf, 6–8 in. (15–20 cm) leaf spread

CULTURE: Easy

LIGHT: Medium

TEMPERATURE: Intermediate to warm

POTTING MEDIUM: Medium epiphytic mix

CULTURAL TIPS: Grow in similar conditions as phalaenopsis, but does not require as much warmth and prefers slightly more light.

Doritis pulcherrima var. *champornensis*

PRONUNCIATION: dor-RYE-tiss pull-KAIR-i-mah var. cham-por-NEN-siss

ORIGIN: Southeast Asia

DESCRIPTION AND QUALITIES: This orchid resembles a small phalaenopsis, to which it is closely related. All forms usually carry their color and upright flower spikes to their offspring when they are hybridized with phalaenopsis.

FLOWER: 1 in. (2.5 cm), usually in shades of pink to dark purple, sometimes white, on an upright inflorescence of 12 in. (30 cm) or more

SEASON OF BLOOM: Spring to summer

MATURE SIZE, HABIT: Dwarf; leaves spread to 6 in. (15 cm).

CULTURE: Easy

LIGHT: Low to medium

TEMPERATURE: Intermediate to warm

POTTING MEDIUM: Fine to medium epiphytic mix

CULTURAL TIPS: Likes growing conditions similar to phalaenopsis, but with slightly more light and dryness between waterings.

HISTORY: Originally collected in Vietnam. First described by John Lindley in 1833.

Dracula sodiroi subsp. *erythrocodon*

PRONUNCIATION: DRACK-you-lah soh-DEER-oh-eye subsp. air-rith-roh-KOH-don

Both petals of *Doritis pulcherrima* var. *champornensis* have the same coloration and shape as the lip of the orchid. This type of flower is called *peloric*. Some consider such flowers freaks, while others consider them delightful mutations.

Dracularis sodiroi subsp. *erythrocodon* is a popular species with bell-shaped flowers.

ORIGIN: Ecuador

DESCRIPTION AND QUALITIES: This successive bloomer comes from wet forests.

FLOWER: 1 in. (2.5 cm), orange, bell-shaped, downfacing

A dramatic orchid, *Dracula venefica* has striking markings.

SEASON OF BLOOM: Variable
MATURE SIZE, HABIT: Dwarf, 6 in. (15 cm)
CULTURE: Intermediate
LIGHT: Medium
TEMPERATURE: Cool to intermediate
POTTING MEDIUM: Fine, well-draining
CULTURAL TIPS: Keep in high humidity—60 percent or more.
HISTORY: Named after the person first recorded as having collected this orchid, Father Alois Sodiro.

Dracula venefica

PRONUNCIATION: DRACK-you-lah veh-NIF-i-kah
ORIGIN: Colombia, Ecuador
DESCRIPTION AND QUALITIES: This species displays "typical" dracula features—furry, triangular flowers with prominent markings, articulating lips, and long tails.
FLOWER: Approximately 5 in. (12.5 cm) from tip to tip
SEASON OF BLOOM: Variable
MATURE SIZE, HABIT: Dwarf, 6 in. (15 cm)
CULTURE: Intermediate
LIGHT: Medium
TEMPERATURE: Cool to intermediate
POTTING MEDIUM: Well-draining mix and container
HISTORY: Discovered in Colombia in 1981.

Dracuvallia Blue Boy

PRONUNCIATION: drack-you-VALL-ee-ah
ORIGIN: *Masdevallia uniflora* × *Dracula chimaera*. Registered by Pui Y. Chin in 1991.
DESCRIPTION AND QUALITIES: Most growers report that this orchid is more vigorous and easier to grow than either of its parents.
FLOWER: Sparkling cerise, approximately 4 in. (10 cm) from tip to tip
SEASON OF BLOOM: Spring to summer
MATURE SIZE, HABIT: Dwarf, 6 in. (15 cm)
CULTURE: Intermediate
LIGHT: Medium

Dracuvallia 'Blue Boy' Cow Hollow AM/AOS is a brilliantly colored hybrid. Grown by J & L Orchids.

TEMPERATURE: Cool to intermediate
POTTING MEDIUM: Fine, well-
draining

Dryadella lilliputana

PRONUNCIATION: dry-ah-DELL-ah
lill-i-pew-TAH-nah
SYNONYM: *Masdevallia lilliputana*
ORIGIN: Brazil
DESCRIPTION AND QUALITIES: This
miniscule orchid was once known
as a masdevallia, to which it is related. One of the smallest of all orchids in this group, it is also one of
the most difficult to grow. The flowers of this species are best viewed
with magnifying glass. Leaves grow
in tight clusters.
FLOWER: Creamy yellow with a
spotted lip, $1/4$ in. (6 mm) wide and
less than $1/2$ in. (1 cm) long
SEASON OF BLOOM: Winter to
spring
MATURE SIZE, HABIT: Miniature,
leaves are $1/2$ in. (1 cm) long
CULTURE: Challenging
LIGHT: Medium
TEMPERATURE: Cool to intermediate
POTTING MEDIUM: Fine, well-
draining
CULTURAL TIPS: Usually grown in
small clay pots. Always keep cool
and damp with high humidity and
ample ventilation.
HISTORY: Discovered by Gustavo
Edwall in 1906 in São Paulo, Brazil.

Dyakia hendersoniana

PRONUNCIATION: dye-ah-KEE-ah
hen-der-soh-nee-AH-nah
SYNONYM: *Ascocentrum hendersoniana*
ORIGIN: Borneo
DESCRIPTION AND QUALITIES: This
member of the vandaceous group is

Dryadella lilliputana
species name hints at
its miniature stature.

The perky, brilliantly
colored flowers of
Dyakia hendersoniana
put on a show.
Grown by Parkside
Orchid Nursery.

small but mighty. The dependable bloomer produces many brightly colored flowers for up to two
months. It will flower in a 2 in. (5 cm) pot.
FLOWER: Mildly fragrant, 1 in. (2.5 cm), in clusters
of up to 30. Color varies from salmon pink to magenta with a white spur.

SEASON OF BLOOM: Spring to summer
MATURE SIZE, HABIT: Miniature, rarely
reaches 4 in. (10 cm)
CULTURE: Easy
LIGHT: Medium
TEMPERATURE: Intermediate to warm
POTTING MEDIUM: Fine or medium mix,
well-draining

The flower of *Encyclia
citrina* resembles an
upside-down tulip.

Encyclia polybulbon
is an easy to grow,
hardy, fragrant
orchid. Grown by
J & L Orchids.

CULTURAL TIPS: Can be grown in pots or
baskets.
RELATED SPECIES, HYBRIDS: Related to all
Ascocentrum species

Encyclia citrina
PRONUNCIATION: en-SICK-lee-ah si-TRY-
nah
SYNONYMS: *Euchile citrina, Cattleya citrina*
ORIGIN: Mexico
DESCRIPTION AND QUALITIES: This species
is found in dry oak or pine forests and is
related to *Encyclia mariae*, another small
orchid. Considered difficult to grow and
bloom.
FLOWER: One to two lemon-scented, 3–3^1/$_2$
in. (7.5–9.0 cm), pendant, waxy, bright yel-
low with orange in the center of the lips
SEASON OF BLOOM: Variable
MATURE SIZE, HABIT: Dwarf, 1^1/$_2$–2^1/$_2$ in.
(4–6 cm) pseudobulbs with narrow, 7–10
in. (18–25 cm), gray-green leaves
CULTURE: Challenging
LIGHT: Medium
TEMPERATURE: Cool to intermediate
POTTING MEDIUM: Usually mounted
CULTURAL TIPS: Keep this plant cool and
dry during the winter to encourage
flowering.
HISTORY: First discovered in Mexico in the
17th century.

Encyclia polybulbon
PRONUNCIATION: en-SICK-lee-ah pol-ee-
BULB-on
SYNONYM: *Dinema polybulbon*
ORIGIN: Central America
DESCRIPTION AND QUALITIES: This rambling species will form mats. Mature plants
in good conditions will almost always be in
flower. This hardy orchid can tolerate a
temperature drop to freezing.
FLOWER: Fragrant, 1 in. (2.5 cm) across,
orange brown marked with burgundy. Lips
are creamy white.

SEASON OF BLOOM: Spring to summer
MATURE SIZE, HABIT: Miniature, low-growing, creeping, reaches $2^1/_2$ in. (6 cm)
CULTURE: Easy
LIGHT: Medium to high
TEMPERATURE: Cool to intermediate
POTTING MEDIUM: Usually mounted on cork or tree fern
HISTORY: Introduced into cultivation in England in 1841.

Epidendrum porpax

PRONUNCIATION: eh-pih-DEN-drum PORE-packs
SYNONYMS: *Neolehmannia porpax, Epidendrum peperomia*
ORIGIN: Mexico to Peru
DESCRIPTION AND QUALITIES: Miniature clumping species is easy to grow.
FLOWER: Waxy, 1 in. (2.5 cm) across, shades of green with a brown lip. Solid green also known.
SEASON OF BLOOM: Spring to summer
MATURE SIZE, HABIT: Miniature, 2 in. (5 cm), low growing, mat forming
CULTURE: Intermediate
LIGHT: Medium
TEMPERATURE: Intermediate
POTTING MEDIUM: Usually mounted on cork or tree fern

Epidendrum Yoko

PRONUNCIATION: eh-pih-DEN-drum
ORIGIN: Unknown parentage. Unregistered.
DESCRIPTION AND QUALITIES: This cute import was brought to the United States from Japan. The flowers are said to last two months. Unlike most epidendrums, this one is small and fits in the windowsill or under lights.
FLOWER: 2 in. (5 cm), bright magenta, clustered on 4 in. (10 cm) spike
SEASON OF BLOOM: Spring to summer
MATURE SIZE, HABIT: Dwarf, 6 in. (15 cm)

The waxy flowers of *Epidendrum porpax* keep for weeks. Grown by Parkside Orchid Nursery.

Epidendrum Yoko 'Yokohama' is an exceptional hybrid because of its size and long-lasting flowers. Grown by J & L Orchids.

A typical *Eria* flower displays colorful markings.

Haraella odorata is a miniature with a lot of character and a sweet fragrance.

Eria extinctoria, Eria maingayi, Eria microchilos, Eria muscicola, Eria pannea, Eria reptans, and *Eria reticosa*. This genus is closely related to *Dendrobium*.

FLOWER: To 1 in. (2.5 cm), usually smaller
SEASON OF BLOOM: Spring to summer
MATURE SIZE, HABIT: Dwarf, 3–4 in. (7.5–10.0 cm)
CULTURE: Intermediate
LIGHT: Medium
TEMPERATURE: Intermediate
POTTING MEDIUM: Fine, well-draining

Haraella odorata

PRONUNCIATION: hah-rah-ELL-ah oh-dor-AH-tah
ORIGIN: Taiwan
DESCRIPTION AND QUALITIES: This miniature gem will flower almost constantly if it is treated well. Leaves are dark green.
FLOWER: Pale green, $1/2$ in. (1 cm) across, usually borne singly on a $1/4$ in. (6 mm) inflorescence. Sweet citrus fragrance.
SEASON OF BLOOM: Summer to fall
MATURE SIZE, HABIT: Miniature, leaves to to 2 in. (5 cm)
CULTURE: Intermediate
LIGHT: Medium
TEMPERATURE: Intermediate
POTTING MEDIUM: Fine textured in well-draining small clay pots
CULTURAL TIPS: Frequently grown mounted on tree fern. Appreciates high humidity.
HISTORY: Described by Kyushu Kudos in Formosa (Taiwan) in 1930.

Hawkinsara Kat Golden Eye

PRONUNCIATION: hawk-inz-ARE-ah
ORIGIN: *Cattleytonia* Jamaica Red × *Sophrolaeliocattleya* Mahalo Jack. Registered by Kendolie Agri-Tech Company in 2003.
DESCRIPTION AND QUALITIES: A floriferous hybrid.
FLOWER: Purple-red with yellow throats, $2^1/2$ in. (6 cm) across, usually borne in clus-

CULTURE: Easy
LIGHT: Medium to high
TEMPERATURE: Intermediate
POTTING MEDIUM: Fine, well-draining

Eria

PRONUNCIATION: EAR-ee-ah
ORIGIN: Malaysia
DESCRIPTION AND QUALITIES: Although many *Eria* species are large, the genus includes some small to miniature species, such as *Eria clavata, Eria cylindrostachya, Eria dalzellii, Eria dasyphylla, Eria exilis,*

ters. The grex is also found in other colors, including red.

SEASON OF BLOOM: Variable
MATURE SIZE, HABIT: Dwarf, 5 in. (12.5 cm)
CULTURE: Easy
LIGHT: Medium
TEMPERATURE: Intermediate
POTTING MEDIUM: Medium mix, well-draining

Hawkinsara Koolau Sunset

PRONUNCIATION: hawk-inz-ARE-ah
ORIGIN: *Sophrolaeliocattleya* Mae Hawkins × *Cattleytonia* Keith Roth. Registered by W. A. Chang in 1984.
DESCRIPTION AND QUALITIES: This hybrid inherited a double dose of red from both parents. Its wide lip comes from *Cattleytonia* Keith Roth.
FLOWER: 3 in. (7.5 cm) across, usually borne in a small cluster
SEASON OF BLOOM: Winter to spring
MATURE SIZE, HABIT: Compact, 8–10 in. (20–25 cm)
CULTURE: Easy
LIGHT: Medium
TEMPERATURE: Intermediate
POTTING MEDIUM: Medium mix, well-draining

Hawkinsara Sogo Doll

PRONUNCIATION: hawk-inz-ARE-ah
ORIGIN: *Laeliocatonia* Peggy San × *Sophrolaeliocattelya* Katsy Noda. Registered by Sogo in 1994.
DESCRIPTION AND QUALITIES: The color in the lip is replicated in the petals, referred to as *splash petals*. A striking flower.
FLOWER: 3 in. (7.5 cm) across
SEASON OF BLOOM: Winter to spring

Hawkinsara Kat Golden Eye has a splash of yellow in the throat of its purple-red flowers.

Flowers of *Hawkinsara* Koolau Sunset 'Hawaii' AM/AOS are a rich and velvety red.

Hawkinsara Sogo Doll 'Little Angel' HCC/AOS has a complex parentage with a show-stopping flower.

MATURE SIZE, HABIT: Compact, 8–10 in. (20–25 cm)
CULTURE: Easy
LIGHT: Medium
TEMPERATURE: Intermediate
POTTING MEDIUM: Medium mix, well-draining

Holcoglossum kimballianum resembles a miniature vanda.

Holcoglossum kimballianum

PRONUNCIATION: hole-koh-GLOSS-um kim-bal-ee-AH-num

ORIGIN: Burma, Thailand, China

DESCRIPTION AND QUALITIES: This orchid is related to vandas. Although it is not difficult to grow, it can be slow to flower, sometimes taking up to six months after the flower spike emerges.

FLOWER: 2 in. (5 cm), creamy white petals and purple-pink lips, borne 15 or more per inflorescence on a mature plant

SEASON OF BLOOM: Spring

MATURE SIZE, HABIT: Dwarf, with slow vertical growth. Six or more 6 in. (15 cm) tall, semi-terete leaves.

CULTURE: Easy

LIGHT: Medium to high

TEMPERATURE: Cool to intermediate

POTTING MEDIUM: Medium mix, well-draining. Frequently mounted on cork or tree fern.

CULTURAL TIPS: Likes a short period of dryness during the winter.

HISTORY: Discovered by Boxall in Burma and first described in 1899.

RELATED SPECIES, HYBRIDS: Also desirable are *Holcoglossum amesianum* and *Hlcgl. quasipinifolium*, both with cultural requirements similar to *Hlcgl. kimballianum*.

Howeara Lava Burst

PRONUNCIATION: how-ee-ARE-ah

ORIGIN: *Howeara* Mini-Primi × *Rodriguezia lanceolata*. Registered by Puanani in 1993.

DESCRIPTION AND QUALITIES: One of the easiest, most rewarding dwarf orchids to grow. For little effort, it rewards you with a spray of brilliantly colored, long-lasting flowers. A highly recommended beginner's orchid. Parent *Howeara* Mini-Primi has long been popular because of its ease of culture.

FLOWER: 1 in. (2.5 cm) wide and high, fiery red with bright orange-yellow markings on the lip, borne on frequently branched, 12 in. (30 cm) inflorescence
SEASON OF BLOOM: Spring to summer
MATURE SIZE, HABIT: Dwarf, 8 in. (20 cm)
CULTURE: Easy
LIGHT: Medium
TEMPERATURE: Intermediate
POTTING MEDIUM: Fine-textured epiphytic mix

Ionopsis paniculata
PRONUNCIATION: eye-oh-NOP-siss pah-nick-you-LAH-tah
ORIGIN: South America
DESCRIPTION AND QUALITIES: This orchid, commonly found in the South American tropics, can grow into an impressive specimen.
FLOWER: $^{1}/_{2}$ in. (1 cm), 6 in. (15 cm) inflorescence
SEASON OF BLOOM: Spring to summer
MATURE SIZE, HABIT: Dwarf, 4–5 in. (10.0–12.5 cm)
CULTURE: Intermediate
LIGHT: Medium
TEMPERATURE: Intermediate to warm
POTTING MEDIUM: Usually mounted
CULTURAL TIPS: Keep damp and in high humidity.
RELATED SPECIES, HYBRIDS: *Ionopsis satyrioides, Inps. utriculoides*

Isabelia virginalis
PRONUNCIATION: iz-ah-BELL-ee-ah ver-jin-AL-iss
ORIGIN: Brazil
DESCRIPTION AND QUALITIES: This easy to grow miniature has a low, creeping habit.
FLOWER: Creamy, with white and rose column, less than $^{1}/_{2}$ in. (1 cm) in diameter, borne singly
SEASON OF BLOOM: Spring to summer
MATURE SIZE, HABIT: Miniature, 3 in. (7.5 cm)

The fire in the flower is apparent in *Howeara* Lava Burst 'Puanani' AM/AOS.

From a distance, flowers of *Ionopsis paniculata* resemble large snowflakes.

Isabelia virginalis grows into attractive mats of flowers and brown fibers.

Elegant sprays of sweet-smelling, long-lasting pink flowers are the main features of the complex hybrid *Iwanagaara* Appleblossom 'Fangtastic'.

CULTURE: Intermediate
LIGHT: Medium
TEMPERATURE: Intermediate
POTTING MEDIUM: Fine mix in a shallow pot or mount on cork or tree fern
HISTORY: Described by Barbosa Rodrigues in the late 19th century.
RELATED SPECIES, HYBRIDS: *Isabelia pulchella*

Iwanagaara Appleblossom

PRONUNCIATION: eye-wan-ah-GAR-ah
ORIGIN: *Dialaelia* Snowflake × *Brassolaelio-cattleya* Orange Nugget. Registered by Rod McLellan Company in 1992.
DESCRIPTION AND QUALITIES: A grex with a great deal of flower color variation in the offspring. This genus has parents from four different genera—*Brassavola*, *Cattleya*, *Diacrium*, and *Laelia*.
FLOWER: Fragrant, 3¹/₂ in. (9 cm), light pink with darker pink flares and gold in throats, on tall, elegant sprays

SEASON OF BLOOM: Spring
MATURE SIZE, HABIT: Compact, to 18 in.
(46 cm)
CULTURE: Intermediate
LIGHT: Medium to high
TEMPERATURE: Intermediate
POTTING MEDIUM: Medium cattleya mix
HISTORY: The Hawaiian Iwanaga family
created these hybrids and gave the genus
its name.
RELATED SPECIES, HYBRIDS: Other superior
clones of this grex include the yellow-
orange flowered *Iwanagaara* Appleblossom
'Golden Elf'.

Kefersteinia laminata

PRONUNCIATION: kef-er-STY-nee-ah
SYNONYM: *Zygopetalum forcipatum*
ORIGIN: Colombia, Ecuador
DESCRIPTION AND QUALITIES: Many of the
30 or so species within this genus are
small growers.
FLOWER: 1 in. (2.5 cm), greenish white,
with speckles of dark red, and dark bur-
gundy–marked lip, borne below the leaves
SEASON OF BLOOM: Winter to spring
MATURE SIZE, HABIT: Compact, 12 in.
(30 cm)
CULTURE: Intermediate
LIGHT: Medium
TEMPERATURE: Intermediate
POTTING MEDIUM: Fine, well-draining
RELATED SPECIES, HYBRIDS: *Kefersteinia
graminea, Kefst. lojae, Kefst. sanguinolenta,
Kefst. tolimensis*

Laelia dayana

PRONUNCIATION: LAY-lee-ah day-AH-nah
SYNONYM: *Laelia pumila* var. *dayana*
ORIGIN: Brazil
DESCRIPTION AND QUALITIES: This species
is not often collected. It frequently has
drooping petals and reflexing flower parts.
FLOWER: Colors variable, from rosy pink to
mauve, 2 in. (5 cm) across. Lip is purple,

Kefersteinia laminata is an uncommon *Zygopetalum* relative.

The parallel dark red veining in the lip of *Laelia dayana* is striking.

with a white throat with prominent red
veins.
SEASON OF BLOOM: Spring to summer
MATURE SIZE, HABIT: Dwarf, 6 in. (15 cm)
CULTURE: Intermediate
LIGHT: Medium
TEMPERATURE: Intermediate
POTTING MEDIUM: Usually mounted, but

The bright yellow pixie flowers of *Laelia esalqueana* sparkle in strong light.

can be grown in pots in medium textured, well-draining mix

CULTURAL TIPS: A dry winter rest helps trigger early spring flowering.

HISTORY: Discovered in 1876 by Boxall in Brazil.

RELATED SPECIES, HYBRIDS: *Laelia pumila, L. praestans*

Laelia esalqueana

PRONUNCIATION: LAY-lee-ah ess-al-kay-AH-nah

ORIGIN: Brazil

DESCRIPTION AND QUALITIES: This baby-sized laelia has been used as a parent to breed mini-catts. Its leaves are thick and succulent.

FLOWER: Bright orange-yellow, 1^1/4 in. (3 cm) across

SEASON OF BLOOM: Spring to summer

MATURE SIZE, HABIT: Miniature, to 3 in. (7.5 cm)

CULTURE: Intermediate

LIGHT: Medium to high

TEMPERATURE: Cool to intermediate

POTTING MEDIUM: Fine, well-draining. Use of clay pot insures that the medium dries adequately between waterings.

CULTURAL TIPS: Should have dry winter rest to trigger spring blooming. During this period, plant can be misted to prevent pseudobulbs from shriveling.

HISTORY: First described by Almiro Blumenschein in 1960. It was thought extinct until it was later rediscovered by Jack Fowlie.

Laelia perrinii

PRONUNCIATION: LAY-lee-ah per-IN-ee-eye

SYNONYMS: *Cattleya perrinii, Cattleya intermedia* var. *angustifolia*

ORIGIN: Central Brazil

DESCRIPTION AND QUALITIES: An uncommonly grown species. A white form of this species is rare.

FLOWER: Lavender, with light, spicy scent, 6 in. (15 cm), with trumpet-shaped lips, edged with deep violet and white in the throat. Several color forms include a white (*Laelia perrinii* var. *alba*) and a blue (*L. perrinii* var. *coerulea*).

SEASON OF BLOOM: Fall

MATURE SIZE, HABIT: Compact, to 10 in. (25 cm)

CULTURE: Easy

LIGHT: Medium to high

TEMPERATURE: Intermediate

POTTING MEDIUM: Medium grade epiphytic mix

CULTURAL TIPS: Naturally grows in areas with warm, wet summers and cooler, drier winters

HISTORY: Described by James Bateman in 1847, who named it after a gardener named Perrin.

Laelia pumila var. coerulea

PRONUNCIATION: LAY-lee-ah PEW-mi-lah var. seh-ROO-lee-ah

SYNONYMS: *Cattleya pumila, Bletia pumila*

ORIGIN: Brazil

DESCRIPTION AND QUALITIES: Popular in its own right, the species is frequently used in breeding programs to provide offspring with a dwarf habit.

FLOWER: Short inflorescence, with one or two mildly scented flowers of 3–4 in. (8–10 cm) across. As large as the entire plant, the petals and sepals are purple to lavender with a darker lip, though various color forms exist.

SEASON OF BLOOM: Variable

MATURE SIZE, HABIT: Dwarf, to 8 in. (20 cm)

CULTURE: Intermediate

LIGHT: Medium to high

TEMPERATURE: Intermediate

POTTING MEDIUM: Medium grade, fast-draining epiphytic mix in pots, or mounted

CULTURAL TIPS: Grow on the dry side during the winter.

HISTORY: Originally described by William Hooker in 1839.

Laelia sincorana

PRONUNCIATION: LAY-lee-ah sink-or-AH-han

SYNONYM: *Cattleya grosvenori*

ORIGIN: Brazil

DESCRIPTION AND QUALITIES: *Laelia sincorana* became more commonly available in the United States in the 1980s. When large and well established, it produces multiple stunning flowers. This species is used as a parent in mini-catt breeding to impart its small stature and fragrance to its offspring.

FLOWER: Fragrant, purple-red, to 4 in. (10 cm) across, large for the size of the plant

SEASON OF BLOOM: Winter to spring

The flower of *Laelia perrinii* is unusually large for the size of the plant.

A fine blue flower graces *Laelia pumila* var. *coerulea*.

Laelia sincorana provides rich red-purple flowers on dwarf plants.

MATURE SIZE, HABIT: Dwarf, 4–5 in. (10.0–12.5 cm), with short, squat, almost globular pseudobulbs

CULTURE: Intermediate

The influence of *Broughtonia* (crossed with *Laelia* to produce *Laeliocatonia*) is seen in the large lip of *Laeliocatonia* Sacramento Splash 'orchidPhile' AM/AOS.

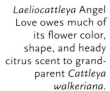

Laeliocattleya Angel Love owes much of its flower color, shape, and heady citrus scent to grandparent *Cattleya walkeriana*.

LIGHT: Medium to high
TEMPERATURE: Intermediate
POTTING MEDIUM: Frequently mounted since its roots prefer to dry out between waterings
HISTORY: First discovered by Schlechter in 1917, it was later thought extinct until rediscovered by Jack Fowlie in 1975.
RELATED SPECIES, HYBRIDS: *Laelia pumila*

Laeliocatonia Sacramento Splash

PRONUNCIATION: lay-lee-oh-kah-TOE-nee-ah
ORIGIN: *Cattleya* Little Dipper × *Laeliocatonia* Peggy San. Registered by Gold Country in 2001.
DESCRIPTION AND QUALITIES: Dramatic splash petals make this a flamboyant hybrid.

FLOWER: 2 in. (5 cm) across, borne in clusters
SEASON OF BLOOM: Winter to spring
MATURE SIZE, HABIT: Dwarf, 8 in. (20 cm)
CULTURE: Easy
LIGHT: Medium
TEMPERATURE: Intermediate
POTTING MEDIUM: Medium grade epiphytic mix

Laeliocattleya Angel Love

PRONUNCIATION: lay-lee-oh-KAT-lee-ah
ORIGIN: *Laeliocattleya* Puppy Love × *Cattleya* Angelwalker. Bred by Orchid Center and registered by Kokusai in 1988.
DESCRIPTION AND QUALITIES: Long-lasting flowers on a neat plant. It inherits its small habit from grandparent *Cattleya walkeriana*.
FLOWER: 4 in. (10 cm), citrus-scented, pink, with a frilled lip and golden to yellow throat
SEASON OF BLOOM: Variable
MATURE SIZE, HABIT: Dwarf
CULTURE: Intermediate
LIGHT: Medium
TEMPERATURE: Intermediate
POTTING MEDIUM: Medium grade epiphytic mix

Laeliocattleya Angel's Treasure

PRONUNCIATION: lay-lee-oh-KAT-lee-ah
ORIGIN: *Cattleya* Tropical Angel × *Laeliocattleya* Tiny Treasure. Registered by J. Woltman in 1991.
DESCRIPTION AND QUALITIES: Flower clusters on a small plant are hallmarks of this hybrid.
FLOWER: 3 in. (7.5 cm), lavender-pink with yellow throats
SEASON OF BLOOM: Winter to spring
MATURE SIZE, HABIT: Compact
CULTURE: Easy
LIGHT: Medium
TEMPERATURE: Intermediate

Laeliocattleya Angel's Treasure is known for its soft and airy flowers.

POTTING MEDIUM: Medium grade epiphytic mix

Laeliocattleya Carolyn Reid

PRONUNCIATION: lay-lee-oh-KAT-lee-ah
ORIGIN: *Cattleya aurantiaca* × *Laeliocattleya* Twinkle Star. Registered by G. Crocker for Reid in 1972.
DESCRIPTION AND QUALITIES: Glowing red flowers are always in demand. As a bonus, this variety is fragrant, an uncommon quality in red cattleya hybrids. It is also more heat tolerant than most red cattleya hybrids, because it does not have the cool-loving species *Sophronitis coccinea*, the most commonly used species to impart red flower color, as one of its parents.
FLOWER: Fragrant, 3 in. (7.5 cm), orange-red, in clusters
SEASON OF BLOOM: Winter to spring
MATURE SIZE, HABIT: Dwarf, 8 in. (20 cm)
CULTURE: Intermediate

Laeliocattleya Carolyn Reid 'Lynchburg' has shimmering red flowers.

LIGHT: Medium
TEMPERATURE: Intermediate
POTTING MEDIUM: Medium grade epiphytic mix

The blazing orange-red flowers of *Laeliocattleya* Fire Dance 'Patricia' appear in winter to spring.

Laeliocattleya Green Veil 'Dressy' has elegant green flowers.

Laeliocattleya Fire Dance

PRONUNCIATION: lay-lee-oh-KAT-lee-ah
ORIGIN: *Cattleya aurantiaca* × *Laeliocattleya* Fire Island. Registered by Beal in 1984.
DESCRIPTION AND QUALITIES: Adding much appreciated color in the winter, this rapidly growing plant matures into a spectacular and fragrant specimen.
FLOWER: Fragrant clusters, 3 in. (7.5 cm) across, red-orange with darker lips
SEASON OF BLOOM: Winter to spring
MATURE SIZE, HABIT: Compact, 10–12 in. (25–30 cm)
CULTURE: Easy
LIGHT: Medium
TEMPERATURE: Intermediate
POTTING MEDIUM: Medium grade epiphytic orchid mix

Laeliocattleya Green Veil

PRONUNCIATION: lay-lee-oh-KAT-lee-ah
ORIGIN: *Laeliocattleya* Cuiseag × *Cattleya* Landate. Registered by Dogashima in 1991.
DESCRIPTION AND QUALITIES: As green as any orchid flower gets.
FLOWER: 2^{1}/$_{2}$ in. (6 cm), fragrant, lime-green, with white and purple lips
SEASON OF BLOOM: Winter to spring
MATURE SIZE, HABIT: Compact, 12 in. (30 cm)
CULTURE: Easy
LIGHT: Medium
TEMPERATURE: Intermediate
POTTING MEDIUM: Medium grade epiphytic orchid mix

Laeliocattleya Hsinying Excell

PRONUNCIATION: lay-lee-oh-KAT-lee-ah
ORIGIN: *Laeliocattleya* Excellescombe × *Laelia briegeri*. Registered by Ching Hua in 2000.
DESCRIPTION AND QUALITIES: This pixie plant with gorgeously marked flowers performs perfectly in a bright windowsill. Frequently will flower twice a year. Stiff, upright leaves.
FLOWER: Clusters of two to four, 3 in. (7.5 cm), soft pink with darker pink flares and a dark red lip with yellow throat
SEASON OF BLOOM: Winter to spring
MATURE SIZE, HABIT: Dwarf, 6–7 in. (15–18 cm)
CULTURE: Easy
LIGHT: Medium to high
TEMPERATURE: Intermediate
POTTING MEDIUM: Medium grade epiphytic orchid mix

Laeliocattleya Irene's Song

PRONUNCIATION: lay-lee-oh-KAT-lee-ah

ORIGIN: *Laeliocattleya* Mari's Song × *Laelio-cattleya* Irene Finney. Registered by Norman's Orchids in 1999.

DESCRIPTION AND QUALITIES: This gorgeous, splash-petalled cattleya hybrid is both sweetly scented and gloriously colored.

FLOWER: Fragrant, 3½ in. (9 cm) wide, lavender, with splashes of white on the petals and bright yellow lips marked with red

SEASON OF BLOOM: Variable

MATURE SIZE, HABIT: Compact, 8–10 in. (20–25 cm)

CULTURE: Easy

LIGHT: Medium

TEMPERATURE: Intermediate

POTTING MEDIUM: Medium mix

Laeliocattleya Love Knot var. *coerulea*

PRONUNCIATION: lay-lee-oh-KAT-lee-ah Love Knot var. seh-ROO-lee-ah

ORIGIN: *Laelia sincorana* × *Cattleya walkeriana*. Registered by J. Miura in 1984.

DESCRIPTION AND QUALITIES: The flower of this hybrid is as large as the entire plant. It inherits a delightful fragrance from *Cattleya walkeriana*.

FLOWER: Various colors, most common is lavender-pink, 3 in. (7.5 cm) across with white lips edged in darker purple-pink

SEASON OF BLOOM: Winter to spring

MATURE SIZE, HABIT: Dwarf, 4 in. (10 cm)

CULTURE: Easy

LIGHT: Medium

TEMPERATURE: Intermediate

POTTING MEDIUM: Medium grade epiphytic orchid mix

Laeliocattleya Mari's Song

PRONUNCIATION: lay-lee-oh-KAT-lee-ah

ORIGIN: *Laeliocattleya* Irene Finney × *Cattleya* Cherry Chip. Bred by K. Takagi and registered by Suwada Orchids in 1992.

DESCRIPTION AND QUALITIES: This com-

Laeliocattleya Hsinying Excell is a petite beauty.

Laeliocattleya Irene's Song 'Montclair' HCC/AOS is a star offspring of the popular *Lc.* Mari's Song.

Laeliocattleya Love Knot var. *coerulea* blooms in a 3 in. (7.5 cm) pot.

Laeliocattleya Mari's Song is a favorite among small orchid growers because of its compact habit and colorful show.

Laeliocattleya Mini Purple 'Princess Road' is a popular hybrid.

TEMPERATURE: Intermediate
POTTING MEDIUM: Cattleya mix

Laeliocattleya Mini Purple

PRONUNCIATION: lay-lee-oh-KAT-lee-ah

ORIGIN: *Cattleya walkeriana* × *Laelia pumila*. Registered by M. Yamada in 1965.

DESCRIPTION AND QUALITIES: This dependable and frequent bloomer is one of the more fragrant mini-catts.

FLOWER: Fragrant, 3 in. (7.5 cm). This grex can vary widely in its color forms from white to yellow to shades of pink to dark purple; some flowers are even bicolored.

SEASON OF BLOOM: Variable

MATURE SIZE, HABIT: Dwarf, 5 in. (12.5 cm)

CULTURE: Easy

LIGHT: Medium

pact, splash-petalled orchid is popular, with several colorful and fragrant varieties available.

FLOWER: Fragrant, 3¹/₂ in. (9 cm), white with bright magenta flares and lip, pink sepals, and yellow throat

SEASON OF BLOOM: Variable

MATURE SIZE, HABIT: Compact

CULTURE: Easy

LIGHT: Medium to high

An older hybrid, *Laeliocattleya* Rojo is frequently found in contemporary collections.

TEMPERATURE: Intermediate
POTTING MEDIUM: Medium orchid bark or coco chip mixes

Laeliocattleya Rojo

PRONUNCIATION: lay-lee-oh-KAT-lee-ah
ORIGIN: *Cattleya aurantiaca* × *Laelia milleri*. Registered by Rod McLellan Company in 1965.
DESCRIPTION AND QUALITIES: One of the first, bright red, small, multiple-flowering hybrids, it is still used frequently as a parent for next generation hybrids.
FLOWER: 2^1/$_2$ in. (6 cm), orange-red, borne in clusters
SEASON OF BLOOM: Winter to spring
MATURE SIZE, HABIT: Compact, 12 in. (30 cm)
CULTURE: Easy
LIGHT: Medium
TEMPERATURE: Intermediate

A rich lavender flower with a delightful scent makes *Laeliocattleya* Tsiku Hibiscus a choice orchid.

POTTING MEDIUM: Medium orchid bark or coco chip mixes

Laeliocattleya Tsiku Hibiscus

PRONUNCIATION: lay-lee-oh-KAT-lee-ah
ORIGIN: *Laeliocattleya* Mini Purple × *Laeliocattleya* Aloha Case. Registered by Tsiku Taiwan Orchids in 2000.
DESCRIPTION AND QUALITIES: This orchid shows a

strong influence from the species *Cattleya walkeriana*, with its flower shape, color, and fragrance.

FLOWER: Fragrant, 3 in. (7.5 cm), deep lavender-pink with darker lips

SEASON OF BLOOM: Winter to spring

MATURE SIZE, HABIT: Dwarf, 6–8 in. (15–20 cm)

CULTURE: Easy

LIGHT: Medium

TEMPERATURE: Intermediate

POTTING MEDIUM: Medium orchid bark or coco chip mixes

Lepanthes maduroi

PRONUNCIATION: leh-PAN-theez mah-DUR-oh-eye

Lepanthes maduroi is rarely seen.

Lepanthes ribes 'Wow' is a dark colored miniature.

ORIGIN: Panama

DESCRIPTION AND QUALITIES: Like most of the species in this genus, you need a magnifying glass to appreciate the delicate beauty of these flowers.

FLOWER: $^1/_2$ in. (1 cm), bronze colored, rounded

SEASON OF BLOOM: Spring to summer

MATURE SIZE, HABIT: Miniature, $2^1/_2$ in. (6 cm)

CULTURE: Challenging

LIGHT: Medium

TEMPERATURE: Cool to intermediate

POTTING MEDIUM: Usually mounted, or in small pots with fine, well-draining media

CULTURAL TIPS: Keep evenly moist with high humidity.

Lepanthes ribes

PRONUNCIATION: leh-PAN-theez RYE-beez

ORIGIN: Colombia

DESCRIPTION AND QUALITIES: Named for its resemblance to the red gooseberry (*Ribes* spp.), this beautiful species has a reputation for being temperamental. Try some of the other *Lepanthes* first.

FLOWER: $^1/_2$ in. (1 cm), red-striped, pouch or bucket-shaped, produced from the middle of the leaf

SEASON OF BLOOM: Variable

MATURE SIZE, HABIT: Miniature, 3 in. (7.5 cm)

CULTURE: Challenging

LIGHT: Medium

TEMPERATURE: Cool to intermediate

POTTING MEDIUM: Usually grown mounted, or in small pots with fine, well-draining media

CULTURAL TIPS: Keep evenly moist with high humidity.

Leptotes bicolor

PRONUNCIATION: lep-TOH-teez BY-kull-ur

SYNONYM: *Bletia bicolor, Leptotes glaucophylla*

ORIGIN: Brazil

DESCRIPTION AND QUALITIES: Only two species in this genus are commonly grown; this is the larger flowering of the two.

FLOWER: Vanilla scented, 2 in. (5 cm), bright white with purple-pink lips

SEASON OF BLOOM: Winter to spring

MATURE SIZE, HABIT: Miniature, 3 in. (7.5 cm)

CULTURE: Intermediate

LIGHT: Medium

TEMPERATURE: Intermediate

POTTING MEDIUM: Usually grown mounted, or in small pots with fine, well-draining media

CULTURAL TIPS: Water generously when in active growth.

HISTORY: Discovered by William Harrison in Rio de Janeiro and described in 1833 by John Lindley.

Leptotes unicolor

PRONUNCIATION: lep-TOH-teez YOU-ni-kull-ur

ORIGIN: Brazil

DESCRIPTION AND QUALITIES: *Leptotes unicolor* is half the size of *Lpt. bicolor* in both plant and flower.

FLOWER: Fragrant, 1–2 in. (2.5–5.0 cm), pink to almost white

SEASON OF BLOOM: Winter to spring

Leptotes bicolor presents a small but colorful flower.

Leptotes unicolor is the smallest in this genus.

Lycaste aromatica has sunny yellow flowers before new leaves emerge in the spring.

MATURE SIZE, HABIT: Miniature, 1^1/$_2$ in. (4 cm)
CULTURE: Intermediate
LIGHT: Medium
TEMPERATURE: Intermediate to warm
POTTING MEDIUM: Usually grown mounted, or in small pots with fine, well-draining media
CULTURAL TIPS: Water generously when in active growth.

Lycaste aromatica

PRONUNCIATION: lye-KASS-tee a-roh-MAT-i-kah
SYNONYMS: *Colax armaticus, Lycaste suaveolens*
ORIGIN: Mexico
DESCRIPTION AND QUALITIES: An easily grown and popular lycaste because of its bright flowers and strong cinnamon fragrance.
FLOWER: Fragrant, golden yellow, 2^1/$_2$ in. (6 cm), borne in groups of 30 or more at the base of the pseudobulbs

SEASON OF BLOOM: Winter to spring
MATURE SIZE, HABIT: Compact, leaves 12 in. (30 cm)
CULTURE: Easy
LIGHT: Medium
TEMPERATURE: Intermediate
POTTING MEDIUM: Medium grade orchid bark or coco chunks
HISTORY: First collected by Lord Napier in Mexico and sent to the Royal Botanical Garden Edinburgh, where it flowered in 1826.

Lycaste campbellii

PRONUNCIATION: lye-KASS-tee kam-BELL-ee-eye
ORIGIN: Panama, Colombia
DESCRIPTION AND QUALITIES: A compact, uncommon lycaste with fragrant flowers that open before new growth starts in the spring.
FLOWER: 1 in. (2.5 cm), light yellow, borne on short scapes of 3–4 in. (7.5–10.0 cm)
SEASON OF BLOOM: Winter to spring

Lycaste campbellii has butter-yellow, fragrant flowers.

MATURE SIZE, HABIT: Compact, leaves to 12 in. (30 cm) tall
CULTURE: Intermediate
LIGHT: Medium
TEMPERATURE: Intermediate to warm
POTTING MEDIUM: Medium grade orchid bark or coco chunks

Macodes petola

PRONUNCIATION: mah-KOH-deez PET-oh-lah
SYNONYM: *Neottia petola*
ORIGIN: Philippines
DESCRIPTION AND QUALITIES: Most orchids are not noted for the beauty of their foliage, but this one is a clear exception. The veins in its leaves glitter like gold. The flowers are not of much interest compared to its glorious foliage.
FLOWER: 8 in. (20 cm) inflorescence, covered with small brownish, insignificant flowers

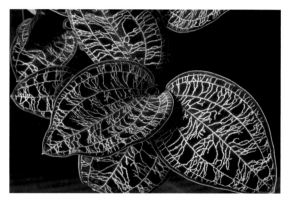

The leaf veins of *Macodes petola* sparkle in bright light.

SEASON OF BLOOM: Spring to summer
MATURE SIZE, HABIT: Dwarf, 6 in. (15 cm), leaves 4 in. (10 cm) long
CULTURE: Intermediate
LIGHT: Low
TEMPERATURE: Warm
POTTING MEDIUM: Sphagnum moss
CULTURAL TIPS: Always keep damp and in high humidity.
HISTORY: Originally described as *Neottia petola* by C. L. Blume in 1825.

A fine specimen plant, *Masdevallia* Angel Frost shows off its colorful blooms.

Masdevallia caloptera flowers resemble birds taking off in flight.

FLOWER: 2 in. (5 cm), tangerine-orange, with a frosted look; can have white or maroon hairs. Color varies.
SEASON OF BLOOM: Variable
MATURE SIZE, HABIT: Dwarf, 6 in. (15 cm)
CULTURE: Intermediate
LIGHT: Low to medium
TEMPERATURE: Cool to intermediate
POTTING MEDIUM: Fine, well-draining
CULTURAL TIPS: If you are new to growing masdevallias, try a hybrid like this one first. They are easier to grow and are more temperature tolerant than most of the species.

Masdevallia Angel Frost

PRONUNCIATION: maz-deh-VALL-ee-ah
ORIGIN: *Masdevallia veitchiana* × *Masdevallia strobelii*. Registered by J & L Orchids in 1982.
DESCRIPTION AND QUALITIES: A classic masdevallia hybrid. The many varieties offered vary in color.

Masdevallia caloptera

PRONUNCIATION: maz-deh-VALL-ee-ah kal-OP-tur-ah
ORIGIN: Ecuador
DESCRIPTION AND QUALITIES: Strik-

Masdevallia calosiphon 'J & L' grows into a handsome plant. Grown by J & L Orchids.

ing in bloom, the species name means beautiful wings, which is appropriate. Dark green leaves are tipped with purple.

FLOWER: White, cupped, $^3/_4$ in. (2 cm), striped in burgundy, with bright yellow tails. Borne in groups of six or more on a 6 in. (15 cm) inflorescence.

SEASON OF BLOOM: Spring to summer

MATURE SIZE, HABIT: Dwarf, 5 in. (12.5 cm)

CULTURE: Intermediate

LIGHT: Low to medium

TEMPERATURE: Cool to intermediate

POTTING MEDIUM: Fine, well-draining

HISTORY: Described in 1874.

RELATED SPECIES, HYBRIDS: For a complete treatment of this fascinating group, consult the excellent book *Masdevallias: Gems of the Orchid World* by Mary E. Gerritsen and Ron Parsons.

Masdevallia calosiphon

PRONUNCIATION: maz-deh-VALL-ee-ah kal-oh-SYE-fun

ORIGIN: Ecuador

DESCRIPTION AND QUALITIES: This species makes an especially handsome plant when grown to specimen size.

FLOWER: Butter-yellow, 1 in. (2.5 cm)

SEASON OF BLOOM: Winter to spring

MATURE SIZE, HABIT: Miniature, 3 in. (7.5 cm)

CULTURE: Intermediate

LIGHT: Low to medium

TEMPERATURE: Cool

POTTING MEDIUM: Fine, well-draining

Masdevallia coccinea

PRONUNCIATION: maz-deh-VALL-ee-ah kok-SIN-ee-ah

ORIGIN: Colombia, Panama

DESCRIPTION AND QUALITIES: One of the taller and more spectacular masdevallias comes in various color forms, including red, white, and yellow, but is usually a brilliant lilac-purple. Considered one of the easier masdevallias to grow and flower.

The brilliant flower of *Masdevallia coccinea* makes this plant a standout.

The excellent *Masdevallia* Copper Angel 'Orange Sherbet' HCC/AOS. Grown by J & L Orchids.

A well grown plant will yield larger and better colored flowers on longer stems.
FLOWER: Usually lavender-purple, 3 in. (7.5 cm) across, borne singly on an inflorescence to 18 in. (46 cm) tall
SEASON OF BLOOM: Spring to summer
MATURE SIZE, HABIT: Compact, 7–10 in. (18–25 cm)
CULTURE: Intermediate
LIGHT: Low to medium
TEMPERATURE: Cool
POTTING MEDIUM: Fine, well-draining
HISTORY: Discovered in 1842 by Jean Linden in the Colombian Andes.

Masdevallia Copper Angel

PRONUNCIATION: maz-deh-VALL-ee-ah
ORIGIN: *Masdevallia triangularis* × *Masdevallia veitchiana*. Registered by J & L Orchids in 1982.
DESCRIPTION AND QUALITIES: A vigorous, profuse-blooming hybrid, whose varieties have won many awards. Considered one of the best masdevallia hybrids.
FLOWER: Flowers in this grex can vary from golden yellow to orange red, 3 in. (7.5 cm) or more long, and 2 in. (5 cm) wide, borne singly on erect stems.
SEASON OF BLOOM: Winter to spring
MATURE SIZE, HABIT: Dwarf, 4–5 in. (10.0–12.5 cm)
CULTURE: Intermediate
LIGHT: Low to medium
TEMPERATURE: Cool to intermediate
POTTING MEDIUM: Fine, well-draining
RELATED SPECIES, HYBRIDS: Copper Angel has spawned many hybrids, including Copper Cherub.

Masdevallia decumana

PRONUNCIATION: maz-deh-VALL-ee-ah deck-you-MAH-nah
ORIGIN: Peru
DESCRIPTION AND QUALITIES: The flowers of this masdevallia are huge compared to

Masdevallia decumana has big, showy flowers. Grown by J & L Orchids.

the petite plant, with an almost iridescent quality. This species can flower more than once per year.

FLOWER: 2 in. (5 cm), speckled, borne singly on a short inflorescence

SEASON OF BLOOM: Spring to summer

MATURE SIZE, HABIT: Dwarf, 3–4 in. (7.5–10.0 cm)

CULTURE: Intermediate

LIGHT: Low to medium

TEMPERATURE: Cool to intermediate

POTTING MEDIUM: Fine, well-draining

CULTURAL TIPS: Keep constantly moist.

HISTORY: First collected by Konigers in 1979 in northeast Peru.

Masdevallia Elven Magic

PRONUNCIATION: maz-deh-VALL-ee-ah

ORIGIN: *Masdevallia davisii* × *Masdevallia infracta*. Bred by Mark Pendleton and registered by Orchid Zone in 1992.

DESCRIPTION AND QUALITIES: Brightly colored and vigorous growing hybrid masdevallia.

This *Masdevallia* Elven Magic flower has a small mealy bug in its lower throat.

FLOWER: Clear, orange-red, 2$^1/_2$ in. (6 cm) high and wide, borne singly on erect stems
SEASON OF BLOOM: Winter to spring
MATURE SIZE, HABIT: Dwarf, 4–5 in. (10.0–12.5 cm)
CULTURE: Intermediate
LIGHT: Low to medium
TEMPERATURE: Cool to intermediate
POTTING MEDIUM: Fine, well-draining

The flower of *Masdevallia erinacea* looks otherworldly.

Look closely to see the bumpy "glands" on the flowers of *Masdevallia glandulosa*.

Masdevallia erinacea
PRONUNCIATION: maz-deh-VALL-ee-ah air-i-NAY-see-ah
SYNONYM: *Masdevallia horrida*
ORIGIN: Costa Rica, Panama
DESCRIPTION AND QUALITIES: Latin epithet means hedgehog, a fitting name for its spiny little flower with lots of character.
FLOWER: $^1/_2$ in. (1 cm), prickly, dark red, globular, and topped in yellow. Sepals have bright yellow tails.
SEASON OF BLOOM: Summer
MATURE SIZE, HABIT: Miniature, 1$^3/_4$ in. (4.5 cm) tall leaves grow in tufts
CULTURE: Intermediate
LIGHT: Low to medium
TEMPERATURE: Intermediate to warm
POTTING MEDIUM: Fine, well-draining

Masdevallia glandulosa
PRONUNCIATION: maz-deh-VALL-ee-ah gland-you-LOH-sah
ORIGIN: Peru, Ecuador
DESCRIPTION AND QUALITIES: This charming species had the added feature of a delicate clove fragrance, an unusual quality for masdevallias.
FLOWER: $^3/_4$ in. (2 cm), bell-shaped, purple-pink, with a gold throat striped with red veins. Multiple inflorescences per growth. The interior of the flower has hairs, while the outer flower has small gladular bumps.
SEASON OF BLOOM: Winter
MATURE SIZE, HABIT: Dwarf, 5 in. (12.5 cm)
CULTURE: Intermediate
LIGHT: Low to medium
TEMPERATURE: Intermediate
POTTING MEDIUM: Fine, well-draining
CULTURAL TIPS: During damp conditions, remove the spent blossoms to prevent

them from molding. This is good advice for all masdevallias that are grown in damp environments.

HISTORY: This species was first collected in 1978 in Peru.

Masdevallia Golden Monarch

PRONUNCIATION: maz-deh-VALL-ee-ah

ORIGIN: *Masdevallia* Golden Angel × *Masdevallia* Monarch. Registered by Golden Gate Orchids in 2000.

DESCRIPTION AND QUALITIES: The blazing yellow flowers are impossible to ignore.

FLOWER: Large, clear yellow, flat, to 3 in. (7.5 cm) or more long and 2 in. (5 cm) wide, borne singly on erect stems

SEASON OF BLOOM: Winter to spring

MATURE SIZE, HABIT: Dwarf, 4–5 in. (10.0–12.5 cm)

CULTURE: Intermediate

LIGHT: Low to medium

TEMPERATURE: Cool to intermediate

POTTING MEDIUM: Fine, well-draining

Masdevallia ignea

PRONUNCIATION: maz-deh-VALL-ee-ah IG-nee-ah

ORIGIN: Colombia

DESCRIPTION AND QUALITIES: This orchid's name was derived from the Latin word *igneus*, meaning fire-red—clearly an appropriate name. *Masdevallia ignea* 'Naranja' has particularly striking stripes.

FLOWER: 2 in. (5 cm), borne singly on 12 in. (30 cm) inflorescence

SEASON OF BLOOM: Spring to summer

MATURE SIZE, HABIT: Dwarf, 6 in. (15 cm)

CULTURE: Challenging

LIGHT: Low to medium

TEMPERATURE: Cool

POTTING MEDIUM: Fine, well-draining mix in pots or mounted on slabs

CULTURAL TIPS: Must be kept constantly moist, cool, and in high humidity.

Masdevallia mendozae

PRONUNCIATION: maz-deh-VALL-ee-ah men-DOH-zay

ORIGIN: Ecuador

DESCRIPTION AND QUALITIES: This showy

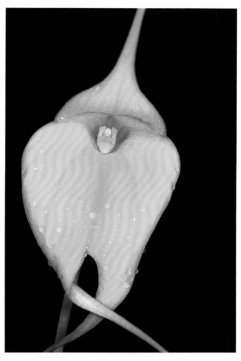

Masdevallia Golden Monarch flowers are outstanding. Grown by J & L Orchids.

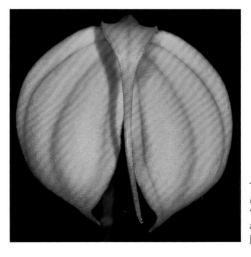

The flower of *Masdevallia ignea* 'Naranja' resembles a lava flow. Grown by J & L Orchids.

and heavily flowering species is supposedly pollinated by moths or hummingbirds.

FLOWER: Yellow to orange, tubular, glossy, 1 in. (2.5 cm) long, with short tails

SEASON OF BLOOM: Spring to summer

MATURE SIZE, HABIT: Dwarf, 4–5 in. (10.0–12.5 cm)

CULTURE: Intermediate

LIGHT: Low to medium

TEMPERATURE: Cool to intermediate

POTTING MEDIUM: Fine, well-draining mix in pots or mounted on slabs

The tubular *Masdevallia mendozae* flower is pollinated by moths or hummingbirds.

Masdevallia Pat Akehurst is a must-have hybrid for masdevallia lovers.

HISTORY: Discovered by Hartman E. Mendoza in 1979 in the Ecuadorean Andes.

Masdevallia Pat Akehurst

PRONUNCIATION: maz-deh-VALL-ee-ah

ORIGIN: *Masdevallia* Heathii × *Masdevallia yungasensis*. Registered by Paradise of New Zealand in 1999.

DESCRIPTION AND QUALITIES: A prized hybrid and granddaughter of *Masdevallia ignea*, Pat Akehurst flower colors shimmer. A dependable bloomer.

FLOWER: 3 in. (7.5 cm) wide and tall, orange with orange tails, and dark red, definitive stripes, borne singly on erect stems

SEASON OF BLOOM: Winter to spring

MATURE SIZE, HABIT: Dwarf, 4–5 in. (10.0–12.5 cm)

CULTURE: Intermediate

LIGHT: Low to medium

TEMPERATURE: Cool to intermediate

POTTING MEDIUM: Fine, well-draining

Masdevallia patula

PRONUNCIATION: maz-deh-VALL-ee-ah PAT-you-lah

ORIGIN: Ecuador

DESCRIPTION AND QUALITIES: An uncommon, large flowered, and striking masdevallia.

FLOWER: Long, 4–5 in. (10.0–12.5 cm), yellow and orange, with dark burgundy-red stripes

SEASON OF BLOOM: Winter to spring

MATURE SIZE, HABIT: Dwarf, 4–5 in. (10.0–12.5 cm)

CULTURE: Intermediate

LIGHT: Low to medium

TEMPERATURE: Cool to intermediate

POTTING MEDIUM: Fine, well-draining mix in pots or mounted on slabs

Masdevallia peristeria

PRONUNCIATION: maz-deh-VALL-ee-ah pair-i-STAIR-ee-ah

ORIGIN: Colombia, Ecuador

DESCRIPTION AND QUALITIES: Flowers are long-lasting.

FLOWER: 4 in. (10 cm) tip to tip, red to orange, stiff and waxy

SEASON OF BLOOM: Spring to summer

MATURE SIZE, HABIT: Dwarf, 4–5 in. (10.0–12.5 cm)

CULTURE: Intermediate

LIGHT: Low to medium

TEMPERATURE: Cool

POTTING MEDIUM: Fine, well-draining mix in pots or mounted on slabs

CULTURAL TIPS: This masdevallia is best kept cool and damp.

HISTORY: First collected by Gustav Wallis in 1873 in Colombia.

Masdevallia pinocchio

PRONUNCIATION: maz-deh-VALL-ee-ah pin-OH-kee-oh

ORIGIN: Ecuador

DESCRIPTION AND QUALITIES: The tall dorsal sepal resembles Pinocchio's nose.

FLOWER: 2 in. (5 cm) tall on 6 in. (15 cm) inflorescence

SEASON OF BLOOM: Spring to summer

Masdevallia patula has a large flower for the size of the plant. Grown by J & L Orchids.

The orange flowers of *Masdevallia peristeria* are long-lasting. Grown by Parkside Nursery.

Masdevallia pinocchio 'Lucinda' is a fine selection of this species. Grown by J & L Orchids.

MATURE SIZE, HABIT: Dwarf, 6 in. (15 cm)
CULTURE: Intermediate
LIGHT: Low to medium
TEMPERATURE: Cool to intermediate
POTTING MEDIUM: Fine, well-draining mix
in pots or mounted on slabs
HISTORY: Originally collected by Father
Angel Andreetta and Alexander Hirtz.

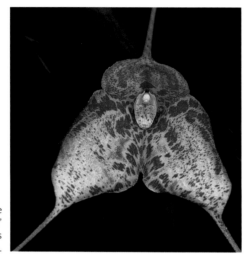

Masdevallia Pixie Leopard flowers' colorful spots are unique.

Masdevallia Pixie Leopard

PRONUNCIATION: maz-deh-VALL-ee-ah
ORIGIN: *Masdevallia* Chaparana × *Masdevallia decumana*. Registered by Mark Pendleton of Orchid Zone in 1997.
DESCRIPTION AND QUALITIES: The wildly marked flower of this hybrid makes it unique.
FLOWER: 3 in. (7.5) wide and tall, with orange tails and prominent and irregular maroon spots, borne singly on erect stems
SEASON OF BLOOM: Winter to spring
MATURE SIZE, HABIT: Dwarf, 4–5 in. (10.0–12.5 cm)
CULTURE: Easy
LIGHT: Low to medium
TEMPERATURE: Cool to intermediate
POTTING MEDIUM: Fine, well-draining

Masdevallia polysticta

PRONUNCIATION: maz-deh-VALL-ee-ah poll-ee-STICK-tah
SYNONYM: *Masdevallia pozoi*
ORIGIN: Ecuador
DESCRIPTION AND QUALITIES: Flowers are

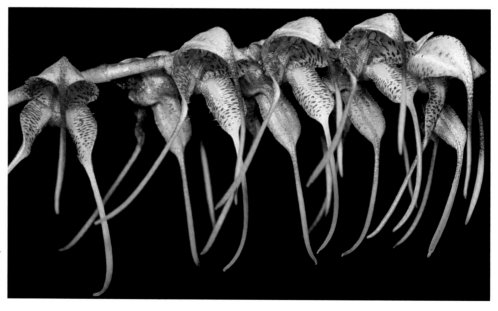

An inflorescence of *Masdevallia polysticta* makes a dramatic statement.

small but plentiful and beautifully marked.

FLOWER: To 15 per inflorescence, $^1/_2$ in. (1 cm) across and $1^1/_2$ in. (4 cm) long, speckled in burgundy, with bright yellow tails

SEASON OF BLOOM: Spring to summer

MATURE SIZE, HABIT: Dwarf, 5 in. (12.5 cm)

CULTURE: Intermediate

LIGHT: Low to medium

TEMPERATURE: Cool to intermediate

POTTING MEDIUM: Fine, well-draining. Does well in sphagnum moss.

CULTURAL TIPS: Always keep damp.

HISTORY: First collected by Benedikt Roezl from northern Peru and described in 1874 by Heinrich Gustav Reichenbach.

Masdevallia tridens

PRONUNCIATION: maz-deh-VALL-ee-ah TRY-denz

ORIGIN: Ecuador

DESCRIPTION AND QUALITIES: When in full bloom, this plant resembles a bunch of small sunbursts.

FLOWER: To 12 per 10 in. (25 cm) inflorescence, $1^1/_2$ in. (4 cm) wide, creamy yellow, with small maroon spots, red lips, and long yellow tails

SEASON OF BLOOM: Winter to spring

MATURE SIZE, HABIT: Dwarf, 8 in. (20 cm)

CULTURE: Intermediate

LIGHT: Low to medium

TEMPERATURE: Cool to intermediate

POTTING MEDIUM: Fine, well-draining. Does well in sphagnum moss.

HISTORY: First collected in 1868 by G. Jameson in Peru and described by Heinrich Gustav Reichenbach in 1879.

Masdevallia venezuelana

PRONUNCIATION: maz-deh-VALL-ee-ah ven-eh-zway-LAH-nah

ORIGIN: Venezuela

DESCRIPTION AND QUALITIES: This petite plant is perfect for a terrarium.

FLOWER: Bright yellow, $^1/_2$ in. (1 cm) across, borne singly

SEASON OF BLOOM: Winter to spring

MATURE SIZE, HABIT: Miniature, 3 in. (7.5 cm)

Masdevallia tridens displays a sunburst of flowers. Grown by J & L Orchids.

Masdevallia venezuelana 'Fox Den' is a petite grower. Grown by J & L Orchids.

A superb specimen of *Maxillaria sanguinea* features blood-red flowers. Grown by Parkside Orchids.

CULTURE: Intermediate
LIGHT: Low to medium
TEMPERATURE: Intermediate
POTTING MEDIUM: Fine, well-draining mix, or mounted on slabs

Maxillaria sanguinea

PRONUNCIATION: macks-ill-AIR-ee-ah san-GWIN-ee-ah
ORIGIN: Panama to Nicaragua
DESCRIPTION AND QUALITIES: The common name, blood-red maxillaria, well describes this dark maxillaria with a growth habit similar to *Maxillaria tenuifolia* but smaller.
FLOWER: Dark red, $5/8$ in. (1.5 cm), with fruity fragrance, borne at the base of the plant
SEASON OF BLOOM: Winter to spring
MATURE SIZE, HABIT: Dwarf, 4–5 in. (10.0–12.5 cm)
CULTURE: Intermediate
LIGHT: Medium
TEMPERATURE: Intermediate to warm
POTTING MEDIUM: Usually grows best if mounted on a raft or slab. Can be grown in pots with a mixture of well-draining media such as shredded tree fern.
CULTURAL TIPS: Likes to be kept moist.
HISTORY: Described by Robert Rolfe in 1895.

Maxillaria tenuifolia

PRONUNCIATION: macks-ill-AIR-ee-ah ten-you-i-FOH-lee-ah
SYNONYM: *Maxillaria gracilifolia*
ORIGIN: Mexico to Costa Rica
DESCRIPTION AND QUALITIES: Found in semi-deciduous forests at low elevations. Fragrance similar to coconuts. One of the most popular of the 200 or so species of *Maxillaria*.
FLOWER: Fragrant, $1^{1}/_{2}$–2 in. (4–5 cm), brick red, borne singly
SEASON OF BLOOM: Summer
MATURE SIZE, HABIT: Compact, 10 in. (25 cm)

CULTURE: Easy
LIGHT: Medium
TEMPERATURE: Intermediate
POTTING MEDIUM: Usually grows best if mounted on a raft or slab. Can be grown in pots with a mixture of well-draining media such as shredded tree fern.
CULTURAL TIPS: Likes to be kept moist.
HISTORY: Discovered in Veracruz, Mexico, by T. Hartweg in 1837.

Mediocalcar decoratum

PRONUNCIATION: mee-dee-oh-KAL-kar deck-or-AH-tum
ORIGIN: New Guinea

Nobody can resist the mouth-watering coconut fragrance of *Maxillaria tenuifolia*.

Mediocalcar decoratum is a low-growing miniature.

Mexicoa ghiesbreghtiana is a neatly growing dwarf plant.

Miltonia Goodale Moir 'Golden Wonder' HCC/AOS is a colorful hybrid from Hawaii.

DESCRIPTION AND QUALITIES: The most commonly grown of the 20 or so species in this genus, with succulent green leaves.
FLOWER: $1/4$ in. (6 mm), bell-shaped, long-lasting, orange with yellow tips
SEASON OF BLOOM: Fall to winter
MATURE SIZE, HABIT: Miniature, 1–2 in. (2.5–5.0 cm), mat forming
CULTURE: Intermediate
LIGHT: Low to medium
TEMPERATURE: Intermediate
POTTING MEDIUM: Best if mounted on a raft or slab

Mexicoa ghiesbreghtiana

PRONUNCIATION: mecks-i-KOH-ah gees-breck-tee-AH-nah
SYNONYM: *Odontoglossum warneri, Oncidium ghiesbreghtiana*
ORIGIN: Mexico
DESCRIPTION AND QUALITIES: This species resembles an oncidium, to which it is closely related.
FLOWER: 1 in. (2.5 cm), with burgundy-brown (or yellow) sepals and petals and yellow lips, on 10 in. (25 cm) spikes
SEASON OF BLOOM: Spring to summer
MATURE SIZE, HABIT: Dwarf, 4–5 in. (10.0–12.5 cm)
CULTURE: Intermediate
LIGHT: Medium
TEMPERATURE: Intermediate
POTTING MEDIUM: Fine, well-draining
HISTORY: Described by John Lindley as *Odontoglossum warneri* in 1845.

Miltonia Goodale Moir

PRONUNCIATION: mill-TOH-nee-ah
ORIGIN: *Miltonia flavescens* × *Miltonia clowesii*. Registered by Goodale Moir in 1954.

DESCRIPTION AND QUALITIES: One of the many hybrids created by this Hawaiian orchid breeder. It is easy to grow and temperature tolerant.

FLOWER: 3 in. (7.5 cm) yellow sepals and petals spotted with burgundy. Lips are white with purple splash.

SEASON OF BLOOM: Winter to spring

MATURE SIZE, HABIT: Compact, 10 in. (25 cm)

CULTURE: Intermediate

LIGHT: Medium

TEMPERATURE: Intermediate

POTTING MEDIUM: Fine, well-draining

Miltonia moreliana

PRONUNCIATION: mill-TOH-nee-ah more-ell-ee-AH-nah

SYNONYM: *Miltonia spectabilis* var. *moreliana*

ORIGIN: Brazil

DESCRIPTION AND QUALITIES: Rich and fragrant flowers make this species stunning.

FLOWER: Plum purple, glossy, 2 in. (5 cm) wide and 4 in. (10 cm) long, with lighter pink lips and dark purple veins

SEASON OF BLOOM: Spring to summer

MATURE SIZE, HABIT: Compact, 8–12 in. (20–30 cm), spreads to 18 in. (46 cm)

CULTURE: Intermediate

LIGHT: Medium

TEMPERATURE: Intermediate

POTTING MEDIUM: Fine, well-draining

CULTURAL TIPS: Always keep damp. This Brazilian miltonia does not require the cool conditions of those from Colombia.

HISTORY: First sent from Brazil to Paris to French grower Morel in 1846.

Miltonia spectabilis

PRONUNCIATION: mill-TOH-nee-ah speck-TAH-bi-liss

ORIGIN: Brazil

DESCRIPTION AND QUALITIES: This elegant species includes some fine white and purple forms that rival the hybrids.

Miltonia moreliana is quite a stunner.

A particularly fine form of *Miltonia spectabilis* shows off its colorful flower.

FLOWER: White tinged with pink, rose-pink lips, and purple columns, 4 in. (10 cm) wide, borne singly on 8 in. (20 cm) inflorescence
SEASON OF BLOOM: Summer to fall
MATURE SIZE, HABIT: Compact, 10 in. (25 cm)
CULTURE: Intermediate

The soft yellow flower of *Miltoniopsis* Golden Butterfly is enchanting.

Miltoniopsis Hajime Ono is a classic waterfall type miltoniopsis hybrid.

LIGHT: Medium
TEMPERATURE: Intermediate
POTTING MEDIUM: Fine, well-draining
CULTURAL TIPS: Always keep damp. This Brazilian miltonia does not require the cool conditions of those from Colombia.
HISTORY: Described by John Lindley in 1837 based on a specimen collected in Brazil by Weddell.

Miltoniopsis Golden Butterfly

PRONUNCIATION: mill-toh-nee-OP-siss
ORIGIN: *Miltoniopsis* Lixos × *Miltoniopsis* Butterfly. Registered by Rod McLellan Company in 1978.
DESCRIPTION AND QUALITIES: This hybrid is popular because of its buttery yellow flower color. Miltoniopsis breeders are working to produce yellows of the same quality as the reds and waterfall types.
FLOWER: Yellow with red and orange markings, 2^1/$_2$ in. (6 cm) wide and 3 in. (7.5 cm) long
SEASON OF BLOOM: Winter to spring
MATURE SIZE, HABIT: Compact, 10 in. (25 cm)
CULTURE: Intermediate
LIGHT: Medium
TEMPERATURE: Intermediate
POTTING MEDIUM: Fine, moisture-retentive

Miltoniopsis Hajime Ono

PRONUNCIATION: mill-toh-nee-OP-siss
ORIGIN: *Miltoniopsis* Martin Orenstein × *Miltoniopsis* Pearl Ono. Registered by Ivan Komoda in 1998.
DESCRIPTION AND QUALITIES: This hybrid shows how far the Hawaiian breeders have progressed in producing truly outstanding waterfall type miltoniopsis hybrids.
FLOWER: Fragrant, 3 in. (7.5 cm) wide and 4 in. (10 cm) long
SEASON OF BLOOM: Winter to spring
MATURE SIZE, HABIT: Compact, 12 in. (30 cm)
CULTURE: Intermediate
LIGHT: Medium

TEMPERATURE: Intermediate
POTTING MEDIUM: Fine, well-draining

Miltoniopsis Maui Pearl

PRONUNCIATION: mill-toh-nee-OP-siss

ORIGIN: *Miltoniopsis* Nicholas Yuen × *Miltoniopsis* Pearl Ono. Registered by Ivan Komoda in 2004.

DESCRIPTION AND QUALITIES: Another fine example of modern miltoniopsis breeding from Hawaii. In general, all of the newer hybrids have larger and more abundant flowers, are more temperature tolerant, and are easier to grow than the species and earlier hybrids.

FLOWER: Fragrant, 3 in. (7.5 cm) wide and 4 in. (10 cm) long

SEASON OF BLOOM: Winter to spring

MATURE SIZE, HABIT: Compact, 12 in. (30 cm)

CULTURE: Intermediate

LIGHT: Medium

TEMPERATURE: Intermediate

POTTING MEDIUM: Fine, well-draining

The clear white *Miltoniopsis* Maui Pearl flower has a burgundy-red mask.

The flower of *Miltoniopsis phalaenopsis* has a brightly marked lip.

Miltoniopsis phalaenopsis

PRONUNCIATION: mill-toh-nee-OP-siss fal-en-OP-siss

SYNONYMS: *Odontoglossum roezlii, Miltonia roezlii*

ORIGIN: Colombia

DESCRIPTION AND QUALITIES: This species is used in breeding to add its waterfall markings to modern hybrids.

FLOWER: White, pansy-shaped, with purple waterfall pattern on lip, $1^3/_4$ in. (4.5 cm) wide, 10 in. (25 cm) inflorescence with three to five flowers. Lily-of-the-valley fragrance.

SEASON OF BLOOM: Winter to spring

MATURE SIZE, HABIT: Compact, 12 in. (30 cm)

CULTURE: Intermediate

LIGHT: Medium

TEMPERATURE: Cool to intermediate

POTTING MEDIUM: Fine mix. Frequently mounted on tree fern or planted in a basket.

CULTURAL TIPS: Provide warm winters and cold summers. Reduce watering during the winter.

HISTORY: Discovered in Colombia in 1850 by Louis Schlim, cousin to Belgium plant explorer Jean Linden, and sent to the Lindens in Belgium.

Miltoniopsis santanaei

PRONUNCIATION: mill-toh-nee-OP-siss san-tah-NAY-eye
SYNONYM: *Miltonia roezlii* var. *alba*
ORIGIN: Venezuela, Colombia, Ecuador
DESCRIPTION AND QUALITIES: An easy-to-grow, warm-tolerant plant, this species is a perfect choice for a windowsill or under lights.

Miltoniopsis santanaei is a temperature tolerant species.
Photo by Marc Herzog.

FLOWER: Fragrant, 2 in. (5 cm) flat, white, pansy-shaped, with a bright yellow flare on the top of the lip
SEASON OF BLOOM: Variable
MATURE SIZE, HABIT: Compact, 10 in. (25 cm)
CULTURE: Easy
LIGHT: Low to medium
TEMPERATURE: Intermediate
POTTING MEDIUM: Fine, moisture-retentive
HISTORY: This species continues to be used extensively as a parent for today's miltoniopsis hybrids. It usually imparts its warmth tolerance and fragrance to its offspring.

Miltoniopsis Venus

PRONUNCIATION: mill-toh-nee-OP-siss
ORIGIN: *Miltoniopsis phalaenopsis* × *Miltoniopsis vexillaria*. First hybridized by the Charlesworth company in 1917.
DESCRIPTION AND QUALITIES: This compact grower offers fragrance and a sparkling floral display. Although its flowers are not as large as some of today's modern hybrids, it is still popular.
FLOWER: Fragrant, 1 in. (2.5 cm) wide and 2 in. (5 cm) tall, pink petals, with yellow-throated lip surrounded by a dark rose-pink blotch and finished with a dazzling waterfall pattern
SEASON OF BLOOM: Summer to fall
MATURE SIZE, HABIT: Compact, 8 to 10 in. (20 to 25 cm) tall with 1 in. (2.5 cm) wide foliage
CULTURE: Intermediate
LIGHT: Medium
TEMPERATURE: Cool to intermediate
POTTING MEDIUM: Fine, well-draining
CULTURAL TIPS: Always keep damp.

A hybrid from the early 20th century, *Miltoniopsis* Venus is still a winner.

Miltoniopsis vexillaria

PRONUNCIATION: mill-toh-nee-OP-siss vecks-i-LAIR-ee-ah
SYNONYMS: *Odontoglossum vexillarium*, *Miltonia vexillaria*

Miltoniopsis vexillaria has luscious pink flowers. Grown by J & L Orchids.

ORIGIN: Colombia, Ecuador

DESCRIPTION AND QUALITIES: This gorgeous pink to white flowering species has been used heavily in breeding modern hybrids.

FLOWER: Four or more, 3 in. (7.5 cm) long, on 12–16 in. (30–40 cm) spike. Color ranges from bright pink to off-white. The lip has yellow markings with dark purple stripes and blotches.

SEASON OF BLOOM: Spring to summer

MATURE SIZE, HABIT: Compact, 9–12 in. (23–30 cm)

CULTURE: Intermediate

LIGHT: Medium

TEMPERATURE: Intermediate

POTTING MEDIUM: Fine, well-draining

CULTURAL TIPS: Keep moist at all times or pleating of the foliage will result.

HISTORY: Discovered in Colombia by Bowman, one of Veitch's plant collectors, in 1866.

The flower of *Mormolyca gracilipes* displays complex colors. Grown by J & L Orchids.

Mormolyca gracilipes

PRONUNCIATION: more-moh-LYE-kah grah-SILL-i-peez

ORIGIN: From Mexico to Brazil, but most commonly found in the Andes

DESCRIPTION AND QUALITIES: Most species in this genus have cinnamon colored to dark brown flowers.
FLOWER: 1¹/₂ in. (4 cm), cinnamon colored, borne singly on 6 in. (15 cm) inflorescence
SEASON OF BLOOM: Spring to summer
MATURE SIZE, HABIT: Dwarf, 5 in. (12.5 cm)
CULTURE: Intermediate
LIGHT: Medium
TEMPERATURE: Intermediate

Flowers of *Nageliella angustifolia* glow like neon. Grown by Parkside Orchid Nursery.

Neofinetia falcata is a delicate beauty, long admired by Asian collectors.

POTTING MEDIUM: Fine mix in pots or mounted
CULTURAL TIPS: Must be kept damp and humid.
HISTORY: Described in 1850.
RELATED SPECIES, HYBRIDS: *Mormolyca peruviana, Mlca. ringens, Mlca. schweinfurthiana*

Nageliella angustifolia

PRONUNCIATION: na-jell-LEE-lah an-guss-ti-FOH-lee-ah
SYNONYM: *Meiracyllium gemma*
ORIGIN: Guatemala
DESCRIPTION AND QUALITIES: The flower is small but bright and glistens in bright light.
FLOWER: ³/₄ in. (2 cm), rose-purple, 2 in. (5 cm) inflorescence
SEASON OF BLOOM: Spring to summer
MATURE SIZE, HABIT: Miniature, 2¹/₂ in. (6 cm)
CULTURE: Intermediate
LIGHT: Medium
TEMPERATURE: Intermediate
POTTING MEDIUM: Fine mix
HISTORY: Genus was named in honor of Otto Nagel, who collected orchids extensively in Mexico.
RELATED SPECIES, HYBRIDS: *Nageliella purpurea*

Neofinetia falcata

PRONUNCIATION: nee-oh-fin-AY-tee-ah fal-KAH-tah
SYNONYM: *Angraecum falcatum*
ORIGIN: Japan
DESCRIPTION AND QUALITIES: This species has produced many intergeneric vandaceous hybrids noted for their small growth habit, fragrance, and ease of bloom in a bright windowsill. The foliage is keel shaped, and flowers last a month or two.

FLOWER: To 12 or more, snow-white, waxy, 1 in. (2.5 cm) wide and tall, with 2 in. (5 cm) spur. Other flower color forms and variegated foliage known.

SEASON OF BLOOM: Summer to fall

MATURE SIZE, HABIT: Dwarf, with mono-podial habit that is variable in size, 3–6 in. (7.5–15.0 cm) high. Foliage 4–6 in. (10–15 cm) long. The plant forms multiple growths or clumps.

CULTURE: Intermediate

LIGHT: Medium

TEMPERATURE: Intermediate to warm

POTTING MEDIUM: Mounted in a basket or grown in sphagnum moss, or in cattleya mix in pots

CULTURAL TIPS: Reduce water in the winter.

HISTORY: Once the exclusive property of the royal family of Japan, its cultivation dates to the Edo period (1603–1867). It was first described in 1784.

Neostylis Lou Sneary

PRONUNCIATION: nee-oh-STY-liss

ORIGIN: *Neofinetia falcata* × *Rhynchostylis coelestis*. Registered by Hajimi Ono in 1970.

DESCRIPTION AND QUALITIES: This hybrid is easy to grow and bloom (frequently more than once a year) and takes up little grow-ing space. A must-have in any miniature orchid collection. 'Blue Moon' is one of the most fragrant Lou Sneary clones, perfect for a windowsill or under lights.

FLOWER: 1 in. (2.5 cm), fragrant, in various colors from creamy whites to shades of pink to purple-blue, borne in clusters. 'Blue Moon' is lavender-blue; 'Pinky' AM/AOS is deliciously fragrant, creamy white, richly marked in pink, with bright fuchsia-pink lips.

SEASON OF BLOOM: Variable

MATURE SIZE, HABIT: Dwarf, leaves spread 8 in. (20 cm)

Neostylis Lou Sneary is one of the best hybrids from *Neofinetia falcata*.

Nobody has enough blue-flowering plants, and few of them are as fragrant as *Neostylis* Lou Sneary 'Blue Moon'.

Neostylis Lou Sneary 'Pinky' AM/AOS is a floriferous prize-winning selection from two fragrant parents.

CULTURE: Easy
LIGHT: Medium
TEMPERATURE: Intermediate to warm
POTTING MEDIUM: Medium grade epiphytic mix
CULTURAL TIPS: Grow in pots or baskets.

Octomeria

PRONUNCIATION: ock-toh-MEER-ee-ah
ORIGIN: Central and South America
DESCRIPTION AND QUALITIES: Most of the species in this genus have fleshy, stiff leaves and small flowers. These orchids are related to pleurothallis and are generally not difficult to grow and flower.
FLOWER: Color varies from cream to white to yellow
SEASON OF BLOOM: Winter to spring

MATURE SIZE, HABIT: Dwarf, but variable, 3–4 in. (7.5–10.0 cm)

CULTURE: Intermediate

LIGHT: Medium

TEMPERATURE: Intermediate

POTTING MEDIUM: Medium grade epiphytic mix

RELATED SPECIES, HYBRIDS: *Octomeria decumbens, Octmr. complanata, Octmr. gracilis, Octmr. integrilabia, Octmr. minor, Octmr. nana, Octmr. steyermarkii*

Odontonia Vesta

PRONUNCIATION: oh-don-TOH-nee-ah

ORIGIN: *Odontonia* Dora × *Miltonia* William Pitt. Registered by the Charlesworth company in 1928.

DESCRIPTION AND QUALITIES: This is one of my favorite odontonia hybrids because of its gaily colored flowers on compact plants.

An unidentified *Octomeria* specimen displays tiny flowers. Grown by Parkside Orchid Nursery.

An older hybrid, *Odontonia* Vesta 'Charm' is still a top performer.

Odontoglossum cervantesii has a crisp white flower.

OPPOSITE:
Odontoglossum crocidipterum 'Mountainside'. Grown by Mountain Orchids.

FLOWER: Sweet rose scented, 3 in. (7.5 cm) wide and 3^1/$_2$ in. (9 cm) long, white marked with rose-red splashes on petals and sepals. Also marked in darker red and yellow.
SEASON OF BLOOM: Winter to spring
MATURE SIZE, HABIT: Compact, 10–12 in. (25–30 cm)
CULTURE: Intermediate
LIGHT: Medium
TEMPERATURE: Intermediate
POTTING MEDIUM: Fine, well-draining

Odontoglossum cervantesii

PRONUNCIATION: oh-don-toh-GLOSS-um sur-van-TEZ-ee-eye
SYNONYM: Lemboglossum cervantesii
ORIGIN: Mexico
DESCRIPTION AND QUALITIES: A fragrant, attractive Mexican native.
FLOWER: 1^1/$_2$ in. (4 cm), white, with small maroon spots on 8 in. (20 cm) spike. Also a pink-flowered form.
SEASON OF BLOOM: Spring to summer
MATURE SIZE, HABIT: Dwarf, 6–8 in. (15–20 cm)
CULTURE: Intermediate
LIGHT: Medium
TEMPERATURE: Cool to intermediate
POTTING MEDIUM: Fine, well-draining

CULTURAL TIPS: Requires abundant water throughout active growing season.

Odontoglossum crocidipterum

PRONUNCIATION: oh-don-toh-GLOSS-um kroh-si-DIP-ter-um
ORIGIN: Colombia, Venezuela
DESCRIPTION AND QUALITIES: This hard to find but fetching odontoglossum produces showers of sweetly scented flowers.
FLOWER: Creamy colored, sprinkled with burgundy spots, 2 in. (5 cm) across, borne in 12 in. (30 cm) sprays of up to a dozen. Lips are sometimes yellow.
SEASON OF BLOOM: Spring
MATURE SIZE, HABIT: Compact, 10 in. (25 cm)
CULTURE: Intermediate
LIGHT: Medium to high
TEMPERATURE: Cool to intermediate
POTTING MEDIUM: Fine, well-draining
CULTURAL TIPS: Does best with cool temperatures, ample air circulation, and high humidity.
RELATED SPECIES, HYBRIDS: Odontoglossum cervantesii, Odm. ehrenbergii, Odm. galeottianum, Odm. oerstedii, Odm. stellatum

Odontoglossum krameri

PRONUNCIATION: oh-don-toh-GLOSS-um KRAY-mer-eye
ORIGIN: Costa Rica
DESCRIPTION AND QUALITIES: This small orchid has an attractive and long-lasting flower.
FLOWER: Light to dark pink, 1^1/$_2$ in. (4 cm) across, borne on 8 in. (20 cm) inflorescence
SEASON OF BLOOM: Winter to spring
MATURE SIZE, HABIT: Dwarf, 6 in. (15 cm)
CULTURE: Intermediate
LIGHT: Medium to high
TEMPERATURE: Cool to intermediate
POTTING MEDIUM: Fine well-draining
HISTORY: First collected in Costa Rica by Kramer, one of the collectors for Veitch,

Flowers of
*Odontoglossum
krameri* are
long-lasting.

The *Odontoglossum
wyattianum* flower
combines unusual
colors. Grown by
Parkside Orchids.

and described by Heinrich Gustav
Reichenbach in 1868.

Odontoglossum wyattianum

PRONUNCIATION: oh-don-toh-GLOSS-um
wye-at-ee-AH-num
SYNONYMS: *Odontoglossum youngii, Rhynchostele rossii*
ORIGIN: Peru, Ecuador
DESCRIPTION AND QUALITIES: The color
combination of the flower is unusual yet
handsome. Even though this orchid was
discovered in the early 1900s, it is only
recently appearing in more collections in
the United States.
FLOWER: 2 in. (5 cm) wide and 3 in. (7.5
cm) long, warm brown petals and sepals
marked with burgundy red. Lip is white
with purple-red.
SEASON OF BLOOM: Winter to spring
MATURE SIZE, HABIT: Compact, 10–12 in.
(25–30 cm)
CULTURE: Intermediate
LIGHT: Medium to high
TEMPERATURE: Cool to intermediate
POTTING MEDIUM: Fine
CULTURAL TIPS: Keep evenly moist.
HISTORY: Described by G. Wilson in 1928.
RELATED SPECIES, HYBRIDS: *Odontoglossum
harryanum*

Oerstedella endresii

PRONUNCIATION: ore-stay-DELL-ah en-
DRESS-ee-eye
ORIGIN: Costa Rica
DESCRIPTION AND QUALITIES: Some of the
species in this genus resemble epidendrums, to which they are closely related.
This species is one of the smallest and
blooms various times of the year. Most
within this genus are hardy and can sur-
vive short stints of temperatures close to
freezing. They frequently sprout smaller
plants at their base so quickly form
clumps.

FLOWER: Fragrant, ¹/₂ in. (1 cm), with pink to bluish lips, borne in clusters
SEASON OF BLOOM: Variable
MATURE SIZE, HABIT: Dwarf, 8 in. (20 cm). Reedlike stems form tight clusters.
CULTURE: Easy
LIGHT: Medium
TEMPERATURE: Cool to intermediate
POTTING MEDIUM: Fine, well-draining
CULTURAL TIPS: Plants should never be allowed to go completely dry.
HISTORY: Common name derived from German orchid collector Endres in the 1800s.
RELATED SPECIES, HYBRIDS: *Oerstedella pumila* (green, creamy white), *Orstdl. centradenia* (pink)

Oncidium cheirophorum

PRONUNCIATION: on-SID-ee-um kay-ROFF-er-um
ORIGIN: Colombia
DESCRIPTION AND QUALITIES: Frequently used as a parent to lend its fragrance and habit. Closely related to *Oncidium ornithorhynchum.*
FLOWER: ¹/₂ in. (1 cm), bright yellow, on branched, arching spray
SEASON OF BLOOM: Winter to spring
MATURE SIZE, HABIT: Dwarf, 5 in. (12.5 cm)
CULTURE: Easy
LIGHT: Medium
TEMPERATURE: Intermediate
POTTING MEDIUM: Fine to medium orchid mix
CULTURAL TIPS: Easy to grow and bloom.
HISTORY: Discovered by the famous Lithuanian plant collector Josef von Warscewicz; described by Heinrich Gustav Reichenbach in 1852.
RELATED SPECIES, HYBRIDS: *Oncidium barbatum, Onc. bifolium, Onc. concolor, Onc. cornigerum, Onc. crista-galli, Onc. dasystyle, Onc. dayanum, Onc. edwallii, Onc. endocharis, Onc. fuscopetalum, Onc. gracile, Onc.*

Oerstedella endresii is one of the smallest of the genus. Grown by J & L Orchids.

Oncidium cheirophorum is a bright and cheery, fragrant oncidium.

The stately flower of
Oncidium crispum
has a musty scent.

A shower of
flowers pours from
Oncidium Kukoo.

harrisonianum, Onc. heteranthum, Onc. hians, Onc. hookeri, Onc. hydrophyllum, Onc. limminghei, Onc. loefgrenii, Onc. macronix, Onc. macropetalum, Onc. meirax, Onc. micropogon, Onc. morenoi, Onc. nanum, Onc. pubes, Onc. pulchellum, Onc. pumilum, Onc. reisii, Onc. tetrapetalum, Onc. triquetrum, Onc. uniflorum, Onc. viperinum, Onc. waluweva

Oncidium crispum

PRONUNCIATION: on-SID-ee-um KRIS-pum
ORIGIN: Brazil
DESCRIPTION AND QUALITIES: The flower is quite attractive, but its musty scent is not one of its assets.
FLOWER: 3 in. (7.5 cm), rust-red, yellow, and orange markings on the lip; borne on long inflorescence
SEASON OF BLOOM: Spring to summer
MATURE SIZE, HABIT: Compact, leaves 6–8 in. (15–20 cm)
CULTURE: Intermediate
LIGHT: Medium to high
TEMPERATURE: Intermediate to warm
POTTING MEDIUM: Medium grade epiphytic mix
HISTORY: Introduced and described by the Loddiges in 1832.

Oncidium Kukoo

PRONUNCIATION: on-SID-ee-um
SYNONYM: *Zelenkocidium Kukoo*
ORIGIN: *Oncidium onustum* × *Oncidium cheirophorum*. Registered by Kugust in 1963.
DESCRIPTION AND QUALITIES: A great pairing of two superior species—the *Oncidium cheirophorum* parent decreased the length of the inflorescence and sometimes imparts its fragrance.
FLOWER: 1 in. (2.5 cm) across, clear yellow
SEASON OF BLOOM: Spring to summer
MATURE SIZE, HABIT: Dwarf, 4–5 in. (10.0–12.5 cm)

CULTURE: Intermediate
LIGHT: Medium
TEMPERATURE: Intermediate
POTTING MEDIUM: Fine to medium grade orchid mix, or can be mounted

Oncidium longipes
PRONUNCIATION: on-SID-ee-um LAWN-ji-peez
SYNONYM: *Oncidium janeirense*
ORIGIN: Brazil
DESCRIPTION AND QUALITIES: *Oncidium longipes* has been popular because it grows quickly into a specimen plant and is easy to bloom.
FLOWER: Cinnamon or anise seed–floral scent, yellow, ³/₄–1 in. (2.5–3.0 cm) across; sepals and petals dark yellow to reddish brown and lip is bright yellow. Frequently blooms twice a year.
SEASON OF BLOOM: Fall
MATURE SIZE, HABIT: Dwarf, to 6 in. (15 cm)
CULTURE: Easy
LIGHT: Medium
TEMPERATURE: Intermediate
POTTING MEDIUM: Fine to medium
HISTORY: Described by John Lindley in 1851 from a plant collected in Rio de Janeiro.

Oncidium onustum
PRONUNCIATION: on-SID-ee-um oh-NUS-tum
SYNONYM: *Zelenkoa onusta*
ORIGIN: Ecuador
DESCRIPTION AND QUALITIES: There are no clearer yellow flowers than those displayed by this species. As a result, it is highly valued in any collection and is used frequently in breeding.
FLOWER: Yellow, ³/₄ in. (2 cm) wide by 1 in. (2.5 cm) long, borne on a inflorescence of 15 in. (38 cm) or more
SEASON OF BLOOM: Fall to winter
MATURE SIZE, HABIT: Dwarf, leaves 4–5 in. (10.0–12.5 cm)

CULTURE: Intermediate
LIGHT: Medium to high
TEMPERATURE: Intermediate
POTTING MEDIUM: Usually grown mounted on tree fern or cork
CULTURAL TIPS: Should be allowed to dry off after new growth appears to stimulate flowering.

Oncidium longipes grows quickly but does not require a large growing area.

The sparkling flowers of *Oncidium onustum* are clear yellow.

A select cultivar of this species, *Oncidium ornithorhynchum* 'Lilac Blossom', is from Hawaiian orchid nursery Ha'iku Maui Orchids. Photo by Marc Herzog.

Oncidium ornithorhynchum

PRONUNCIATION: on-SID-ee-um ore-nith-oh-RINK-um

ORIGIN: Mexico, Guatemala, El Salvador, Costa Rica

DESCRIPTION AND QUALITIES: Highly recommended for beginning growers because of its ease of culture, dependable blooming, and sweet fragrance.

FLOWER: 1 in. (2.5 cm) across, lavender-pink, produced by the hundreds on a mature plant

SEASON OF BLOOM: Spring to summer

MATURE SIZE, HABIT: Dwarf, 6–8 in. (15–20 cm)

CULTURE: Easy

LIGHT: Medium

TEMPERATURE: Intermediate

POTTING MEDIUM: Fine to medium grade orchid mix

HISTORY: First described by F. H. A. von Humboldt in 1815.

Oncidium Twinkle

PRONUNCIATION: on-SID-ee-um

ORIGIN: *Oncidium cheirophorum* × *Oncidium ornithorhynchum*. Registered by W. W. G. Moir in 1958.

DESCRIPTION AND QUALITIES: The ease of growth, fragrance, and flower make this high-performance cross a must-have for miniature orchid lovers.

FLOWER: Profusion of flowers 1 in. (2.5 cm) in highly variable colors from creamy whites and soft yellows to pinks and scarlet reds. 'Red Fantasy' is a dark-flowered form, somewhat vanilla-scented.

SEASON OF BLOOM: Variable

MATURE SIZE, HABIT: Dwarf, 6–8 in. (15–20 cm)

CULTURE: Easy

LIGHT: Medium

TEMPERATURE: Intermediate to warm

POTTING MEDIUM: Fine to medium grade orchid mix

CULTURAL TIPS: Highly recommended as a beginner's orchid because it is easy to grow and bloom.

HISTORY: The original Twinkle was registered by the famed Hawaiian orchid hybridizer Goodale Moir in 1958.

Ornithocephalus manabina

PRONUNCIATION: ore-nith-oh-SEFF-ah-lus man-ah-BEE-nah

ORIGIN: South America

DESCRIPTION AND QUALITIES: *Ornicephalus* is commonly called bird head orchid, and if you use a mag-

Oncidium Twinkle 'Fragrance Fantasy' is in flower for a month or more.

Combining two outstanding dwarf species resulted in this winning result, *Oncidium* Twinkle 'Red Fantasy'.

Ornithocephalus manabina flowers are small but charming. Grown by J & L Orchids.

This newly opened *Paphiopedilum armeniacum* flower will get larger, rounder, and brighter as it matures.

Paphiopedilum Armeni White has soft white flowers that emit a delicate citrus fragrance.

HISTORY: First described by Calaway Dodson in 1984.

Paphiopedilum armeniacum

PRONUNCIATION: paff-ee-oh-PEA-di-lum are-men-ee-AH-kum

ORIGIN: Yunnan province of China

DESCRIPTION AND QUALITIES: This species has opened the door for new avenues of paphiopedilum breeding because of its yellow color. Leaves are deeply marbled with purple underneath.

FLOWER: 3 in. (7.5 cm) wide, soft to bright yellow, borne solitary on 6–8 in. (15–20 cm) scape

SEASON OF BLOOM: Winter to spring

MATURE SIZE, HABIT: Dwarf, 3 in. (7.5 cm), leaves spread to 4 in. (10 cm)

CULTURE: Intermediate

LIGHT: Low to medium

TEMPERATURE: Intermediate

POTTING MEDIUM: Fine, well-draining

CULTURAL TIPS: Allow to dry out slightly during winter and lower temperature to about 50°F (10°C) to trigger early spring blooming.

HISTORY: First described by Chen and Lie in 1982.

Paphiopedilum Armeni White

PRONUNCIATION: paff-ee-oh-PEA-di-lum

ORIGIN: *Paphiopedilum armeniacum* × *Paphiopedilum delenatii*. Registered by H. Kubo in 1987.

DESCRIPTION AND QUALITIES: This vigorous, easy blooming hybrid is one of the most popular yet to be produced from *Paphiopedilum armeniacum*. It is curious that a cross of a yellow-flowered parent and a pink-flowered parent produces white offspring. Foliage is an attractive dark-patterned green.

FLOWER: Fragrant, $3^{1}/_{2}$ in. (9 cm), creamy white, one or two per scape on 18 in. (46 cm) stalk

nifying glass to look at the center of the flower at the column of the orchid, you can see the resemblance. Although flowers are small, they are charming and can last for months. Foliage is fan shaped.

FLOWER: Crystalline white, $1/_4$ in. (6 mm), borne on a 2 in. (5 cm) inflorescence

SEASON OF BLOOM: Variable

MATURE SIZE, HABIT: Miniature, 2 in. (5 cm) across

CULTURE: Intermediate

LIGHT: Low to medium

TEMPERATURE: Intermediate to warm

POTTING MEDIUM: Mounted or potted in fine, well-draining media

CULTURAL TIPS: Keep constantly damp.

SEASON OF BLOOM: Spring to summer
MATURE SIZE, HABIT: Dwarf, 6 in. (15 cm),
with 8–10 in. (20–25 cm) spread
CULTURE: Easy
LIGHT: Low
TEMPERATURE: Intermediate
POTTING MEDIUM: Fine, well-draining

Paphiopedilum bellatulum

PRONUNCIATION: paff-ee-oh-PEA-di-lum
bell-AT-you-lum
ORIGIN: Burma, Thailand, Laos
DESCRIPTION AND QUALITIES: Used fre-
quently in hybridizing because of its large
round flowers. Unfortunately, most of its
hybrids suffer from short, weak flower
stems. Leaves are succulent, tessellated,
and dark purple underneath.
FLOWER: White, 3 in. (7.5 cm), with dark
purple spots that in better forms are almost round
SEASON OF BLOOM: Spring to summer
MATURE SIZE, HABIT: Dwarf, 4 in. (10 cm),
leaf spread 12 in. (30 cm)
CULTURE: Intermediate
LIGHT: Low to medium
TEMPERATURE: Intermediate
POTTING MEDIUM: Fine, well-draining
CULTURAL TIPS: Keep drier than most
paphiopedilums. They can be killed by too
much water and growing conditions that
are too warm.
HISTORY: First imported into England in
1888 by Low and Company

Paphiopedilum Buena Bay

PRONUNCIATION: paff-ee-oh-PEA-di-lum
ORIGIN: *Paphiopedilum* Yerba Buena ×
Paphiopedilum Saint Ouens Bay. Registered
by Kevin Porter of Curved Air Orchids in
1992.
DESCRIPTION AND QUALITIES: This hybrid
displays the classic round shape for which
breeders of complex hybrid paphiopedilums are always striving. The primarily

Paphiopedilum bellatulum is a delightful species with beautifully marked foliage.

Paphiopedilum Buena Bay 'Golden' has become a classic and coveted complex hybrid.

white dorsal, inherited from *Paphiopedilum*
Yerba Buena, makes it a standout. Purple
vertical and horizontal stripes in the dorsal
and petals show the influence of *Paph.*
spicerianum.
FLOWER: $3^1/2$ in. (9 cm), round; 'Golden'
has white dorsal sepal and warm yellow
petals
SEASON OF BLOOM: Winter to spring
MATURE SIZE, HABIT: Compact, 9 in. (23
cm) tall with 12 in. (30 cm) leaf spread
CULTURE: Easy
LIGHT: Low to medium
TEMPERATURE: Intermediate
POTTING MEDIUM: Fine, well-draining

Ease of culture and attractive foliage have made *Paphiopedilum callosum* a popular selection.

Paphiopedilum charlesworthii displays a stunning pink dorsal sepal.

Paphiopedilum callosum

PRONUNCIATION: paff-ee-oh-PEA-di-lum kah-LOH-sum
ORIGIN: Laos, Cambodia, Thailand
DESCRIPTION AND QUALITIES: One of the first paphiopedilums that I grew, this vigorous grower is a dependable bloomer. The dark purple-red forms have been important in producing the vinicolored (deep purple-red) hybrids popular today. The leaves are attractively marbled.
FLOWER: Shape is variable, most 3 in. (7.5 cm) long and 2 in. (5 cm) wide, blends of green, burgundy, and white

SEASON OF BLOOM: Winter to spring
MATURE SIZE, HABIT: Dwarf, 5 in. (12.5 cm), leaf spread 10 in. (25 cm)
CULTURE: Easy
LIGHT: Low to medium
TEMPERATURE: Intermediate
POTTING MEDIUM: Fine, well-draining
HISTORY: Discovered by Alexander Regnier of France in 1885.

Paphiopedilum charlesworthii

PRONUNCIATION: paff-ee-oh-PEA-di-lum charles-WORTH-ee-eye
ORIGIN: Southeast Asia
DESCRIPTION AND QUALITIES: Difficult to find, but worth the search. Its wide pink dorsal makes it distinctive and prized both as a species and as a parent. Can be slow growing, but once established it is easy to grow. A specimen sized, blooming plant is breathtaking.
FLOWER: $2^1/_2$–3 in. (6.0–7.5 cm). Dorsal sepal is various shades of pink, 2–$2^1/_2$ in. (5–6 cm) wide and tall. A white form, *Paphiopedilum charlesworthii* var. *album*, is rare, expensive, and gorgeous.
SEASON OF BLOOM: Fall
MATURE SIZE, HABIT: Dwarf, 5 in. (12.5 cm)
CULTURE: Easy
LIGHT: Low to medium
TEMPERATURE: Intermediate
POTTING MEDIUM: Fine, well-draining
CULTURAL TIPS: For best flowering, provide a 20°F (10°C) differential between day and evening temperatures.
HISTORY: Discovered by R. Moore in 1893.

Paphiopedilum concolor

PRONUNCIATION: paff-ee-oh-PEA-di-lum KON-kull-er
ORIGIN: Southeast Asia
DESCRIPTION AND QUALITIES: A commonly offered and easy to grow, dainty species. Particularly handsome foliage.
FLOWER: Intensity of color varies from

creamy yellow to strong yellow, 2–2¹/₂ in. (5–
6 cm) across with small burgundy speckles
SEASON OF BLOOM: Spring to summer
MATURE SIZE, HABIT: Miniature, 3 in.
(7.5 cm)
CULTURE: Intermediate
LIGHT: Low to medium
TEMPERATURE: Intermediate
POTTING MEDIUM: Fine, well-draining
CULTURAL TIPS: Will bloom more depend-
ably if kept on the cool and dry side during
the winter. This species is sensitive to salts
so do not over-fertilize.
HISTORY: Discover by Reverend Parish in
1859.

*Paphiopedilum con-
color* is known for its
colorful spots.

Paphiopedilum Deception II
PRONUNCIATION: paff-ee-oh-PEA-di-lum
ORIGIN: *Paphiopedilum niveum* × *Paphiope-
dilum delenatii*. Registered by Cooke in
1942.
DESCRIPTION AND QUALITIES: The flower of
this hybrid resemble a large *Paphiopedilum
niveum*, though it is easier to grow. A nice
white to add to any collection. Leaves are
tessellated with dark purple undersides.
FLOWER: 3 in. (7.5 cm), bright white, with a
light dusting of purple speckles
SEASON OF BLOOM: Variable
MATURE SIZE, HABIT: Dwarf, 5 in. (12.5 cm)
CULTURE: Easy
LIGHT: Low to medium
TEMPERATURE: Intermediate
POTTING MEDIUM: Fine, well-draining

Paphiopedilum
Deception II has
lightly speckled
white flowers.

Paphiopedilum delenatii
PRONUNCIATION: paff-ee-oh-PEA-di-lum
dell-ah-NAT-ee-eye
SYNONYM: *Cypripedium delenatii*
ORIGIN: Vietnam
DESCRIPTION AND QUALITIES: A new form
of this species was discovered from Vietnam in the 1990s. This more vigorous and
easier grower is most often sold today. Gorgeous mottled, dark green foliage.

*Paphiopedilum
delenatii* is one of
the few fragrant Asian
lady's slipper orchids.

FLOWER: Fragrant, 3 in. (7.5 cm), pale pink
with darker pink pouch
SEASON OF BLOOM: Variable
MATURE SIZE, HABIT: Compact, foliage 4 in.
(10 cm) long

Large-flowering, compact *Paphiopedilum* Delrosi is a French hybrid.

Down-swept petals are the hallmark of *Paphiopedilum fairrieanum*.

Paphiopedilum Delrosi

PRONUNCIATION: paff-ee-oh-PEA-di-lum
ORIGIN: *Paphiopedilum delenatii* × *Paphiopedilum rothschildianum*. Registered by Vacherot and Lecoufle in 1961.
DESCRIPTION AND QUALITIES: Since this illustrious French orchid growing establishment kept *Paphiopedilum delenatii* in cultivation, it seems fitting that the French be the first to register this hybrid. Like most *Paph. rothschildianum* hybrids, this one is grand. Unlike many others, it is a compact grower. Plants of the cross being sold today are usually from newer forms of *Paph. delenatii* and *Paph. rothschildianum* and bloom quicker and easier. Leaves are lightly tessellated.
FLOWER: 4 in. (10 cm) or more across, white with red veins and dark pink pouch
SEASON OF BLOOM: Winter to spring
MATURE SIZE, HABIT: Compact, 6 in. (15 cm), leaves are 12 in. (30 cm) long
CULTURE: Intermediate
LIGHT: Medium
TEMPERATURE: Intermediate
POTTING MEDIUM: Fine, well-draining

Paphiopedilum fairrieanum

PRONUNCIATION: paff-ee-oh-PEA-di-lum fair-ee-AH-num
ORIGIN: India
DESCRIPTION AND QUALITIES: This adorable species is used frequently as a parent to add its exotic flower shape to its offspring. It is easy to grow and makes a striking specimen plant. The albino form has white flowers with dark green veins and elegant marking.
FLOWER: 2 in. (5 cm) across and veined in dark red, with down-swept petals
SEASON OF BLOOM: Winter to spring
MATURE SIZE, HABIT: Dwarf, 3 in. (7.5 cm), leaves spread 10 in. (25 cm)
CULTURE: Easy
LIGHT: Low to medium

CULTURE: Easy
LIGHT: Low
TEMPERATURE: Intermediate
POTTING MEDIUM: Fine mix
CULTURAL TIPS: Easy to grow with other paphiopedilums.
HISTORY: First discovered in northern Vietnam by a French army officer in 1914. Until the early 1990s, most of the species available for sale originated from plants raised from seed by the famous French orchid nursery of Vacherot and Lecoufle.

TEMPERATURE: Cool to intermediate
POTTING MEDIUM: Fine, well-draining
CULTURAL TIPS: Keeping it cool and drier during winter months will result in better blooming.
HISTORY: Was first flowered by Reid in England in 1857. In the early 1900s it was rare in cultivation, highly desirable, and expensive.

Paphiopedilum Fanaticum

PRONUNCIATION: paff-ee-oh-PEA-di-lum
ORIGIN: *Paphiopedilum malipoense* × *Paphiopedilum micranthum*. Registered by Paphanatics in 1999.
DESCRIPTION AND QUALITIES: Some slipper specialists regard this orchid as a separate species, not a hybrid, but most paphiopedilum experts consider it a hybrid.
FLOWER: 2^1/$_2$ in. (6 cm) across, usually green, with red veins and pink ballooned pouches
SEASON OF BLOOM: Winter to spring
MATURE SIZE, HABIT: Dwarf, 4 in. (10 cm)
CULTURE: Easy
LIGHT: Low to medium
TEMPERATURE: Intermediate
POTTING MEDIUM: Fine, well-draining

Paphiopedilum Gloria Naugle

PRONUNCIATION: paff-ee-oh-PEA-di-lum
ORIGIN: *Paphiopedilum rothschildianum* × *Paphiopedilum micranthum*. Registered by Mr. and Mrs. J. Naugle for Orchid House in 1993.
DESCRIPTION AND QUALITIES: The blending of outstanding parents yields great results—a large, gorgeous flower on a small plant with well-marked foliage.
FLOWER: Relatively large for the size of the plant, 4 in. (10 cm) or more across, green with red veins and dark pink pouch
SEASON OF BLOOM: Winter to spring
MATURE SIZE, HABIT: Dwarf, 6 in. (15 cm), leaf spread 10 in. (25 cm)

Paphiopedilum Fanaticum has a dramatically marked flower.

Paphiopedilum Gloria Naugle has a glorious flower.

CULTURE: Easy
LIGHT: Low to medium
TEMPERATURE: Intermediate
POTTING MEDIUM: Fine, well-draining

Paphiopedilum Hsinying Fairbre

PRONUNCIATION: paff-ee-oh-PEA-di-lum
ORIGIN: *Paphiopedilum* Macabre × *Paphiopedilum fairrieanum*. Registered by Ching Hua in 2004.
DESCRIPTION AND QUALITIES: The downswept petals show the strong influence of parent *Paphiopedilum fairrieanum*. The desirable, dark red coloring is usually called *vinicolor*.
FLOWER: Waxy, burgundy red, 2^1/$_2$ in. (6 cm) wide and 3 in. (7.5 cm) long, color intensity varies

The glossy flower of *Paphiopedilum* Hsinying Fairbre looks as though it has been varnished.

Paphiopedilum Joyce Hasegawa displays a soft white, elegant flower.

SEASON OF BLOOM: Spring
MATURE SIZE, HABIT: Dwarf, 5 in. (12.5 cm)
CULTURE: Easy
LIGHT: Low to medium
TEMPERATURE: Intermediate
POTTING MEDIUM: Fine, well-draining

Paphiopedilum Joyce Hasegawa

PRONUNCIATION: paff-ee-oh-PEA-di-lum
ORIGIN: *Paphiopedilum delenatii* × *Paphiopedilum emersonii*. Registered by Paphanatics in 1991.

DESCRIPTION AND QUALITIES: This fragrant hybrid resembles a large *Paphiopedilum delenatii*.
FLOWER: Large, white, with blush of pink on pouch, 3 in. (7.5 cm) across
SEASON OF BLOOM: Variable
MATURE SIZE, HABIT: Dwarf, 4 in. (10 cm)
CULTURE: Intermediate
LIGHT: Low to medium
TEMPERATURE: Intermediate
POTTING MEDIUM: Fine, well-draining

Paphiopedilum Kowloon

PRONUNCIATION: paff-ee-oh-PEA-di-lum
ORIGIN: *Paphiopedilum* New Era × *Paphiopedilum purpuratum*. Bred by G. Boyd and registered by Stewart, Inc., in 1977.
DESCRIPTION AND QUALITIES: This mini *Paphiopedilum* hybrid is vigorous and easy to grow and quickly becomes a nice specimen plant.
FLOWER: 3 in. (7.5 cm) spread, dorsal is white with green stripes, petals are green and purple, and pouch is light red
SEASON OF BLOOM: Spring to summer
MATURE SIZE, HABIT: Dwarf, 3 in. (7.5 cm)
CULTURE: Easy
LIGHT: Low to medium
TEMPERATURE: Intermediate to warm
POTTING MEDIUM: Fine, well-draining

Paphiopedilum Langley Pride

PRONUNCIATION: paff-ee-oh-PEA-di-lum
ORIGIN: *Paphiopedilum* Euryostom × *Paphiopedilum* Maginot. Registered by Black and Flory in 1947.
DESCRIPTION AND QUALITIES: This complex hybrid is typical of some of the finer spotted hybrids, which have been out of vogue in recent times but are starting to receive new attention. I obtained a division of this plant many years ago. Unfortunately, I damaged the roots (probably from overwatering) and it took a long time to recover. In fact, I owned this orchid for 26 years be-

fore it bloomed. Luckily, it is now healthy and blooms each year.

FLOWER: 4 in. (10 cm) across, dorsal is white with a flush of green and prominent dark burgundy spots, petals and pouch are suffused in red

SEASON OF BLOOM: Winter to spring

MATURE SIZE, HABIT: Compact, 9 in. (23 cm)

CULTURE: Easy

LIGHT: Low to medium

TEMPERATURE: Intermediate

POTTING MEDIUM: Fine, well-draining

Paphiopedilum Kowloon is a charming, dwarf growing slipper orchid.

Paphiopedilum Lynleigh Koopowitz

PRONUNCIATION: paff-ee-oh-PEA-di-lum

ORIGIN: *Paphiopedilum delenatii* × *Paphiopedilum malipoense*. Registered by Paphanatics in 1991.

DESCRIPTION AND QUALITIES: This elegant *Paphiopedilum* primary hybrid offers a delicate raspberry scent and gorgeous marbled foliage. It is easier to grow and bloom than either of its parents.

FLOWER: 3 in. (7.5 cm) across, soft creamy lime with maroon dusting, light pink pouch with darker pink or purple staminode

SEASON OF BLOOM: Variable

MATURE SIZE, HABIT: Dwarf, 4 in. (10 cm)

CULTURE: Intermediate

LIGHT: Low

TEMPERATURE: Intermediate

POTTING MEDIUM: Fine, well-draining

Paphiopedilum Langley Pride 'Burlingame' HCC/ AOS has a huge, showy flower.

Paphiopedilum Magic Lantern

PRONUNCIATION: paff-ee-oh-PEA-di-lum

ORIGIN: *Paphiopedilum micranthum* × *Paphiopedilum delenatii*. Bred by Terry Root and registered by Orchid Zone in 1990.

DESCRIPTION AND QUALITIES: One of the most popular dwarf growing slipper hybrids because of its rich flower color and beautifully marked foliage.

FLOWER: $2^1/_2$–3 in. (6.0–7.5 cm) wide, color varies from light pink to raspberry with darker red veins

Paphiopedilum Lynleigh Koopowitz has become a favorite.

Paphiopedilum Magic Lantern is brilliantly colored.

Paphiopedilum malipoense is a collector's treasure.

Paphiopedilum Maudiae represents the ultimate in slipper orchids for grace and style.

SEASON OF BLOOM: Spring to summer
MATURE SIZE, HABIT: Dwarf, 4 in. (10 cm)
CULTURE: Easy
LIGHT: Low to medium
TEMPERATURE: Intermediate
POTTING MEDIUM: Fine, well-draining

Paphiopedilum malipoense

PRONUNCIATION: paff-ee-oh-PEA-di-lum mal-i-poh-EN-see
ORIGIN: China, Vietnam
DESCRIPTION AND QUALITIES: This unusual green-flowered variety is valued both as a species and as a parent to impart its large flower size and apple green color to its offspring. The foliage is mottled green.
FLOWER: Raspberry scented, $3^1/_2$ in. (9 cm) across, light or dark green with burgundy veins more or less pronounced. Prominent, dark purple staminode. Scape to 18 in. (46 cm).
SEASON OF BLOOM: Spring to summer
MATURE SIZE, HABIT: Dwarf, 4 in. (10 cm)
CULTURE: Intermediate
LIGHT: Low to medium
TEMPERATURE: Intermediate
POTTING MEDIUM: Fine, well-draining
HISTORY: Introduced by K. M. Feng in 1947.

Paphiopedilum Maudiae

PRONUNCIATION: paff-ee-oh-PEA-di-lum
ORIGIN: *Paphiopedilum callosum* × *Paphiopedilum lawrenceanum*. Registered by Mansell and Hatcher at Charlesworth & Company in 1900.
DESCRIPTION AND QUALITIES: Probably the single most popular slipper orchid in the world due to its elegant, long-lasting flower; gorgeous foliage; and vigorous growth.
FLOWER: Size varies depending on the selection; most are at least 3 in. (7.5 cm) across. Flowers are frequently referred to as *albino* since they have no red pigments

but are white with green veins and pouch.
Also found in dark red variations.
SEASON OF BLOOM: Winter to spring
MATURE SIZE, HABIT: Compact, 9 in. (23 cm)
CULTURE: Easy
LIGHT: Low to medium
TEMPERATURE: Intermediate
POTTING MEDIUM: Fine, well-draining

Paphiopedilum Mint Chocolate

PRONUNCIATION: paff-ee-oh-PEA-di-lum
ORIGIN: *Paphiopedilum godefroyae* × *Paphio-
pedilum malipoense*. Registered by Terry
Root at Orchid Zone in 1994.
DESCRIPTION AND QUALITIES: This delight-
ful, small growing paphiopedilum has
charming, subtly colored flowers.
FLOWER: Creamy white to light green,
3 in. (7.5 cm) across, with dark burgundy
veining
SEASON OF BLOOM: Winter to spring
MATURE SIZE, HABIT: Dwarf, 4 in. (10 cm)
CULTURE: Easy
LIGHT: Low to medium
TEMPERATURE: Intermediate
POTTING MEDIUM: Fine, well-draining

Paphiopedilum moquettianum

PRONUNCIATION: paff-ee-oh-PEA-di-lum
moh-kett-ee-AH-num
ORIGIN: Java, Indonesia
DESCRIPTION AND QUALITIES: This adaptable slipper orchid provides a long blooming period, since each flower is long last-
ing and flowers are borne in sequence.
Leaves are plain green to lightly marked.
FLOWER: Similar to *Paphiopedilum glaucophyllum*, 2^1/$_2$ in. (6 cm) across with cork-
screw petals. Dorsal sepal is apple green
with a dusting of burgundy speckles, slipper is rose-pink.
SEASON OF BLOOM: Spring
MATURE SIZE, HABIT: Compact, 9 in. (23
cm), leaves to 12 in. (30 cm) or more
CULTURE: Easy

A newer primary
hybrid, *Paphio-
pedilum* Mint
Chocolate

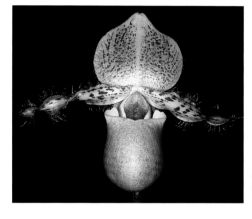

*Paphiopedilum
moquettianum*
sparkles in
bright light.

LIGHT: Low to medium
TEMPERATURE: Intermediate
POTTING MEDIUM: Fine, well-draining
HISTORY: Introduced by J. J. Smith in 1906.

Paphiopedilum Norito Hasegawa

PRONUNCIATION: paff-ee-oh-PEA-di-lum
ORIGIN: *Paphiopedilum malipoense* × *Paphiopedilum armeniacum*. Registered by Terry
Root at Orchid Zone in 1992.
DESCRIPTION AND QUALITIES: The flower
shape of this newer hybrid resembles a
larger form of *Paphiopedilum armeniacum*.
FLOWER: 3 in. (7.5 cm) across, color varies
from greens to light pink, to creamy white,
to yellow
SEASON OF BLOOM: Winter to spring

Paphiopedilum Norito Hasegawa flowers are a brilliant yellow.

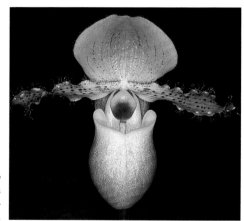

Paphiopedilum Pinocchio has charming, long-lasting flowers.

Paphiopedilum primulinum is favored for its buttery yellow sequential flowers.

MATURE SIZE, HABIT: Compact, 9 in. (23 cm)
CULTURE: Easy
LIGHT: Medium
TEMPERATURE: Intermediate to warm
POTTING MEDIUM: Fine, well-draining

Paphiopedilum Pinocchio

PRONUNCIATION: paff-ee-oh-PEA-di-lum
ORIGIN: *Paphiopedilum glaucophyllum* × *Paphiopedilum primulinum*. Registered by Marcel Lecoufle in 1977.
DESCRIPTION AND QUALITIES: This popular, easy hybrid has small, colorful flowers that are borne sequentially to put on a show for months.
FLOWER: 2–2^1/$_2$ in. (5–6 cm), borne in succession, lime green dorsal, red striped petals, bright pink pouch
SEASON OF BLOOM: Spring to summer
MATURE SIZE, HABIT: Dwarf, 5 in. (12.5 cm)
CULTURE: Easy
LIGHT: Low to medium
TEMPERATURE: Intermediate
POTTING MEDIUM: Fine, well-draining

Paphiopedilum primulinum

PRONUNCIATION: paff-ee-oh-PEA-di-lum prim-you-LYE-num
ORIGIN: Sumatra, Indonesia
DESCRIPTION AND QUALITIES: Easy to grow and sequentially blooming, frequently used to produce small, multi-flowering hybrids. Plain green foliage.
FLOWER: 2 in. (5 cm) across, green to yellow
SEASON OF BLOOM: Spring to summer
MATURE SIZE, HABIT: Dwarf, 4 in. (10 cm), leaves 12 in. (30 cm) long
CULTURE: Easy
LIGHT: Low to medium
TEMPERATURE: Intermediate
POTTING MEDIUM: Fine, well-draining
CULTURAL TIPS: If grown in subdued light, flowers tend to be greenish; they are more yellow when grown in brighter light.
RELATED SPECIES, HYBRIDS: *Paphiopedilum*

primulinum var. *purpurascens* has darker coloration, and *Paph. primulinum* var. *aureum* is a yellow form.

HISTORY: Introduced by Liem in 1972.

Paphiopedilum S. Gratix

PRONUNCIATION: paff-ee-oh-PEA-di-lum

ORIGIN: *Paphiopedilum bellatulum* × *Paphiopedilum godefroyae*. Registered by S. Gratix in 1898.

DESCRIPTION AND QUALITIES: This old hybrid was made before the turn of the 20th century, yet it is still included in collections today. This variety is also used in hybridizing to produce white-flowered offspring.

FLOWER: 3 in. (7.5 cm) across, white, covered with dark burgundy spots

SEASON OF BLOOM: Winter to spring

MATURE SIZE, HABIT: Miniature, 3 in. (7.5 cm)

CULTURE: Easy

LIGHT: Low to medium

TEMPERATURE: Intermediate

POTTING MEDIUM: Fine, well-draining

CULTURAL TIPS: Let it dry between waterings. Like its parents, it can rot if kept too wet.

Paphiopedilum spicerianum

PRONUNCIATION: paff-ee-oh-PEA-di-lum spice-er-ee-AH-num

ORIGIN: India, Burma

DESCRIPTION AND QUALITIES: This distinctive slipper orchid has a special beauty and has been extensively used in breeding, due to its clear white, wide dorsal sepal. Its hybrids usually carry the telltale purple vertical stripe and wide, usually white, dorsal. Leaves are dark green and semi-glossy.

FLOWER: 2 in. (5 cm) across, dorsal sepal is bright white with purple vertical stripe. Petals and slipper are blends of olive green and brown. The prominent staminode is dark purple.

Paphiopedilum S. Gratix is a dwarf grower with spotted white flowers.

The fabulous white dorsal sepal with a purple vertical stripe quickly identifies this orchid as *Paphiopedilum spicerianum*.

SEASON OF BLOOM: Winter to spring

MATURE SIZE, HABIT: Dwarf, 9 in. (23 cm)

CULTURE: Easy

LIGHT: Low to medium

TEMPERATURE: Intermediate

POTTING MEDIUM: Fine, well-draining

HISTORY: Introduced from India into cultivation in England in 1878.

Brightly spotted, wide petals are the definitive features of *Paphiopedilum sukhakulii*.

Paphiopedilum Vanda M. Pearman is a longtime favorite.

Paphiopedilum sukhakulii

PRONUNCIATION: paff-ee-oh-PEA-di-lum sook-ah-KOOL-ee-eye

ORIGIN: Thailand

DESCRIPTION AND QUALITIES: One of the easiest of the paphiopedilums to grow and bloom. This species has been more difficult to find for sale of late but it has commonly been used in hybrids. Leaves are handsomely marked.

FLOWER: Petals are green with maroon spots and hairs, 3 in. (7.5 cm) across; lip is dark red; and dorsal sepal is white with red veins

SEASON OF BLOOM: Spring to summer

MATURE SIZE, HABIT: Dwarf, 9 in. (23 cm) tall, leaves spread 8 in. (20 cm)

CULTURE: Easy

LIGHT: Low to medium

TEMPERATURE: Intermediate

POTTING MEDIUM: Fine, well-draining

HISTORY: Discovered by Prasong Sakhakul in 1964 in Thailand.

Paphiopedilum Vanda M. Pearman

PRONUNCIATION: paff-ee-oh-PEA-di-lum

ORIGIN: *Paphiopedilum bellatulum* × *Paphiopedilum delenatii*. Registered by S. Farnes in 1939.

DESCRIPTION AND QUALITIES: This old classic has a stunning flower and foliage to match. The highly recommended beginner orchid is easier to grow than both its parents. New crossings of it are being made today using *Paphiopedilum delenatii* selections that, hopefully, will make this hybrid easier to bloom.

FLOWER: 3 in. (7.5 cm) or more across, light pink, with darker pink speckles

SEASON OF BLOOM: Winter to spring

MATURE SIZE, HABIT: Compact, 5 in. (12.5 cm), 10 in. (25 cm) leaf spread

CULTURE: Easy

LIGHT: Low to medium

TEMPERATURE: Intermediate

Flowers of *Phalaenopsis* Ambo Buddha 'SW' shimmer in the light.

POTTING MEDIUM: Fine, well-draining

CULTURAL TIPS: The plants bloom better when they are permitted to become larger plants. Do not be too eager to divide them.

Phalaenopsis Ambo Buddha

PRONUNCIATION: fal-en-OP-siss

ORIGIN: *Phalaenopsis* Brother Buddha × *Phalaenopsis amboinensis*. Registered by Brother in 1993.

DESCRIPTION AND QUALITIES: The fact that this *Phalaenopsis* hybrid is offered in many clones attests to its popularity.

FLOWER: 2^1/$_2$ in. (6 cm) across, lightly fragrant, thick and glossy, yellow with an overlay of dark red spots and bars, red lip

SEASON OF BLOOM: Winter to spring

MATURE SIZE, HABIT: Dwarf, 4 in. (10 cm), leaf spread of 12 in. (30 cm)

CULTURE: Easy

LIGHT: Low to medium

TEMPERATURE: Warm

POTTING MEDIUM: Sphagnum moss, medium bark, or coco chunk mixes

Phalaenopsis bellina is used extensively as a parent to impart its waxy substance, color, and fragrance to its progeny.

Phalaenopsis bellina

PRONUNCIATION: fal-en-OP-siss bell-EE-nah

SYNONYMS: *Phalaenopsis violacea* 'Borneo', *Phalaenopsis violacea* var. *bellina*

ORIGIN: Malaysia, East Malaysia

Phalaenopsis borneensis is a rare species.

DESCRIPTION AND QUALITIES: This important species is valuable as a parent to produce small hybrids with waxy flowers borne on short inflorescences. Glossy green leaves.

FLOWER: Fragrant, waxy, greenish with purple markings, borne sequentially

SEASON OF BLOOM: Variable

MATURE SIZE, HABIT: Compact, leaves 8–10 in. (20–25 cm) long

CULTURE: Intermediate

LIGHT: Low to medium

TEMPERATURE: Warm

POTTING MEDIUM: Sphagnum moss, medium bark, or coco chunk mixes

CULTURAL TIPS: Smaller seedling plants can be susceptible to crown rot. Ensure that the growing point of the plant is dry in evening. Do not cut off the flower spike after the flower fades because new flowers form on the same inflorescence.

HISTORY: Discovered by Teijsmann in 1859.

Phalaenopsis borneensis

PRONUNCIATION: fal-en-OP-siss bore-nee-EN-siss

ORIGIN: Borneo

DESCRIPTION AND QUALITIES: This species is frequently confused with *Phalaenopsis cornu-cervi*.

FLOWER: 2 in. (5 cm), waxy, yellow-green, barred in dark brown and borne sequentially

SEASON OF BLOOM: Winter to summer

MATURE SIZE, HABIT: Compact, 10 in. (25 cm) leaf spread

CULTURE: Intermediate

LIGHT: Low to medium

TEMPERATURE: Warm

POTTING MEDIUM: Sphagnum moss, medium bark, or coco chunk mixes

Phalaenopsis Caribbean Sunset

PRONUNCIATION: fal-en-OP-siss

ORIGIN: *Phalaenopsis* Cassandra × *Phalae-*

nopsis Mambo. Bred by Fred K. Thorton and registered by Thorton's in 1970.
DESCRIPTION AND QUALITIES: A delightful red hybrid with a delicate, roselike scent.
FLOWER: 2 in. (5 cm), abundant; this grex can have colors from soft pinks to rosy reds and light purple reds
SEASON OF BLOOM: Variable
MATURE SIZE, HABIT: Dwarf, leaves 6 in. (15 cm) long
CULTURE: Easy
LIGHT: Low
TEMPERATURE: Warm
POTTING MEDIUM: Sphagnum moss, medium bark, or coco chunk mixes
HISTORY: 'Sweet Fragrance' is part of a phalaenopsis fragrance series offered by Norman's Orchids.

Phalaenopsis cornu-cervi
PRONUNCIATION: fal-en-OP-siss kore-noo-SURV-eye
SYNONYMS: *Phalaenopsis lamelligera, Phalaenopsis devriesiana*

ORIGIN: India, Java
DESCRIPTION AND QUALITIES: This easily grown species is highly variable and used frequently in hybridizing to impart its waxy texture and barred patterns to its offspring.
FLOWER: 2 in. (5 cm) across, waxy, from greenish to yellow, brown barred
SEASON OF BLOOM: Summer
MATURE SIZE, HABIT: Dwarf, 3 in. (7.5 cm), leaves spread 10 in. (25 cm)

Phalaenopsis Caribbean Sunset 'Sweet Fragrance' is sweetly scented.

Phalaenopsis cornu-cervi 'Rhegan' flowers look as though they have been varnished.

The white form of *Phalaenopsis equestris* is dazzling.

CULTURE: Easy

LIGHT: Low to medium

TEMPERATURE: Warm

POTTING MEDIUM: Sphagnum moss, medium bark, or coco chunk mixes

HISTORY: First brought into England in 1864 by the famous Parish and Low orchid purveyors.

Phalaenopsis equestris

PRONUNCIATION: fal-en-OP-siss eh-KWESS-triss

SYNONYMS: *Phalaenopsis rosea, Stauroglottis equestris*

ORIGIN: Philippines

DESCRIPTION AND QUALITIES: This species has been widely used as a parent to produce small, multiple branching, flowering offspring. It contributes striping and colored lips to hybrids. Similar to *Phalaenopsis lindenii*.

FLOWER: 1 in. (2.5 cm) across, color variable, from light to dark pink, sometimes white, with darker lips, or striped

SEASON OF BLOOM: Winter to spring

MATURE SIZE, HABIT: Dwarf, 3 in. (7.5 cm), leaf spread 6 in. (15 cm)

CULTURE: Easy

LIGHT: Low to medium

TEMPERATURE: Warm

POTTING MEDIUM: Sphagnum moss, medium bark, or coco chunk mixes

CULTURAL TIPS: Do not cut off the flower spikes as they frequently bloom again. This species frequently forms *keikis* (baby plants) on the flowering spikes.

HISTORY: First collected on the island of Luzon in the Philippines in 1843.
RELATES SPECIES, HYBRIDS: *Phalaenopsis lindenii*

Phalaenopsis Kilby Cassviola

PRONUNCIATION: fal-en-OP-siss
ORIGIN: *Phalaenopsis* Cassandra × *Phalaenopsis violacea*. Registered by C. Taylor in 1997.
DESCRIPTION AND QUALITIES: This compact growing phalaenopsis has glistening white, spice-scented flowers. As plants get older, they produce branching flower spikes that make an attractive display.
FLOWER: 2^1/$_2$ in. (6 cm), spicy scented, clear white, with a yellow flush and light brown barring on the lower sepals and throat
SEASON OF BLOOM: Variable
MATURE SIZE, HABIT: Compact
CULTURE: Intermediate
LIGHT: Low
TEMPERATURE: Warm
POTTING MEDIUM: Sphagnum moss, medium bark, or coco chunk mixes
HISTORY: Bred using the white *Phalaenopsis violacea* var. *alba*. 'Sweet Fragrance' is one of the series of fragrant phalaenopsis from Norman's Orchids.

Phalaenopsis Kung's Gelb Lishian

PRONUNCIATION: fal-en-OP-siss
ORIGIN: *Phalaenopsis* Yungho Gelbliambo × *Phalaenopsis* Hsu Li-Shian. Registered by Kung's in 2001.
DESCRIPTION AND QUALITIES: A strikingly handsome flower on a compact plant make this hybrid a welcome addition to any collection.
FLOWER: 2^1/$_2$ in. (6 cm) across, bright yellow with prominent, wide, dark burgundy bars
SEASON OF BLOOM: Winter to spring
MATURE SIZE, HABIT: Compact, 4 in. (10 cm), 12 in. (30 cm) leaf spread

Flowers of *Phalaenopsis* Kilby Cassviola 'Sweet Fragrance' are sparkling white.

Phalaenopsis Kung's Gelb Lishian flowers are brilliantly marked.

CULTURE: Easy
LIGHT: Medium
TEMPERATURE: Warm
POTTING MEDIUM: Sphagnum moss, medium bark, or coco chunk mixes

Phalaenopsis Kuntrarti Rarashati

PRONUNCIATION: fal-en-OP-siss
ORIGIN: *Phalaenopsis equestris* × *Phalaenopsis venosa*. Registered by A. Kolopaking in 1986.
DESCRIPTION AND QUALITIES: This cute, heavily and frequently flowering primary hybrid is petite enough to be included in any miniature orchid collection. Its small stature is from parent *Phalaenopsis equestris* and the fragrance is inherited from *Phal. venosa*.

The flowers of *Phalaenopsis* Kuntrarti Rarashati 'Joy' have a luminous quality.

FLOWER: Fragrant, 1 in. (2.5 cm), light pink and lightly striped, with a touch of yellow at the base of the lip, borne on 6 in. (15 cm) inflorescence
SEASON OF BLOOM: Variable
MATURE SIZE, HABIT: Dwarf, 10 in. (25 cm) leaf spread, slow vertical growth
CULTURE: Easy
LIGHT: Low to medium
TEMPERATURE: Warm
POTTING MEDIUM: Fine to medium epiphytic mix

Phalaenopsis Little Mary

PRONUNCIATION: fal-en-OP-siss
ORIGIN: *Phalaenopsis* Mary Tuazon × *Phalaenopsis equestris*. Registered by R. Takase in 1986.
DESCRIPTION AND QUALITIES: Popular at orchid shows because of its uniquely marked flower and small size.
FLOWER: 2$^{1}/_{2}$ in. (6 cm) across, dark pink,

with darker pink picotee-like markings on the edge of the petals
SEASON OF BLOOM: Winter to spring
MATURE SIZE, HABIT: Dwarf
CULTURE: Easy
LIGHT: Low to medium
TEMPERATURE: Warm
POTTING MEDIUM: Sphagnum moss, medium bark, or coco chunk mixes

Phalaenopsis lobbii

PRONUNCIATION: fal-en-OP-siss LOBB-ee-eye
SYNONYM: *Phalaenopsis parishii* var. *lobbii*
ORIGIN: Eastern Himalayas
DESCRIPTION AND QUALITIES: One of the smallest of all *Phalaenopsis* species, it can be a reluctant grower. Its charming flowers and miniature growth habit make it useful as a parent for small hybrids.
FLOWER: White, slightly reflexed, $^{1}/_{2}$ in. (1 cm) across, red-orange lip with yellow

Phalaenopsis Little Mary 'Cherry Blossom' displays tight sprays of flowers.

markings. Various forms display different lip colors and markings.

SEASON OF BLOOM: Spring to summer
MATURE SIZE, HABIT: Miniature, $1^1/2$ in. (4 cm) leaves, with 5 in. (12.5 cm) spread
CULTURE: Intermediate
LIGHT: Low to medium
TEMPERATURE: Warm
POTTING MEDIUM: Fine orchid mix
CULTURAL TIPS: Keep evenly moist.
HISTORY: Named in honor of plant collector Thomas Lobb.

Phalaenopsis mannii

PRONUNCIATION: fal-en-OP-siss MANN-ee-eye
SYNONYM: *Phalaenopsis oxalis*
ORIGIN: India, Vietnam
DESCRIPTION AND QUALITIES: This *Phalaenopsis* species requires low light and tolerates high temperatures. Flowers last to three months.

Phalaenopsis lobbii is a true miniature.

FLOWER: Mandarin orange fragrance, 10 to 15 waxy, star-shaped, 1–2 in. (2.5–5.0 cm) across, borne on a pendulous spike. Sepals and petals yellow to bronze; petals frequently marked with red blotches. Lip is purple and white.
SEASON OF BLOOM: Winter to spring

Flowers of *Phalaenopsis mannii* are long-lasting and waxy.

Brilliant bars of color mark the flowers of *Phalaenopsis mariae* 'Chappy'.

MATURE SIZE, HABIT: Compact, leaf spread 6–18 in. (15–46 cm)
CULTURE: Intermediate
LIGHT: Low
TEMPERATURE: Warm

POTTING MEDIUM: Sphagnum moss, medium bark, or coco chunk mixes
HISTORY: Named after the first collector of this species, Gustav Mann.

Phalaenopsis mariae

PRONUNCIATION: fal-en-OP-siss mah-REE-ay
ORIGIN: Philippines
DESCRIPTION AND QUALITIES: This brilliantly colored species deserves to be in more collections. Used in hybridizing to impart its strong dark red bars and red coloration to its offspring. Somewhat rare in cultivation. Sometimes confused with *Phalaenopsis bastiani*.
FLOWER: Lightly fragrant, 2 in. (5 cm) across, creamy white with dark red to burgundy barring
SEASON OF BLOOM: Winter to spring

MATURE SIZE, HABIT: Dwarf, 4 in. (10 cm), leaves spread 12 in. (30 cm)
CULTURE: Intermediate
LIGHT: Low to medium
TEMPERATURE: Warm
POTTING MEDIUM: Sphagnum moss, medium bark, or coco chunk mixes
HISTORY: F. W. Burbidge of the English Veitch orchid establishment found this orchid on an island in the Philippines. Its name was first published in 1883.

Phalaenopsis Mini Mark

PRONUNCIATION: fal-en-OP-siss
ORIGIN: *Phalaenopsis* Micro Nova × *Phalaenopsis philippinensis.* Registered by Breckenridge in 1992.
DESCRIPTION AND QUALITIES: A delightful *Phalaenopsis* with a delicate scent.
FLOWER: 1^1/$_4$ in. (3 cm), white with dark red speckles and orange and yellow lip
SEASON OF BLOOM: Variable
MATURE SIZE, HABIT: Dwarf, leaf spread 6 in. (15 cm)
CULTURE: Easy
LIGHT: Low to medium
TEMPERATURE: Warm
POTTING MEDIUM: Sphagnum moss, medium bark, or coco chunk mixes

Phalaenopsis Nobby's Amy

PRONUNCIATION: fal-en-OP-siss
ORIGIN: *Phalaenopsis* Be Glad × *Phalaenopsis* Rothschildiana. Registered by Nobby Orchids in 1998.
DESCRIPTION AND QUALITIES: This hybrid inherits its habit from *Phalaenopsis* Be Glad, which inherited its size from *Phal. equestris.*
FLOWER: 2^1/$_2$ in. (6 cm), creamy white with suffusions of yellow and pink

Phalaenopsis Mini Mark 'Holm' is a lovely phalaenopsis with a delicate floral scent. Photo by Marc Herzog.

The unusual peloric flower form of *Phalaenopsis* Nobby's Amy

SEASON OF BLOOM: Winter to spring
MATURE SIZE, HABIT: Dwarf, 4 in. (10 cm), 10 in. (25 cm) leaf span
CULTURE: Easy
LIGHT: Low to medium
TEMPERATURE: Warm
POTTING MEDIUM: Sphagnum moss, medium bark, or coco chunk mixes

Phalaenopsis Orchid World

PRONUNCIATION: fal-en-OP-siss
ORIGIN: *Phalaenopsis* Malibu Imp × *Phalaenopsis* Deventeriana. Registered by Orchid World International in 1984.
DESCRIPTION AND QUALITIES: If you enjoy fragrant phalaenopsis, look for any of the clones of this grex or hybrid.

Phalaenopsis Orchid World 'Roman Holiday' AM/AOS is a fabulous orchid that is compact, brightly colored, and fragrant.

Phalaenopsis Penang Girl is richly colored and sweetly scented.

Phalaenopsis Perfection Is 'Chen' AM/AOS has a gorgeous flower with a strong, spicy scent.

clones of this popular, fragrant variety are available.
FLOWER: 2^1/$_2$ in. (6 cm), heavy, orange-yellow overlaid with red
SEASON OF BLOOM: Winter to spring
MATURE SIZE, HABIT: Compact, 4 in. (10 cm), leaf spread 10 in. (25 cm)
CULTURE: Easy
LIGHT: Low to medium
TEMPERATURE: Warm
POTTING MEDIUM: Sphagnum moss, medium bark, or coco chunk mixes

Phalaenopsis Perfection Is

PRONUNCIATION: fal-en-OP-siss
ORIGIN: *Phalaenopsis* Golden Peoker × *Phalaenopsis* Black Eagle. Registered by Howard Ginsberg in 1999.
DESCRIPTION AND QUALITIES: One of my favorite compact, fragrant phalaenopsis. The waxy flowers are always presented well and last a long time. This superior clone is frequently offered by various phalaenopsis specialists.
FLOWER: Spicy fragrance, 2^1/$_2$ in. (6 cm), heavy, flat yellow, covered with burgundy-red spots
SEASON OF BLOOM: Variable

FLOWER: Fragrant, 2^1/$_2$ in. (6 cm), bright yellow, with dark red stripes and markings
SEASON OF BLOOM: Winter to spring
MATURE SIZE, HABIT: Compact, slow vertical growth. Will take several years to exceed 6 in. (15 cm) in height.
CULTURE: Easy
LIGHT: Low to medium
TEMPERATURE: Warm
POTTING MEDIUM: Medium grade epiphytic mix or sphagnum moss

Phalaenopsis Penang Girl

PRONUNCIATION: fal-en-OP-siss
ORIGIN: *Phalaenopsis violacea* × *Phalaenopsis venosa*. Registered by Ooi Leng Soon in 1984.
DESCRIPTION AND QUALITIES: Many selected

Phalaenopsis Sogo Twinkle is an ideal dwarf-sized plant.

MATURE SIZE, HABIT: Compact
CULTURE: Easy
LIGHT: Low
TEMPERATURE: Warm
POTTING MEDIUM: Medium orchid mix or sphagnum moss

Phalaenopsis Sogo Twinkle

PRONUNCIATION: fal-en-OP-siss
ORIGIN: *Phalaenopsis* Be Tris × *Phalaenopsis* Sogo Tris. Registered by Sogo in 1999.
DESCRIPTION AND QUALITIES: This fine hybrid produces plenty of small flowers on a branched spike that does not need to be staked. Its growth habit and branched flower spikes are inherited from grandparent *Phalaenopsis equestris*.
FLOWER: 2 in. (5 cm) across, dark pink with white edging
SEASON OF BLOOM: Winter to spring
MATURE SIZE, HABIT: Dwarf, 3 in. (7.5 cm),

leaf spread 8 in. (20 cm)
CULTURE: Easy
LIGHT: Medium
TEMPERATURE: Warm
POTTING MEDIUM: Sphagnum moss, medium bark, or coco chunk mixes

Phalaenopsis Valentinii

PRONUNCIATION: fal-en-OP-siss
ORIGIN: *Phalaenopsis cornu-cervi* × *Phalaenopsis violacea*. Registered in 1959.
DESCRIPTION AND QUALITIES: This older hybrid is still popular, with long-lasting, sweetly scented flowers.
FLOWER: Fragrant, waxy, brownish orange with dark pink overlay, 2 in. (5 cm) or more across
SEASON OF BLOOM: Winter to spring
MATURE SIZE, HABIT: Dwarf, 3 in. (7.5 cm), leaf spread 10 in. (25 cm)
CULTURE: Easy

Phalaenopsis Valentinii has a waxy, fragrant flower.

A fine *Phalaenopsis violacea* orchid displays vibrant flower colors.

Phalaenopsis violacea 'Blue Chip' is a superb "blue" form.

LIGHT: Low to medium
TEMPERATURE: Warm
POTTING MEDIUM: Sphagnum moss, medium bark, or coco chunk mixes

Phalaenopsis violacea

PRONUNCIATION: fal-en-OP-siss vye-oh-LAY-see-ah
SYNONYM: *Phalaenopsis violacea 'Malayan Type'*
ORIGIN: Malaysia, Indonesia
DESCRIPTION AND QUALITIES: This species has a compact habit and brightly colored, fragrant flowers. It is used in hybridizing to pass both characteristics to its offspring. A bit more challenging to grow than some of the other *Phalaenopsis* species, it is worth the effort. Glossy, light green leaves. 'Blue Chip' a gorgeous clone developed by H. P. Norton of Orchidview in South Carolina.
FLOWER: Fragrant, 2 in. (5 cm) across, larger on selected forms, color variable from white to light and dark pink, and rarely shades of lavender blue. 'Blue Chip' is more than 2 in. (5 cm) across, solid lavender-blue that is among the bluest to date, with a darker lip and touch of yellow in the throat.
SEASON OF BLOOM: Variable
MATURE SIZE, HABIT: Compact, 4 in. (10 cm), leaf spread 12 in. (30 cm)
CULTURE: Intermediate
LIGHT: Low to medium
TEMPERATURE: Warm
POTTING MEDIUM: Sphagnum moss, medium bark, or coco chunk mixes
CULTURAL TIPS: Do not remove the old flower spike because new flowers will arise from it.

Phalaenopsis Yungho Gelb Canary

PRONUNCIATION: fal-en-OP-siss
ORIGIN: *Phalaenopsis* Gelblieber × *Phalaenopsis* Princess Kaiulani. Registered by Yung-Ho in 1995.

DESCRIPTION AND QUALITIES: This much loved, fragrant hybrid was one of the first to show clear yellow flowers. Many of its superior clones are starting to appear on the market.

FLOWER: Yellow

SEASON OF BLOOM: Winter to spring

MATURE SIZE, HABIT: Compact

CULTURE: Easy

LIGHT: Low to medium

TEMPERATURE: Warm

POTTING MEDIUM: Sphagnum moss, medium bark, or coco chunk mixes

Phalaenopsis Yungho Gelb Canary 'GT' is as bright as sunshine.

Phragmipedium Hanne Popow

PRONUNCIATION: frag-mi-PEA-dee-um

ORIGIN: *Phragmipedium besseae* × *Phragmipedium schlimii*. Registered by H. Doll in 1991.

DESCRIPTION AND QUALITIES: This hybrid has been used frequently as a parent for newer crosses.

FLOWER: Sequential bloomer, $2^1/2$ in. (6 cm) wide, variable in color, from light to dark pink, to shades of red and orange, with a bright yellow staminode

SEASON OF BLOOM: Winter to spring

MATURE SIZE, HABIT: Compact, 12 in. (30 cm) or taller

CULTURE: Intermediate

LIGHT: Medium

TEMPERATURE: Intermediate

POTTING MEDIUM: Frequently grown in long-fibered sphagnum moss

CULTURAL TIPS: Growing medium should always stay damp.

Phragmipedium schlimii

PRONUNCIATION: frag-mi-PEA-dee-um SHLIM-ee-eye

SYNONYM: *Cypripedium schlimii*

Phragmipedium Hanne Popow is a popular hybrid.

ORIGIN: Colombia

DESCRIPTION AND QUALITIES: Although most species and hybrids in this popular genus tend to be large plants, this fragrant one is a beautiful exception.

FLOWER: Fragrant, 2 in. (5 cm), white with pink pouch, borne successively along a 12 in. (30 cm) inflorescence

SEASON OF BLOOM: Spring

MATURE SIZE, HABIT: Compact, to 18 in. (46 cm) but frequently smaller

CULTURE: Intermediate

LIGHT: Low to medium

TEMPERATURE: Intermediate

POTTING MEDIUM: Frequently grown in long-fibered sphagnum moss

Phragmipedium schlimii is one of the few fragrant phragmipediums.

The blood-red flowers of *Pleurothallis cardiothallis* emerge from the centers of its heart-shaped leaves.

FLOWER: Dark scarlet-red, $^1/_2$ in. (1 cm) long, emerges from the center of the leaf
SEASON OF BLOOM: Summer to fall
MATURE SIZE, HABIT: Dwarf, 6 in. (15 cm)
CULTURE: Intermediate
LIGHT: Medium
TEMPERATURE: Intermediate
POTTING MEDIUM: Fine, well-draining mix, or mounted

Pleurothallis mystax

PRONUNCIATION: ploor-oh-THAL-iss MISS-tacks
SYNONYM: *Stelis mystax*
ORIGIN: Panama
DESCRIPTION AND QUALITIES: The species name and common name, mustached pleurothallis, refers to the flower's resemblance to a mustache.
FLOWER: $^3/_4$ in. (2 cm), dark red
SEASON OF BLOOM: Summer to fall
MATURE SIZE, HABIT: Miniature, 2 in. (5 cm)
CULTURE: Intermediate
LIGHT: Medium
TEMPERATURE: Cool to intermediate
POTTING MEDIUM: Fine, well-draining mix, or mounted
HISTORY: First described by Carlyle Luer in 1976.

Pleurothallis pterophora

PRONUNCIATION: ploor-oh-THAL-iss tear-OFF-er-ah
SYNONYM: *Trichosalpinx pterophora*
ORIGIN: Brazil
DESCRIPTION AND QUALITIES: Small, but prolific, long-lasting flowers emit a sweet rose or lily-of-the-valley fragrance. It blooms more than once a year and flowers repeatedly on older growths.
FLOWER: Scented, $^1/_4$ in. (6 mm), on 5 in. (12.5 cm) inflorescence
SEASON OF BLOOM: Spring to summer
MATURE SIZE, HABIT: Dwarf, 4 in. (10 cm)

CULTURAL TIPS: Growing medium should always stay damp.
HISTORY: Discovered by L. J. Schlim in 1852.

Pleurothallis cardiothallis

PRONUNCIATION: ploor-oh-THAL-iss kar-dee-oh-THAL-iss
ORIGIN: Ecuador
DESCRIPTION AND QUALITIES: This once rare species is found more frequently in today's collections. The species name is derived from the Greek word *cardia*, meaning heart, and refers to its leaf shape. Leaves are shiny and resemble those of an anthurium. Part of the Pleurothallid Alliance.

Pleurothallis mystax
is an interesting
miniature.

*Pleurothallis
pterophora* is a
prolific bloomer.

A fine specimen of *Pleurothallis sonderana*. Grown by Parkside Orchid Nursery.

CULTURE: Easy
LIGHT: Medium
TEMPERATURE: Intermediate
POTTING MEDIUM: Fine, well-draining mix, or mounted
HISTORY: First described in 1896.

Pleurothallis sonderana

PRONUNCIATION: ploor-oh-THAL-iss sonder-AN-ah
ORIGIN: Brazil
DESCRIPTION AND QUALITIES: This popular and readily available pleurothallis tolerates warm temperatures.
FLOWER: Orange to yellow, $^1/_2$ in. (1 cm) across, borne in small clusters
SEASON OF BLOOM: Fall to winter
MATURE SIZE, HABIT: Miniature, $1^1/_2$ in. (4 cm), clump forming
CULTURE: Intermediate
LIGHT: Medium
TEMPERATURE: Intermediate

POTTING MEDIUM: Fine, well-draining mix, or mounted
CULTURAL TIPS: Should never dry out completely.
HISTORY: Heinrich Gustav Reichenbach described the species more than 100 years ago.

Pleurothallis tribuloides

PRONUNCIATION: ploor-oh-THAL-iss trib-you-LOY-deez
SYNONYM: *Cryptophoranthus acaulis*
ORIGIN: Broad distribution in the New World and Old World tropics
DESCRIPTION AND QUALITIES: This temperature tolerant species is relatively easy to grow.
FLOWER: Fleshy, $^1/_2$ in. (1 cm), bright red, borne on short spikes; dark blue-green seed pods
SEASON OF BLOOM: Winter to spring
MATURE SIZE, HABIT: Miniature, 3 in. (7.5 cm), leaves $2^1/_2$ in. (6 cm), clump forming

CULTURE: Intermediate
LIGHT: Low to medium
TEMPERATURE: Intermediate
POTTING MEDIUM: Fine, well-draining mix, or mounted
HISTORY: Described as *Epidendrum tribuloides* by Olof P. Swartz in 1788.

Pleurothallis truncata

PRONUNCIATION: ploor-oh-THAL-iss trun-KAH-tah
ORIGIN: Panama, Ecuador
DESCRIPTION AND QUALITIES: This standout *Pleurothallis* species has both attractive foliage and striking flowers. Quite the showpiece, it frequently blooms more than once a year. Heart-shaped leaves.
FLOWER: Spherical, hanging on a 10 in. (25 cm) stem, like small beads on a necklace, from the center of the leaf
SEASON OF BLOOM: Spring to summer
MATURE SIZE, HABIT: Dwarf, 6–8 in. (15–20 cm)
CULTURE: Intermediate
LIGHT: Medium
TEMPERATURE: Cool to intermediate
POTTING MEDIUM: Fine, well-draining mix, or mounted

Polystachya bella

PRONUNCIATION: poll-ee-STACK-ee-ah BELL-ah
ORIGIN: Kenya
DESCRIPTION AND QUALITIES: Considered one of the showiest species in the genus, this easy grower's flowers have a fruity, lemony scent.
FLOWER: Fragrant, $1/2$ in. (1 cm), golden yellow to orange, densely borne upside down on an upright inflorescence
SEASON OF BLOOM: Spring to summer
MATURE SIZE, HABIT: Dwarf, 6 in. (15 cm)
CULTURE: Easy
LIGHT: Medium
TEMPERATURE: Cool to intermediate

Pleurothallis tribuloides has a bright red flower.

Pleurothallis truncata flowers resemble little beads.

The upside-down, bell-shaped flowers of *Polystachya bella* are neatly arranged on the inflorescence.

The flowers of *Polystachya* Darling Star are crystalline white. Grown by J & L Orchids.

Polystachya pubescens displays its bright yellow flowers on an upright inflorescence.

Polystachya Darling Star

PRONUNCIATION: poll-ee-STACK-ee-ah
ORIGIN: *Polystachya ottoniana* × *Polystachya virginea*. Registered by Duckitt in 1995.
DESCRIPTION AND QUALITIES: This vigorous growing hybrid has flowers with heavy substance and sweet fragrance.
FLOWER: Fragrant, $3/4$ in. (2 cm), clear white, borne upside down
SEASON OF BLOOM: Spring
MATURE SIZE, HABIT: Dwarf, 6 in. (15 cm)
CULTURE: Intermediate
LIGHT: Medium
TEMPERATURE: Intermediate
POTTING MEDIUM: Fine grade mix

Polystachya pubescens

PRONUNCIATION: poll-ee-STACK-ee-ah pew-BESS-enz
ORIGIN: South Africa
DESCRIPTION AND QUALITIES: This popular species is showy and easy to grow and flower.
FLOWER: Fragrant, 1 in. (2.5 cm) across, bright yellow, borne in sprays of up to 25. Lower sepals are striped in brown and lips have small tufts of hair.
SEASON OF BLOOM: Fall to winter
MATURE SIZE, HABIT: Dwarf, 4 in. (10 cm)
CULTURE: Easy

POTTING MEDIUM: Fine, well-draining mix, or mounted
CULTURAL TIPS: Place pseudobulb toward the back of the pot to allow room for the creeping rhizome.
RELATED SPECIES, HYBRIDS: Most of the 100 species in this genus are dwarf to compact growers, including *Polystachya aconitifolia*, *Pol. brassii*, *Pol. latilabris*, and *Pol. ottoniana*.

The striking orchid *Ponerorchis graminifolia* var. *suzukiana* is hardy to USDA zone 6.

LIGHT: Medium
TEMPERATURE: Intermediate
POTTING MEDIUM: Fine, well-draining mix, or mounted
HISTORY: Introduced into cultivation in England in the mid-19th century.

Ponerorchis graminifolia var. suzukiana

PRONUNCIATION: pone-OR-kiss gram-in-i-FOH-lee-ah var. soo-zoo-kee-AH-nah
ORIGIN: Japanese islands, Korea
DESCRIPTION AND QUALITIES: This charming orchid was awarded the best species in the 2005 New York International Orchid Show. It is hardy to USDA zone 6 and is used in rock gardens, but it can also be grown as an indoor plant in a cool spot. Dark green foliage is beautifully striped in purple.
FLOWER: $^1/_2$ in. (1 cm), borne on a 3 in. (7.5 cm) inflorescence; species has many color forms

SEASON OF BLOOM: Spring to summer
MATURE SIZE, HABIT: Dwarf, 5 in. (12.5 cm)
CULTURE: Intermediate
LIGHT: Medium
TEMPERATURE: Intermediate
POTTING MEDIUM: Use water-retaining medium. Frequently grown in sphagnum moss.
CULTURAL TIPS: Can be grown in similar fashion to *Neofinetia falcata*. It has tubers the size of a pencil eraser. Keep it cooler, around 50°F (10°C), and drier in the winter.

Porroglossum eduardii

PRONUNCIATION: pore-oh-GLOSS-um ed-WAR-dee-eye
ORIGIN: Colombia
DESCRIPTION AND QUALITIES: A rambling grower with brilliantly colored flowers that glisten in the sunlight.
FLOWER: $^1/_2$ in. (1 cm) tall, 5 in. (12.5 cm) inflorescence
SEASON OF BLOOM: Spring to summer

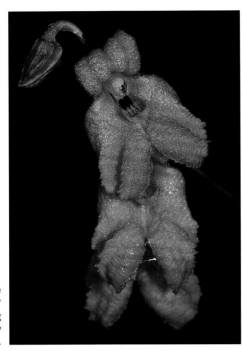

Porroglossum eduardii 'Posada' is a rambling grower. Grown by J & L Orchids.

The flowers of *Porroglossum muscosum* 'Dark Angel' are darker than those of the species. Grown by J & L Orchids.

MATURE SIZE, HABIT: Miniature, 1 in. (2.5 cm), leaves 1 in. (2.5 cm)
CULTURE: Intermediate
LIGHT: Medium
TEMPERATURE: Intermediate
POTTING MEDIUM: Fine, well-draining mix, or mounted
RELATED SPECIES, HYBRIDS: *Porroglossum mordax, Prgm. peruvianum, Prgm. rodrigoi, Prgm. xipheres*

Porroglossum muscosum

PRONUNCIATION: pore-oh-GLOSS-um muss-KOH-sum
ORIGIN: Andes, Ecuador to Venezuela
DESCRIPTION AND QUALITIES: The Latin name means mossy and refers to its fuzzy flower stem.
FLOWER: Single, 1¹/₂ in. (4 cm), on 6 in. (15 cm) inflorescence
SEASON OF BLOOM: Spring to summer
MATURE SIZE, HABIT: Dwarf, 5 in. (12.5 cm)
CULTURE: Intermediate
LIGHT: Medium
TEMPERATURE: Cool to intermediate
POTTING MEDIUM: Fine, well-draining mix, or mounted

Porroglossum sergioi

PRONUNCIATION: pore-oh-GLOSS-um ser-jee-OH-eye
SYNONYM: *Porroglossum sergii*
ORIGIN: Colombia
DESCRIPTION AND QUALITIES: A bright flowering dwarf orchid.
FLOWER: Single, 2 in. (5 cm) lavender-pink, triangular shaped, on 8 in. (20 cm) inflorescence
SEASON OF BLOOM: Spring to summer
MATURE SIZE, HABIT: Dwarf, 5 in. (12.5 cm)
CULTURE: Intermediate
LIGHT: Medium
TEMPERATURE: Intermediate
POTTING MEDIUM: Fine, well-draining mix, or mounted

HISTORY: Name first published as *Porroglossum sergii* in 1975 by Pedro Ortiz.

Potinara Burana Beauty

PRONUNCIATION: pot-in-AR-ah
ORIGIN: *Potinara* Netrasiri Starbright × *Cattleya* Netrasiri Beauty. Registered by P. Buranaraktham in 1996.
DESCRIPTION AND QUALITIES: This popular orchid is frequently offered for sale because it is compact, easy to grow and bloom, and has a pleasant citrus fragrance.
FLOWER: Fragrant, 3 in. (7.5 cm) across, golden yellow with splashes of red on the petals and lips
SEASON OF BLOOM: Winter to spring
MATURE SIZE, HABIT: Compact, 10–12 in. (25–30 cm)
CULTURE: Intermediate
LIGHT: Medium

TEMPERATURE: Intermediate
POTTING MEDIUM: Medium textured orchid mix

Potinara Heavenly Jewel

PRONUNCIATION: pot-in-AR-ah
ORIGIN: *Sophrolaeliocattleya* Tangerine Jewel × *Brassolaeliocattleya* Meditation. Bred by H & R Nurseries in 1989.
DESCRIPTION AND QUALITIES: This dwarf variety packs a great deal of flower power on a small plant.

In the sunlight, *Porroglossum sergioi* sparkles.

Potinara Burana Beauty 'Burana' HCC/AOS is a rewarding orchid to grow.

FLOWER: 3 in. (7.5 cm) across, white with dark red-purple lip and yellow throat
SEASON OF BLOOM: Winter to spring
MATURE SIZE, HABIT: Dwarf, 6 in. (15 cm)
CULTURE: Intermediate
LIGHT: Medium
TEMPERATURE: Intermediate
POTTING MEDIUM: Medium textured orchid mix

Potinara Heavenly Jewel 'Puanani' AM/AOS has a prominent red-purple lip.

Potinara Hoku Gem 'Freckles' HCC/AOS is loaded with cheery flowers.

Potinara Hoku Gem

PRONUNCIATION: pot-in-AR-ah
ORIGIN: *Brassolaelia* Richard Mueller × *Sophrolaeliocattleya* Tangerine Jewel. Registered by H & R Nurseries in 1988.
DESCRIPTION AND QUALITIES: This pert and colorful hybrid has a well-known and popular parent, *Brassolaelia* Richard Mueller.
FLOWER: 2¹/₂ in. (6 cm); somewhat variable flower colorations from clear yellow to golden, from orange-red to scarlet red, with various degress of spotting
SEASON OF BLOOM: Winter to spring
MATURE SIZE, HABIT: Compact, 10 in. (25 cm)
CULTURE: Intermediate
LIGHT: Medium
TEMPERATURE: Intermediate
POTTING MEDIUM: Medium textured orchid mix

Potinara Twentyfour Carat

PRONUNCIATION: pot-in-AR-ah
ORIGIN: *Potinara* Lemon Tree × *Brassolaeliocattleya* Yellow Imp. Registered by Armacost in 1983.
DESCRIPTION AND QUALITIES: There is no clearer yellow-gold than the flower of this hybrid. It stands out wherever it is grown or shown.
FLOWER: Fragrant, 3¹/₂ in. (9 cm) across; some variation in flower color in this grex, from soft yellow to more golden yellow, with varied markings on the lip
SEASON OF BLOOM: Winter to spring
MATURE SIZE, HABIT: Compact, 12 in. (30 cm)
CULTURE: Intermediate
LIGHT: Medium
TEMPERATURE: Intermediate
POTTING MEDIUM: Medium textured orchid mix

Propetalum Ayla

PRONUNCIATION: pro-PET-ah-lum
ORIGIN: *Propetalum* Hiawatha × *Zygopeta-*

lum maxillare. Registered by B. C. Berliner in 2000.

DESCRIPTION AND QUALITIES: This beauty is heavily scented. The flowers closely resemble its *Zygopetalum* parent, but this hybrid is more temperature tolerant and easier to grow and bloom.

FLOWER: Fragrant, $1^1/_2$–2 in. (4–5 cm), white lips with purple flares, yellow petals striped in burgundy-brown

SEASON OF BLOOM: Variable

MATURE SIZE, HABIT: Dwarf, 6–8 in. (15–20 cm)

CULTURE: Intermediate

LIGHT: Medium

TEMPERATURE: Cool to intermediate

POTTING MEDIUM: Fine, well-draining

CULTURAL TIPS: Will bloom best when grown with at least a 20°F (10°C) difference between day and evening temperatures.

Psygmorchis pusilla

PRONUNCIATION: sig-MORE-kiss pew-SILL-ah

ORIGIN: Mexico to Trinidad to Brazil

DESCRIPTION AND QUALITIES: This charming lilliputian plant does not have a history of long life in orchid collections. Closely related to oncidium. Its fleshy leaves grow in a fan pattern.

FLOWER: Sunny yellow, 1 in. (2.5 cm)

SEASON OF BLOOM: Spring to summer

MATURE SIZE, HABIT: Miniature, leaves 3 in. (7.5 cm)

CULTURE: Intermediate

LIGHT: Medium

TEMPERATURE: Intermediate

POTTING MEDIUM: Best mounted

CULTURAL TIPS: Needs to be kept in high humidity with good air movement.

HISTORY: First described in 1753 as

Potinara Twentyfour Carat 'Lea' AM/AOS is as bright as gold.

Propetalum Ayla is an unusual cross with an interesting and fragrant flower.

Psygmorchis pusilla resembles a miniature oncidium, to which it is closely related.

The flowers of *Renanthera monachica* resemble molten lava.

Epidendrum pusillium and has undergone various name changes since then.
RELATED SPECIES, HYBRIDS: *Psygmorchis glossomystax, Psgmrc. gnomus, Psgmrc. pumilio*

Renanthera monachica

PRONUNCIATION: reh-NAN-ther-ah moh-NAH-ki-kah
ORIGIN: Philippines
DESCRIPTION AND QUALITIES: One of the few small growing renantheras, this one fits well in any sunny windowsill. Most species in this genus are huge.
FLOWER: $1^{1}/4$ in. (3 cm), orange-yellow, covered with dark red bars, many borne on an inflorescence that is sometimes branched
SEASON OF BLOOM: Spring to summer
MATURE SIZE, HABIT: Compact, slow to reach 12 in. (30 cm)
CULTURE: Intermediate
LIGHT: High
TEMPERATURE: Intermediate to warm

POTTING MEDIUM: Medium textured, well-draining
CULTURAL TIPS: Most frequently grown in wooden baskets.
HISTORY: First collected in the Philippines by H. M. Curran and described by Oakes Ames in 1915.

Restrepia contorta

PRONUNCIATION: reh-STREP-ee-ah kon-TOR-tah
SYNONYMS: *Humboldiana contorta, Restrepia caucana*
ORIGIN: Colombia, Venezuela
DESCRIPTION AND QUALITIES: The Latin epithet refers to the twisted leaf tips of this brightly colored restrepia.
FLOWER: Single, borne in succession, 2 in. (5 cm) from top to bottom; lip 1 in. (2.5 cm), orange with red markings
SEASON OF BLOOM: Spring to summer
MATURE SIZE, HABIT: Dwarf, 7–8 in. (18–20 cm)

CULTURE: Intermediate
LIGHT: Medium
TEMPERATURE: Intermediate
POTTING MEDIUM: Fine, well-draining mix, or mounted
HISTORY: First described by Carlyle Luer in 1996.
RELATED SPECIES, HYBRIDS: *Restrepia antennifera, Rstp. elegans, Rstp. filamentosa, Rstp. hemsleyana*

Restrepia iris

PRONUNCIATION: reh-STREP-ee-ah EYE-riss
SYNONYM: *Restrepia pulchella*
DESCRIPTION AND QUALITIES: The lip of this restrepia is prominent and darkly marked. It is highly variable in its coloration.
FLOWER: Single flower, 2 in. (5 cm) from top to bottom; 1 in. (2.5 cm) lip creamy yellow with dark maroon markings
SEASON OF BLOOM: Winter to spring
MATURE SIZE, HABIT: Miniature, 3 in. (7.5 cm)
CULTURE: Challenging
LIGHT: Medium
TEMPERATURE: Intermediate
POTTING MEDIUM: Fine, well-draining mix, or mounted
HISTORY: First described by Carlyle Luer in 1980.

Restrepia muscifera

PRONUNCIATION: reh-STREP-ee-ah muss-IF-er-ah
SYNONYM: *Restrepia xanthophthalma*
ORIGIN: Mexico to Panama
DESCRIPTION AND QUALITIES: This species is highly variable in its plant size and flower coloration. It has thick, leathery leaves.
FLOWER: Single, borne in succession, light green, 1 in. (2.5 cm) long; prominent red lips with dark burgundy spots
SEASON OF BLOOM: Winter to spring

The lip of *Restrepia contorta* is most of the flower. Grown by J & L Orchids.

The *Restrepia iris* flower is vibrantly marked. Grown by J & L Orchids.

Restrepia muscifera is a delightful small grower.

Rhyncholaelia digbyana has passed on its unique fringed lip, apple-green flower, compact growth habit, and sumptuous fragrance to many modern hybrids.

MATURE SIZE, HABIT: Dwarf, 4 in. (10 cm), variable in growth habit
CULTURE: Intermediate
LIGHT: Medium
TEMPERATURE: Intermediate
POTTING MEDIUM: Fine, well-draining mix, or mounted
HISTORY: First described by John Lindley in 1842 as *Pleurothallis muscifera*.

Rhyncholaelia digbyana

PRONUNCIATION: rink-oh-LAY-lee-ah dig-bee-AH-nah
SYNONYMS: *Brassavola digbyana, Laelia digbyana*

ORIGIN: Mexico, Belize, Guatemala, Honduras
DESCRIPTION AND QUALITIES: This species is important as a parent to impart its wonderful lemony, lily-of-the-valley fragrance; fringed lip; and large flower size. Ernest Hetherington of Stewart Orchids stated (1986) that "The delightful fragrance blends with other species, such as *Cattleya dowiana*, into a multitude of pleasing fragrances."
FLOWER: Usually borne singly, apple-green with spectacular, unique fringed lip (fimbriated), usually 4–5 in. (10.0–12.5 cm), sometimes to 7 in. (18 cm), across
SEASON OF BLOOM: Spring to summer
MATURE SIZE, HABIT: Compact, 14 in. (36 cm)
CULTURE: Challenging
LIGHT: Medium to high
TEMPERATURE: Intermediate
POTTING MEDIUM: On a slab, or in loose, well-draining medium in a clay pot
CULTURAL TIPS: This orchid likes it on the bright side and should be allowed to dry out well between waterings.
HISTORY: Named after Vincent Digby of Minterne in Dorsetshire, England, who flowered it for the first time in 1845.

Rhyncholaelia glauca

PRONUNCIATION: rink-oh-LAY-lee-ah GLAW-kah
SYNONYM: *Brassavola glauca*
ORIGIN: Mexico, Guatemala, Honduras
DESCRIPTION AND QUALITIES: A popular species because of its sweet fragrance and showy flower.
FLOWER: $2^{1}/_{2}$ in. (6 cm), pale green with white lip
SEASON OF BLOOM: Spring
MATURE SIZE, HABIT: Compact, leaves to 9 in. (23 cm) long
CULTURE: Intermediate
LIGHT: Medium
TEMPERATURE: Warm

A soft creamy green flower, fragrance, and compact plant habit make *Rhyncholaelia glauca* a popular orchid.

Rhynchostele rossii flowers are exotically spotted. Grown by J & L Orchids.

Rodriguezia bahiensis has dazzling white flowers.

POTTING MEDIUM: Medium epiphytic mix
CULTURAL TIPS: This species is not as difficult to grow and bloom as its revered cousin, *Rhyncholaelia digbyana*.
HISTORY: Originally found in Mexico by J. Henchman in the 1800s.

Rhynchostele rossii

PRONUNCIATION: rink-oh-STEEL-ee ROSS-ee-eye
SYNONYMS: *Lemboglossum rossii, Odontoglossum rossii*
ORIGIN: Mexico to Nicaragua
DESCRIPTION AND QUALITIES: Widely distributed in Central America.

FLOWER: To four, 2 in. (5 cm), white, with sepals spotted in maroon and white lips with yellow callus
SEASON OF BLOOM: Spring
MATURE SIZE, HABIT: Dwarf, 5–7 in. (12.5–18.0 cm)
CULTURE: Intermediate
LIGHT: Medium
TEMPERATURE: Cool to intermediate
POTTING MEDIUM: Fine, well-draining
CULTURAL TIPS: Requires abundant water throughout active growing season.

Rodriguezia bahiensis

PRONUNCIATION: roh-dri-GEEZ-ee-ah ba-hee-EN-siss
DESCRIPTION AND QUALITIES: One of 40 *Rodriguezia* species, most of which are small growing plants; related to oncidiums.
FLOWER: Crystalline white, 1 in. (2.5 cm)

Rodrumnia Orchidom Dancer displays its dark, rich flower colors.

MATURE SIZE, HABIT: Miniature, 3 in. (7.5 cm), clump forming
CULTURE: Easy
LIGHT: Medium to high
TEMPERATURE: Intermediate
POTTING MEDIUM: Fine, well-draining

Sarcochilus Cherie

PRONUNCIATION: sar-koh-KYE-lus
ORIGIN: *Sarcochilus* Fitzhart × *Sarcochilus fitzgeraldii*. Registered by W. Upton in 1990.
DESCRIPTION AND QUALITIES: Flowers of this Australian hybrid are variable in color. The hybrid is more vigorous than the species and easier to grow and bloom.
FLOWER: 1 in. (2.5 cm), white, overlaid with dark burgundy-red markings with a touch of yellow in the center
SEASON OF BLOOM: Spring to summer
MATURE SIZE, HABIT: Dwarf, 4–6 in. (10–15 cm)
CULTURE: Intermediate
LIGHT: Medium
TEMPERATURE: Cool to intermediate

Sarcochilus Fitzhart

PRONUNCIATION: sar-koh-KYE-lus
ORIGIN: *Sarcochilus hartmannii* × *Sarcochilus fitzgeraldii*. Registered by I. Butler in 1963.
DESCRIPTION AND QUALITIES: This genus includes 20 species native to Australia. All are diminutive and resemble miniature vandas.
FLOWER: Clear white, with burgundy-red markings in their centers
SEASON OF BLOOM: Spring to summer
MATURE SIZE, HABIT: Dwarf, 4–6 in. (10–15 cm)
CULTURE: Intermediate
LIGHT: Medium
TEMPERATURE: Cool to intermediate
POTTING MEDIUM: Fine, well-draining mix, or mounted

long, with yellow markings at the top of the lip
SEASON OF BLOOM: Spring to summer
MATURE SIZE, HABIT: Dwarf, 6 in. (15 cm)
CULTURE: Easy
LIGHT: Medium to high
TEMPERATURE: Intermediate
POTTING MEDIUM: Fine, well-draining mix, or mounted
RELATED SPECIES, HYBRIDS: *Rodriguezia batemanii, Rdza. candida, Rdza. lanceolata* (syn. *Rdza. secunda*)

Rodrumnia Orchidom Dancer

PRONUNCIATION: roh-dri-SID-ee-um
ORIGIN: *Tolumnia* Fan Dancer × *Rodricidium* Kone's Good Choice. Registered by W. Savage in 2002.
DESCRIPTION AND QUALITIES: This excellent beginner's orchid is easy to grow, compact, and floriferous.
FLOWER: 1³⁄₄ in. (4 cm) long, purple-red with orange, yellow, and darker red markings
SEASON OF BLOOM: Spring to summer

Sarcochilus Cherie
has fine dark flowers.

Sarcochilus Fitzhart
is one of the early
hybrids of this genus.

RELATED SPECIES, HYBRIDS: *Sarco. aequalis* (syn. *Sarco. hartmannii*), *Sarcochilus australis, Sarco. ceciliae, Sarco. falcatus, Sarco. aequalis* (syn. *Sarco. hartmannii*), *Sarco. fitzgeraldii, Sarco. hillii*

Sarcochilus Sweetheart

PRONUNCIATION: sar-koh-KYE-lus

ORIGIN: *Sarcochilus* Fitzhart × *Sarcochilus* Heidi. Cross made by S. Batchelor and registered by R. Clement in 1998.

DESCRIPTION AND QUALITIES: This genus has seen much line breeding and hybridizing, with this hybrid as one of the results. It flowers generously.

FLOWER: 1 in. (2.5 cm), clear white with dark maroon markings on sepals and petals; touches of yellow on the lip

SEASON OF BLOOM: Spring to summer

MATURE SIZE, HABIT: Dwarf, 4–6 in. (10–15 cm)

CULTURE: Intermediate

LIGHT: Medium

TEMPERATURE: Cool to intermediate

Sedirea japonica

PRONUNCIATION: seh-DEER-ee-ah jah-PON-i-kah

ORIGIN: Japan, Korea

DESCRIPTION AND QUALITIES: This delightful plant has long been admired by Asian orchid lovers for its delicate fragrance.

FLOWER: Three to twelve, 1 in. (2.5 cm), cream to green, with purple bars and spots on the lips and sepals

SEASON OF BLOOM: Spring to summer

MATURE SIZE, HABIT: Dwarf, leaves 6 in. (15 cm) long

CULTURE: Intermediate

LIGHT: Medium

TEMPERATURE: Warm

POTTING MEDIUM: Sphagnum moss or fine phalaenopsis mix

CULTURAL TIPS: Grow much like a phalaenopsis but needs slightly more light.

OPPOSITE:
Sarcochilus Sweetheart is a brightly colored hybrid.

Sedirea japonica is a sweetly scented Asian beauty.

HISTORY: Enjoyed and revered by the Japanese for hundreds of years, this orchid is becoming more available in Western countries.

Sigmatostalix radicans

PRONUNCIATION: sig-mat-oh-STAY-licks RAD-i-kanz

ORIGIN: American tropics

DESCRIPTION AND QUALITIES: A dainty and charming miniature, with thin, grasslike foliage and a honey scent. This genus of 20 species is found in the American tropics.

FLOWER: $3/4$ in. (2 cm), white, with greenish sepals and petals, brown column, and white lip

SEASON OF BLOOM: Fall

MATURE SIZE, HABIT: Miniature, leaves 6 in. (15 cm)

CULTURE: Easy

LIGHT: Medium

TEMPERATURE: Intermediate

Sigmatostalix radicans 'HMO's Petite Prince' is a small and delicate orchid. Selection from Ha'iku Maui Orchids in Hawaii. Photo by Marc Herzog.

Sophrocattleya Beaufort 'Elizabeth' AM/AOS is a richly colored mini.

POTTING MEDIUM: Fine mix
RELATED SPECIES, HYBRIDS: *Sigmatostalix amazonica, Sgmx. crescentilabia, Sgmx. graminea, Sgmx. guatemalensis, Sgmx. hymenantha, Sgmx. pandurata, Sgmx. racemifera*

Sophrocattleya Beaufort
PRONUNCIATION: soff-roh-KAT-lee-ah

ORIGIN: *Sophronitis coccinea* × *Cattleya luteola*. Registered in 1963 by Casa Luna.
DESCRIPTION AND QUALITIES: This grex has become a classic of the mini-catts. Even though it was registered in the 1960s, its clones are still appearing on the market and it has proven to be a valuable and productive parent.
FLOWER: $2^{1}/_{2}$ in. (6 cm) across; colors from clear yellow to orange red in this grex
SEASON OF BLOOM: Spring to summer
MATURE SIZE, HABIT: Dwarf, 4 in. (10 cm)
CULTURE: Intermediate
LIGHT: Medium
TEMPERATURE: Intermediate
POTTING MEDIUM: Fine, well-draining

Sophrocattleya Crystelle Smith
PRONUNCIATION: soff-roh-KAT-lee-ah
ORIGIN: *Sophrocattleya* Beaufort × *Cattleya loddigesii*. Registered by Krull-Smith in 1985.
DESCRIPTION AND QUALITIES: This excel-

Sophrocattleya Crystelle Smith 'Aileen' AM/AOS is a gem of a mini.

The flower of *Sophrocattleya* Royal Beau 'Prince' is a delicate pastel color.

lent clone frequently shows up at orchid shows.

FLOWER: $2^1/2$ in. (6 cm) across, from shades of pink to peach tones
SEASON OF BLOOM: Winter to spring
MATURE SIZE, HABIT: Dwarf, 5 in. (12.5 cm)
CULTURE: Easy
LIGHT: Medium
TEMPERATURE: Intermediate
POTTING MEDIUM: Medium mix, well-draining

Sophrocattleya Royal Beau

PRONUNCIATION: soff-roh-KAT-lee-ah
ORIGIN: *Cattleya* Princess Bells × *Sophrocattleya* Beaufort. Registered by H & R Orchids in 1995.
FLOWER: Fragrant, salmon-pink, 3 in. (7.5 cm), with a rose-pink lip and yellow throat
SEASON OF BLOOM: Winter to spring
MATURE SIZE, HABIT: Dwarf, 8 in. (20 cm)
CULTURE: Intermediate
LIGHT: Medium
TEMPERATURE: Intermediate
POTTING MEDIUM: Fine, well-draining

Sophrolaelia Psyche 'Prolific' AM/AOS is an old timer that is still grown today.

Sophrolaelia Psyche

PRONUNCIATION: soff-roh-LAY-lee-ah
ORIGIN: *Laelia cinnabarina* × *Sophronitis coccinea.* Registered by the Charlesworth company in 1902.
DESCRIPTION AND QUALITIES: One of the first of the mini-catts to be bred, its influence is still seen in today's hybrids.
FLOWER: Orange-red with yellow in the lip, 2 in. (5 cm) across
SEASON OF BLOOM: Spring to summer
MATURE SIZE, HABIT: Dwarf, 6 in. (15 cm)
CULTURE: Easy
LIGHT: Medium
TEMPERATURE: Intermediate
POTTING MEDIUM: Medium mix, well-draining

Sophrolaeliocattleya Anzac offers sumptuous saturated color.

Sophrolaeliocattleya Jewel Box 'Dark Waters' AM/AOS is an amazing and highly prized clone.

Sophrolaeliocattleya Anzac

PRONUNCIATION: soff-roh-lay-lee-oh-KAT-lee-ah

ORIGIN: *Sophrolaeliocattleya* Marathon × *Laeliocattleya* Dominiana. Registered by the Charlesworth company in 1921.

DESCRIPTION AND QUALITIES: Another classic, this is one of the early successes of producing a larger cattleya type flower with red coloration.

FLOWER: 5 in. (12.5 cm) across, magenta-red, with slightly darker lip

SEASON OF BLOOM: Winter to spring

MATURE SIZE, HABIT: Compact, 10–12 in. (25–30 cm)

CULTURE: Intermediate

LIGHT: Medium

TEMPERATURE: Intermediate

POTTING MEDIUM: Medium mix, well-draining

Sophrolaeliocattleya Jewel Box

PRONUNCIATION: soff-roh-lay-lee-oh-KAT-lee-ah

ORIGIN: *Cattleya aurantiaca* × *Sophrolaeliocattleya* Anzac. Registered by Stewart, Inc., in 1962.

Sophrolaeliocattleya Jewel Box 'Scheherazade' AM/AOS has bright red flowers.

DESCRIPTION AND QUALITIES: This cross set the standard for compact reds in the Cattleya Alliance, and it is still popular. 'Dark Waters' AM/AOS is slightly less known than 'Scheherazade' AM/AOS but is a superior selection. flower: 3 in. (7.5 cm) across, with some variation in flower color from orange red to scarlet to dark blood red. 'Dark Waters' AM/AOS flowers are darker and petals wider than those of 'Scheherazade', with a velvety sheen; flowers of 'Scheherazade' AM/AOS are clear, solid red.

SEASON OF BLOOM: Winter to spring

MATURE SIZE, HABIT: Compact, 10–12 in. (25–30 cm)

CULTURE: Intermediate

LIGHT: Medium

TEMPERATURE: Intermediate

POTTING MEDIUM: Medium mix, well-draining

Sophrolaeliocattleya Love Fresh is a sunny charmer.

Sophrolaeliocattleya Love Fresh

PRONUNCIATION: soff-roh-lay-lee-oh-KAT-lee-ah

ORIGIN: *Laelia briegeri* × *Sophrocattleya* Beaufort. Registered by Dogashima in 1991.

DESCRIPTION AND QUALITIES: This hybrid will mature in a 4 in. (10 cm) pot and is ideal for a small growing area on a windowsill or under lights.

FLOWER: 2 in. (5 cm) across, orange-yellow, with red ruffled lips, borne in clusters of up to four

SEASON OF BLOOM: Spring to summer

MATURE SIZE, HABIT: Dwarf, 6 in. (15 cm)

CULTURE: Easy

LIGHT: Medium

TEMPERATURE: Intermediate

POTTING MEDIUM: Medium mix, well-draining

CULTURAL TIPS: Plants readily form multiple leads.

Sophrolaeliocattleya Memoria Miyo Takeda blooms two or three times a year.

Sophrolaeliocattleya Memoria Miyo Takeda

PRONUNCIATION: soff-roh-lay-lee-oh-KAT-lee-ah

ORIGIN: *Sophrolaeliocattleya* Little Precious × *Sophrolaeliocattleya* Mahalo Jack. Registered by Norman Mizuno of Ha'iku Maui Orchids in 2002.

DESCRIPTION AND QUALITIES: This impressive plant is undemanding and flowers two or three times a year.

FLOWER: 3 in. (7.5 cm) across, solid rose–dark pink

SEASON OF BLOOM: Winter to spring

MATURE SIZE, HABIT: Dwarf, 6 in. (15 cm)

CULTURE: Easy

Sophrolaeliocattleya Paprika 'Black Magic' HCC/AOS is a favorite.

FLOWER: Fragrant, intense rose-red, 5 in. (12.5 cm) across, with yellow in the throat of the lip
SEASON OF BLOOM: Winter to spring
MATURE SIZE, HABIT: Compact, 10–12 in. (25–30 cm)
CULTURE: Intermediate
LIGHT: Medium
TEMPERATURE: Intermediate
POTTING MEDIUM: Medium mix, well-draining

Sophrolaeliocattleya Sutter Creek

PRONUNCIATION: soff-roh-lay-lee-oh-KAT-lee-ah
ORIGIN: *Sophronitis coccinea* × *Sophrolaeliocattleya* Kauai Starbright. Registered by Gold Country Orchids in 1989.
DESCRIPTION AND QUALITIES: A product of one of today's premier breeders of mini-catts, Alan Koch.
FLOWER: Fragrant, 2½ in. (6 cm) across, golden yellow edged in red—a stunning combination
SEASON OF BLOOM: Winter to spring
MATURE SIZE, HABIT: Dwarf, 5 in. (12.5 cm)
CULTURE: Intermediate
LIGHT: Medium
TEMPERATURE: Intermediate
POTTING MEDIUM: Medium mix, well-draining

Sophrolaeliocattleya Sutter Creek is a diminutive plant with bright sunset colors.

LIGHT: Medium
TEMPERATURE: Intermediate
POTTING MEDIUM: Medium mix, well-draining

Sophrolaeliocattleya Paprika

PRONUNCIATION: soff-roh-lay-lee-oh-KAT-lee-ah
ORIGIN: *Laeliocattleya* Orange Gem × *Sophrolaeliocattleya* Anzac. Registered by Stewart, Inc., in 1960.
DESCRIPTION AND QUALITIES: This beauty has the fragrance of roses.

Sophronitis cernua

PRONUNCIATION: soff-roh-NYE-tiss SURN-you-ah
SYNONYMS: *Sophronitis hoffmannseggii, S. modesta*
ORIGIN: Bolivia, Brazil
DESCRIPTION AND QUALITIES: A charming species, but like the others in this genus, it is considered difficult to grow. If you like miniature cattleya-type orchids but want something easier to grow, try the *Sophronitis* hybrids. The leaves are leathery and frequently gray-green in color.

FLOWER: 1 in. (2.5 cm) across, bright orange-red; various color forms
SEASON OF BLOOM: Winter to spring
MATURE SIZE, HABIT: Miniature, 2 in. (5 cm); flat pseudobulbs lie almost horizontal
CULTURE: Challenging
LIGHT: Medium to high
TEMPERATURE: Intermediate to warm
POTTING MEDIUM: Usually performs best if mounted.
CULTURAL TIPS: Needs to dry off quickly after watering.
HISTORY: Discovered near Rio de Janeiro by William Harrison in 1827.
RELATED SPECIES, HYBRIDS: *Sophronitis brevipedunculata, S. mantiqueirae, S. wittigiana*

Sophronitis cernua is a colorful miniature that is challenging to grow.

Sophronitis coccinea

PRONUNCIATION: soff-roh-NYE-tiss kok-SIN-ee-ah
SYNONYMS: *Cattleya coccinea, Sophronitis grandiflora*
ORIGIN: Brazil
DESCRIPTION AND QUALITIES: One of the best known and most attractive of the *Sophronitis* species, it is used to produce many color variants and clones. This species has been critically important for its contribution of the color red in the Cattleya Alliance hybrids.
FLOWER: Scarlet, 2¹/₂ in. (6 cm), flat, borne singly
SEASON OF BLOOM: Variable
MATURE SIZE, HABIT: Miniature, 3 in. (7.5 cm)
CULTURE: Challenging
LIGHT: Medium
TEMPERATURE: Intermediate
POTTING MEDIUM: Usually performs best if mounted.

The *Sophronitis coccinea* flower is glowing red.

HISTORY: First collected by Michel É. Descourtilz and described by John Lindley as *Cattleya coccinea* in 1864.

Stelis hallii

PRONUNCIATION: STELL-iss HAL-ee-eye
ORIGIN: Peru, Ecuador, Colombia
DESCRIPTION AND QUALITIES: One thousand species of this genus are spread throughout Central and South America; most of their flowers resemble those of *Stelis hallii*. They are closely related to *Pleurothallis*.
FLOWER: ¹/₄ in. (6 mm) across, light lime green, borne on an upright inflorescence
SEASON OF BLOOM: Winter to spring
MATURE SIZE, HABIT: Dwarf, 4 in. (10 cm)
CULTURE: Intermediate

LIGHT: Medium
TEMPERATURE: Intermediate
POTTING MEDIUM: Fine, well-draining mix, or mounted
RELATED SPECIES, HYBRIDS: *Stelis argentata, Stel. gemma, Stel. inaequalis*

Stenocoryne aureo-fulva
PRONUNCIATION: sten-oh-kor-EYE-nee ORE-ee-oh-FULL-vah

SYNONYMS: *Bifrenaria aureo-fulva, Maxillaria stenopetala*
ORIGIN: Brazil
DESCRIPTION AND QUALITIES: This brightly colored, fragrant orchid likes it warm.
FLOWER: To 12, orange, 1 in. (2.5 cm), nodding, borne from the base of the pseudobulbs on a 6–12 in. (15–30 cm) inflorescence
SEASON OF BLOOM: Summer

An attractive specimen of *Stelis hallii*, grown by Parkside Orchid Nursery

MATURE SIZE, HABIT: Dwarf, 6–10 in. (15–25 cm) tall, four-angled pseudobulbs

CULTURE: Intermediate

LIGHT: Medium

TEMPERATURE: Intermediate to warm

POTTING MEDIUM: Fine, well-draining mix, or mounted

CULTURAL TIPS: Prefers ample moisture when actively growing but does best with a drier winter rest.

HISTORY: *Bifrenaria aureo-fulva* was described by Hooker in 1843; *Maxillaria stenopetala* was described by Knowles and Westcott in 1838.

RELATED SPECIES, HYBRIDS: *Stenocoryne melanopoda*, *Stncm. racemosa*, *Stncm. vitellina*

Stenoglottis fimbriata

PRONUNCIATION: sten-oh-GLOT-iss fim-bree-AH-tah

ORIGIN: South Africa

DESCRIPTION AND QUALITIES: A beautiful orchid, not only for its fringed pink and spotted flowers, but for its wavy edged leaves with striking purple spots. The plant will remain in flower for several weeks or longer. This terrestrial tuberous orchid is naturally found in shaded forests. Used by Africans in an enema to relieve flatulence. Leaves are produced in a compact rosette.

FLOWER: $1/2$ in. (1 cm), pink, borne on a 6–12 in. (15–30 cm) inflorescence

SEASON OF BLOOM: Winter to spring

MATURE SIZE, HABIT: Compact, 8 in. (20 cm), leaves 10 in. (25 cm)

CULTURE: Intermediate

LIGHT: Medium

Stenocoryne aureo-fulva flowers resemble pendulous bells.

Stenoglottis fimbriata flowers sparkle.

A pendulous spray of *Symphoglossum sanguineum*. Grown by Parkside Orchid Nursery.

An unnamed *Tolumnia* hybrid shows rich saturated colors.

TEMPERATURE: Intermediate

POTTING MEDIUM: Fine-textured terrestrial orchid mix

CULTURAL TIPS: This orchid goes dormant after it flowers, and its leaves then naturally die back. At this point, the plant should be grown on the dry and cool side for two or three months. After this rest period, new growth will start to appear, and then normal watering and warmer temperatures can be resumed.

HISTORY: First described by John Lindley in 1837.

RELATED SPECIES, HYBRIDS: *Stenoglottis longifolia, Sngl. woodii*

Symphoglossum sanguineum

PRONUNCIATION: sim-foh-GLOSS-um san-GWIN-ee-um

SYNONYMS: *Cochlioda sanguinea, Mesospinidium sanguineum*

ORIGIN: Ecuador, Peru

DESCRIPTION AND QUALITIES: This showy species is not yet commonly found in many collections.

FLOWER: Up to 40, light to dark pink, 1 in. (2.5 cm) long, on arching inflorescence

SEASON OF BLOOM: Fall to winter

MATURE SIZE, HABIT: Compact, 10–12 in. (25–30 cm)

CULTURE: Intermediate

LIGHT: Medium

TEMPERATURE: Cool to intermediate

POTTING MEDIUM: Fine-textured terrestrial orchid mix

HISTORY: Discovered by Professor Jameson in the Ecuadorean Andes around 1850.

Tolumnia hybrid

PRONUNCIATION: toll-um-NEE-ah

ORIGIN: *Tolumnia* Marion Liberty × *Tolumnia* Catherine Wilson. Unregistered hybrid.

SEASON OF BLOOM: Spring to summer

MATURE SIZE, HABIT: Miniature, 3 in. (7.5 cm)

Tolumnia Potpourri 'Scarlet' displays a colorful and graceful spray of flowers.

CULTURE: Intermediate
LIGHT: Medium
TEMPERATURE: Medium
POTTING MEDIUM: Fine, well-draining. Can be mounted.

Tolumnia Potpourri

PRONUNCIATION: toll-um-NEE-ah
ORIGIN: *Tolumnia* Catherine Wilson × *Tolumnia* Redgate. Cross made by S. Taba and registered by Goodale Moir in 1977.
DESCRIPTION AND QUALITIES: A clear red flower is hard to find in *Tolumnia* hybrids, but this one hits the mark.
FLOWER: $1^1/4$ in. (3 cm) long, solid scarlet, edged in white
SEASON OF BLOOM: Spring to summer
MATURE SIZE, HABIT: Miniature, 3 in. (7.5 cm)
CULTURE: Intermediate
LIGHT: Medium
TEMPERATURE: Intermediate

Tolumnia Savanna La Mar is an older hybrid that still sparkles.

POTTING MEDIUM: Fine, well-draining. Can be mounted.

Tolumnia Savanna La Mar

PRONUNCIATION: toll-um-NEE-ah
ORIGIN: *Tolumnia* Red Belt × *Tolumnia* Catherine Wilson. Registered by Goodale Moir in 1967.
DESCRIPTION AND QUALITIES: Goodale Moir was

the premier pioneer breeder of tolumnias (at the time they were called oncidiums). All these hybrids pack many flowers onto small plants.

FLOWER: 1¹/₂ in. (4 cm) long, bright yellow with dark red markings, borne on an upright inflorescence

SEASON OF BLOOM: Spring to summer

The flower of *Trichocentrum tigrinum* displays attractive spots.

Trichoglottis philippinensis 'Pololei' shows off its dark red flower color. Photo by Marc Herzog.

MATURE SIZE, HABIT: Miniature, 3 in. (7.5 cm)

CULTURE: Intermediate

LIGHT: Medium

TEMPERATURE: Intermediate

POTTING MEDIUM: Fine, well-draining. Can be mounted.

Trichocentrum tigrinum

PRONUNCIATION: try-koh-SEN-trum ti-GRY-num

ORIGIN: Ecuador, Peru, Brazil, Central America

DESCRIPTION AND QUALITIES: Twenty species in this genus are now found from Florida to Brazil. Several of them are small growers. They are related to oncidiums.

FLOWER: Fragrant, showy, 2 in. (5 cm), yellow, spotted with brown. Large white lip with rose-colored base.

SEASON OF BLOOM: Spring to summer

MATURE SIZE, HABIT: Dwarf, 4³/₄ in. (12 cm)

CULTURE: Intermediate

LIGHT: Medium to high

TEMPERATURE: Intermediate

POTTING MEDIUM: Fine, well-draining. Can be mounted.

HISTORY: Discovered by Richard Pfau in 1969 in Central America.

RELATED SPECIES, HYBRIDS: *Trichocentrum albo-coccineum, Trctm. capistratum, Trctm. hoegei, Trctm. pfavii, Trctm. pulchrum*

Trichoglottis philippinensis

PRONUNCIATION: trick-oh-GLOTT-iss fill-i-peen-EN-siss

SYNONYMS: *Arachnis philippinensis, Staurochilus philippinensis*

ORIGIN: Philippines

DESCRIPTION AND QUALITIES: Some folks would say that this orchid should not be called a miniature because it will eventually reach 2 ft. (60 cm) tall, but it will flower as abundantly as a short plant. Keep topping and repotting this plant to keep it small. This same approach can be taken for all monopodial orchids.

FLOWER: Ripe apple scented, heavy, dark red (sometimes almost brown), 2 in. (5 cm) across, with a bright pink lip

SEASON OF BLOOM: Winter to spring

MATURE SIZE, HABIT: Compact, can be kept to 12 in. (30 cm)

CULTURE: Intermediate

LIGHT: Medium

TEMPERATURE: Intermediate

POTTING MEDIUM: Medium textured, well-draining

Trichoglottis pusilla

PRONUNCIATION: trick-oh-GLOTT-iss pew-SILL-ah

ORIGIN: Java

DESCRIPTION AND QUALITIES: One of the smallest growing species of this genus.

FLOWER: Fragrant, $^1/_2$ in. (1 cm) across, white with burgundy bars, borne successively

SEASON OF BLOOM: Winter to spring

MATURE SIZE, HABIT: Dwarf, 5 in. (12.5 cm)

CULTURE: Intermediate

LIGHT: Medium

TEMPERATURE: Intermediate

POTTING MEDIUM: Fine, well-draining. Can be mounted.

Trichopilia suavis

PRONUNCIATION: trick-oh-PILL-ee-ah SWAH-viss

SYNONYM: *Trichopilia kienastiana*

ORIGIN: Costa Rica, Panama, Colombia

DESCRIPTION AND QUALITIES: This species puts on an attractive display in a basket, where the fragrant flowers, borne at the bottom of the plant, can cascade.

FLOWER: Fragrant, two to five per pendant inflorescence, usually white, $2^1/_2$ in. (6 cm) across, spotted with red. The lip is tubular with pink and orange spots.

SEASON OF BLOOM: Spring

Trichoglottis pusilla. Grown by J & L Orchids.

Trichopilia suavis is a charming species and considered one of the most attractive in the genus.

MATURE SIZE, HABIT: Dwarf, leaves 16 in. (40 cm); oblong pseudobulbs

CULTURE: Easy

LIGHT: Medium

TEMPERATURE: Intermediate

POTTING MEDIUM: Medium textured, well-draining

CULTURAL TIPS: Frequently grown in baskets.

HISTORY: Discovered by Josef von Warscewicz in Costa Rica in 1848.

RELATED SPECIES, HYBRIDS: *Trichopilia maculata, Trpla. oicophylax, Trpla. subulata, Trpla. tortilis, Trpla. turialbae*

Trisetella hoeijeri

PRONUNCIATION: triss-i-TELL-ah HO-yer-eye

ORIGIN: Ecuador

DESCRIPTION AND QUALITIES: Flowers of this miniature resemble gliders in flight. Twenty species are known in this genus from the Andes. Narrow, medium green leaves.

FLOWER: $1^1/_2$ in. (4 cm) spread, white with dark veins

SEASON OF BLOOM: Variable

MATURE SIZE, HABIT: Miniature, 2 in. (5 cm)

CULTURE: Intermediate

LIGHT: Medium

TEMPERATURE: Cool

POTTING MEDIUM: Fine, well-draining. Can be mounted.

HISTORY: Named in honor of the Swedish explorer who discovered this plant, Thomas Hoijer.

Tuberolabium kotoense

PRONUNCIATION: too-bur-oh-LAY-bee-um koh-toh-EN-see

SYNONYM: *Saccolabium quisumbingii*

ORIGIN: Southeast Asia, including Taiwan and the Philippines

DESCRIPTION AND QUALITIES: This easy,

Trisetella hoeijeri flowers resemble gliders in flight.

fragrant species is commonly found growing on ficus trees in mountainous areas of Taiwan and the Philippines.

FLOWER: Waxy, $^1/_2$ in. (1 cm), white, with purple-tipped lips. Can have 50 or more long-lasting flowers per spike as the plant matures.

SEASON OF BLOOM: Fall to winter

MATURE SIZE, HABIT: Miniature, 3 in. (7.5 cm), leaves to 12 in. (30 cm) long

CULTURE: Easy

LIGHT: Medium

TEMPERATURE: Intermediate to warm

POTTING MEDIUM: Slabs, or in medium bark or coco chunks in pots

The diminutive *Tuberolabium kotoense* can display up to 50 small, sweetly scented flowers.

Vanda coerulea

PRONUNCIATION: VAN-dah seh-ROO-lee-ah

ORIGIN: India, Thailand

DESCRIPTION AND QUALITIES: One of the finest blue flowers to be found in the orchid family that has so many superior clones. It also appears in white and various shades of pink. Used extensively in hybridizing. This plant can grow tall over time. Keep topping (cutting of the top portion of the plant, with roots, and repotting) to maintain a smaller size.

FLOWER: $2^1/_2$ in. (6 cm) across (superior clones can be larger), light or dark blue, some with tessellations

SEASON OF BLOOM: Spring to summer

MATURE SIZE, HABIT: Compact; without topping, can reach 2 ft. (60 cm) or more

CULTURE: Intermediate

LIGHT: High

TEMPERATURE: Warm

Vanda coerulea flowers are a gorgeous blue.

POTTING MEDIUM: Usually grown in a wooden basket with little medium. Can be grown in pots in coarse, well-draining medium.

HISTORY: Discovered by William Griffith in 1837.

RELATED SPECIES, HYBRIDS: *Vanda coerulescens, V. cristata, V. lilacina, V. pumila*

Vanda denisoniana

PRONUNCIATION: VAN-dah den-i-son-ee-AH-nah

SYNONYM: *Vanda henryi*

ORIGIN: Burma, Vietnam

DESCRIPTION AND QUALITIES: This species varies in its flower color. Its pleasant vanilla scent is strongest in the evening.

FLOWER: Fragrant, 2 in. (5 cm) across, yellow-green to pure yellow (usually with brown speckles), to brown

SEASON OF BLOOM: Spring to summer

MATURE SIZE, HABIT: Compact, 6 in. (15 cm). Slow to grow vertically. Leaf spread 12 in. (30 cm).

CULTURE: Intermediate

LIGHT: High

Brown speckles dot the yellow petals of *Vanda denisoniana*.

TEMPERATURE: Warm

POTTING MEDIUM: Usually grown in a wooden basket with little medium. Can be grown in pots with coarse, well-draining medium.

Woodwardara Beverley Lou

PRONUNCIATION: wood-ward-AR-ah

ORIGIN: *Zygoneria* Dynamo × *Zygopabstia* Elfin Jade. Registered by Troweena in 1997.

DESCRIPTION AND QUALITIES: This grex produces a wide range of interesting color combinations.

FLOWER: Fragrant, $2^1/_2$ in. (6 cm) wide, bright green with a white lip with purple markings

SEASON OF BLOOM: Spring

MATURE SIZE, HABIT: Compact, 10–12 in. (25–30 cm)

Woodwardara Beverley Lou flowers display a wild color combination.

CULTURE: Intermediate
LIGHT: Medium to high
TEMPERATURE: Cool to intermediate
POTTING MEDIUM: Fine, well-draining

Yonezawaara hybrid

PRONUNCIATION: yone-zah-WAH-rah
ORIGIN: *Vandofinetia* Virgil × *Rhynchostylis coelestis*. Unregistered hybrid.
DESCRIPTION AND QUALITIES: This hybrid has an interesting combination of parents that produced a compact growing vanda-like plant with sweetly fragrant flowers. Another example in which a *Neofinetia* has been used in breeding a compact growing, fragrant hybrid.

FLOWER: Fragrant, $1^1/_2$ in. (4 cm) across, creamy white petals and sepals with purple-blue lips, six or more borne on a compact spike
SEASON OF BLOOM: Summer to fall
MATURE SIZE, HABIT: Compact, grows vertically slowly. Leaf spread 8 in. (20 cm).
CULTURE: Easy
LIGHT: Medium to high
TEMPERATURE: Intermediate to warm
POTTING MEDIUM: Medium textured. Can be grown in pots or baskets.

A delightful, small growing *Yonezawaara* hybrid is so far unnamed.

Zygoneria
Cosmo-Murray

Zygoneria Cosmo-Murray

PRONUNCIATION: zye-gone-AIR-ee-ah
ORIGIN: *Zygopetalum* Artur Elle × *Neogardneria murrayana*. Registered by Kokusai in 1997.
DESCRIPTION AND QUALITIES: This *Zygoneria* hybrid has beautiful flower markings.
FLOWER: Fragrant, 3 in. (7.5 cm), yellow petals, burgundy-brown spots, and purple flared lips

SEASON OF BLOOM: Winter to spring
MATURE SIZE, HABIT: Compact, 18 in. (46 cm)
CULTURE: Intermediate
LIGHT: Medium to high
TEMPERATURE: Intermediate
POTTING MEDIUM: Medium grade epiphytic mix

ꙮ Orchids by Size

Miniature

Aerangis calantha
Aerangis curnowiana
Aerangis fastuosa
Aerangis luteo-alba var. *rhodosticta*
Aerangis Somasticta
Amesiella philippinensis
Angraecum chamaeanthus
Angraecum humile
Angraecum pusillum
Angraecum rutenbergianum
Angraecum sacciferum
Ascocentrum pumilum
Barbosella cucullata
Bolusiella imbricata
Bolusiella iridifolia
Bolusiella maudiae
Bulbophyllum tingabarinum
Cadetia chionantha
Centroglossa macroceras
Cirrhopetalum yasnae 'Aussie'
Comparettia speciosa
Dendrobium cuthbertsonii orange form
Dendrobium cuthbertsonii pink and white
  form
Dendrobium cuthbertsonii pink form
Dendrobium cuthbertsonii yellow form
Dendrobium laevifolium
Dendrobium masarangense
Dendrobium petiolatum
Dendrobium violaceum
Dipteranthus duchii
Dracula venefica
Dryadella lilliputana
Dyakia hendersoniana

Encyclia polybulbon
Epidendrum porpax
Haraella odorata
Isabelia virginalis
Laelia esalqueana
Laelia lundii
Lepanthes lucifer
Lepanthes maduroi
Lepanthes ribes 'Wow'
Leptotes bicolor
Leptotes unicolor
Masdevallia agaster
Masdevallia calosiphon
Masdevallia erinacea
Masdevallia hirtzii
Masdevallia livingstoneana
Masdevallia peristeria
Masdevallia triangularis
Masdevallia venezuelana
Mediocalcar decoratum
Nageliella angustifolia
Ornithocephalus gladiatus
Ornithocephalus manabina
Phalaenopsis lobbii
Phalaenopsis Mini Mark 'Holm'
Phalaenopsis taenialis
Phalaenopsis tetraspis
Pleurothallis mystax
Pleurothallis sonderana
Pleurothallis tribuloides
Porroglossum eduardii 'Posada'
Psygmorchis pusilla
Restrepia iris
Rodrumnia Orchidom Dancer
Rodrumnia unregistered hybrid

Sigmatostalix graminea
Sigmatostalix radicans 'HMO's Petite
    Prince'
Sophronitis cernua
Sophronitis coccinea
Tolumnia
Tolumnia Potpourri
Tolumnia Savanna La Mar 'Golden Galaxy'
Trisetella hoeijeri
Tuberolabium kotoense

Dwarf

Aerangis articulata
Aerangis biloba
Aerangis brachycarpa
Aerangis citrata
Aerangis clavigera
Aerangis confusa
Aerangis kirkii
Aerangis kotschyana
Aerangis modesta
Aerangis mooreana
Aerangis mystacidii
Aerangis somalensis
Aerangis stylosa
Aeranthes Grandiose
Aerides maculosa
Agasepalum Blue Butterfly
Angraecum cultriforme
Angraecum didieri
Angraecum distichum
Angraecum equitans
Angraecum leonis
Angraecum mauritianum
Angraecum pseudofilicornu
Ascocentrum ampullaceum var. *aurantiacum*
Ascocentrum ampullaceum 'Crownfox'
Ascocentrum ampullaceum 'Thai Snow'
Ascocentrum garayi
Ascofinetia Cherry Blossom
Baptistonia echinata
Barkeria barkeriola
Barkeria chinensis
Barkeria cyclotella
Barkeria dorotheae

Barkeria elegans
Barkeria halbingeri
Barkeria melanocaulon
Barkeria palmeri
Barkeria shoemakeri
Barkeria skinneri
Barkeria spectabilis
Barkeria strophinx
Brassavola nodosa
Brassocattleya Binosa 'Kirk' AM/AOS
Brassolaeliocattleya Arthur Bossin 'Rapture'
Brassolaeliocattleya Orange Treat
Brassolaeliocattleya Yellow Imp
Broughtonia sanguinea
Bulbophyllum annandalei
Bulbophyllum falcatum 'Standing Tall'
    AM/AOS
Bulbophyllum flammula
Bulbophyllum medusae
Cattleya aclandiae
Cattleya Brabantiae
Cattleya Fascelis
Cattleya forbesii
Cattleya luteola
Cattleya Peckhaviensis
Cattleya Pradit Spot 'Black Prince' AM/
    AOS
Cattleya schilleriana
Cattleya walkeriana 'Pinkie'
Cattleya walkeriana var. *semi-alba*
Cattleytonia Maui Maid
Cattleytonia Why Not
Cirrhopetalum
Cirrhopetalum Daisy Chain
Cischweinfia popowiana
Cischweinfia sheenae
Cochlioda rosea
Cochlioda vulcanica
Crepidium mieczyskawi
Darwinara
Darwinara Charm 'Blue Star'
Dendrobium aberrans
Dendrobium aggregatum
Dendrobium bellatulum
Dendrobium Bonnie Riley

Dendrobium Chinsai
Dendrobium cruentum
Dendrobium dichaeoides
Dendrobium Iki
Dendrobium jenkinsii
Dendrobium kingianum
Dendrobium kingianum var. *alba*
Dendrobium kingianum 'Baby Blue'
Dendrobium moniliforme
Dendrobium Nalene Bui
Dendrobium scabrilingue
Dendrobium unicum
Dendrobium williamsonii
Dendrochilum cootesii
Dendrochilum formosanum
Doritaenopsis Musick Surprise
Doritaenopsis Pixie Star 'Norman'
Doritaenopsis Purple Gem
Doritis pulcherrima var. *alba*
Doritis pulcherrima var. *champornensis*
Dracula chestertonii
Dracula sodiroi subsp. *erythrocodon*
Dracuvallia Blue Boy 'Cow Hollow'
    AM/AOS
Encyclia citrina
Epidendrum Yoko 'Yokohama'
Hawkinsara Kat Golden Eye
Hawkinsara Sogo Doll 'Little Angel'
    HCC/AOS
Holcoglossum kimballianum
Howeara Lava Burst 'Puanani' AM/AOS
Ionopsis paniculata
Jumellea confusa
Laelia albida
Laelia dayana
Laelia pumila var. *coerulea*
Laelia pumila 'Snowstorm'
Laelia sincorana
Laeliocatonia Sacramento Splash
    'orchidPhile' AM/AOS
Laeliocattleya Angel Love
Laeliocattleya Carolyn Reid 'Lynchburg'
Laeliocattleya Hsinying Excell
Laeliocattleya Love Knot var. *coerulea*
Laeliocattleya Mini Purple 'Princess Road'

Laeliocattleya Pixie Gold
Laeliocattleya Tsiku Hibiscus
Macodes petola
Masdevallia Angel Frost
Masdevallia caloptera
Masdevallia Confetti
Masdevallia Copper Angel 'Orange
    Sherbet' HCC/AOS
Masdevallia Copper Cherub
Masdevallia decumana
Masdevallia Elven Magic
Masdevallia glandulosa
Masdevallia Golden Monarch
Masdevallia ignea 'Naranja'
Masdevallia mendozae
Masdevallia Pat Akehurst
Masdevallia patula
Masdevallia pinocchio 'Lucinda'
Masdevallia Pixie Leopard
Masdevallia polysticta
Masdevallia Sunset Jaguar
Masdevallia tridens
Maxillaria juergensii
Maxillaria rufescens
Maxillaria sanguinea
Maxillaria tenuifolia
Mexicoa ghiesbreghtiana
Miltoniopsis roezlii
Mormolyca gracilipes
Neofinetia falcata
Neostylis Lou Sneary
Neostylis Lou Sneary 'Blue Moon'
Neostylis Lou Sneary 'Pinky' AM/AOS
Octomeria species
Odontoglossum cervantesii
Odontoglossum krameri
Oerstedella endresii
Oncidium cheirophorum
Oncidium cucullatum
Oncidium Kukoo
Oncidium longipes
Oncidium onustum
Oncidium ornithorhynchum 'Lilac Blossom'
Oncidium Twinkle 'Fragrance Fantasy'
Oncidium Twinkle 'Red Fantasy'

Paphiopedilum Angela
Paphiopedilum ang-thong
Paphiopedilum armeniacum
Paphiopedilum Armeni White
Paphiopedilum Batalinii
Paphiopedilum bellatulum
Paphiopedilum callosum
Paphiopedilum charlesworthii
Paphiopedilum concolor
Paphiopedilum Deception II
Paphiopedilum delenatii
Paphiopedilum fairrieanum
Paphiopedilum Fanaticum
Paphiopedilum F. C. Puddle
Paphiopedilum Fumi's Delight
Paphiopedilum godefroyae
Paphiopedilum henryanum
Paphiopedilum Joyce Hasegawa
Paphiopedilum Kowloon
Paphiopedilum Lynleigh Koopowitz
Paphiopedilum Magic Lantern
Paphiopedilum malipoense
Paphiopedilum micranthum
Paphiopedilum Mint Chocolate
Paphiopedilum Mrs. A W Sutton
Paphiopedilum niveum
Paphiopedilum Pinocchio
Paphiopedilum Pisar
Paphiopedilum primulinum
Paphiopedilum purpuratum
Paphiopedilum Ron Williamson
Paphiopedilum S. Gratix
Paphiopedilum spicerianum
Paphiopedilum sukhakulii
Paphiopedilum Vanda M. Pearman
Paphiopedilum venustum
Paphiopedilum venustum var. *pardinum*
Paphiopedilum wilhelminiae
Paphiopedilum Yellow Butterfly
Phalaenopsis Ambo Buddha 'SW'
Phalaenopsis amboinensis
Phalaenopsis bellina
Phalaenopsis Caribbean Sunset 'Sweet
    Fragrance'
Phalaenopsis cornu-cervi 'Rhegan'

Phalaenopsis equestris
Phalaenopsis Fantasy Musick
Phalaenopsis fasciata
Phalaenopsis hieroglyphica
Phalaenopsis Kilby Cassviola 'Sweet
    Fragrance'
Phalaenopsis Kuntrarti Rarashati 'Joy'
Phalaenopsis Little Mary 'Cherry Blossom'
Phalaenopsis lueddemanniana
Phalaenopsis mannii
Phalaenopsis mariae 'Chappy'
Phalaenopsis modesta
Phalaenopsis Nobby's Amy
Phalaenopsis Sogo Twinkle
Phalaenopsis Valentinii
Phalaenopsis violacea 'Blue Chip'
Phalaenopsis Yungho Gelb Canary 'GT'
Platystele oxyglossa
Pleurothallis cardiothallis
Pleurothallis pterophora
Pleurothallis truncata
Polystachya bella
Polystachya Darling Star
Polystachya pubescens
Ponerorchis graminifolia var. *suzukiana*
Porroglossum muscosum
Porroglossum sergioi
Potinara Heavenly Jewel 'Puanani' AM/
    AOS
Propetalum Ayla
Restrepia contorta
Restrepia muscifera
Rhyncholaelia glauca
Rodriguezia bahiensis
Sarcochilus Burgundy on Ice
Sarcochilus Cherie
Sarcochilus Fitzhart
Sarcochilus hartmannii
Sarcochilus Sweetheart
Sedirea japonica
Sigmatostalix auriculata
Sophrocattleya Beaufort 'Elizabeth'
    AM/AOS
Sophrocattleya Crystelle Smith 'Aileen'
    AM/AOS

Sophrocattleya Royal Beau 'Prince'
Sophrolaelia Psyche 'Prolific' AM/AOS
Sophrolaeliocattleya Love Fresh
Sophrolaeliocattleya Memoria Miyo Takeda
Sophrolaeliocattleya Sutter Creek
Sophronitis coccinea subsp. *orgaoensis*
Stelis hallii
Stenocoryne aureo-fulva
Symphoglossum sanguineum
Tolumnia Margie Crawford
Trichocentrum tigrinum
Trichoglottis pusilla
Trichopilia suavis
Vanda laotica

Compact
Ada aurantiaca 'Cata'
Ada elegantula
Aerangis appendiculata
Aeranthes ramosa
Aerides crassifolia
Aerides fieldingii
Aerides flabellata
Angraecum aporoides
Angraecum compactum
Angraecum germinyanum
Angraecum magdalenae
Angraecum White Emblem 'Shooting Stars'
    AM/AOS
Angranthes Grandalena
Anoectochilus regalis
Anoectochilus roxburghii
Anoectochilus sikkimensis
Ascocenda Dong Tarn 'Robert' AM/AOS
Ascocenda Motes Mandarin 'Mary Motes'
    HCC/AOS
Ascocenda Peggy Foo '#1'
Barkeria lindleyana
Barkeria naevosa
Beardara Henry Wallbrunn
Bifrenaria harrisoniae
Bothriochilus bellus
Brassavola cordata
Brassavola Little Stars
Brassavola tuberculata

Brassia gireoudiana
Brassia ochroleuca
Brassocattleya Cynthia 'Pink Lady'
Brassolaeliocattleya Haw Yuan Beauty
    'Orchis'
Brassolaeliocattleya Keowee
Bulbophyllum ambrosia
Bulbophyllum Jersey
Bulbophyllum lobbii
Bulbophyllum rothschildianum
Catcylaelia John Davison of Bryn Ingli
Cattleya aurantiaca
Cattleya Baby Kay
Cattleya Fort Motte
Cattleya intermedia
Cattleya Landate
Cattleya loddigesii
Cirrhopetalum robustum
Coelogyne cristata
Coelogyne fimbriata
Coelogyne lawrenceana
Coelogyne ochracea
Coelogyne pandurata
Cycnoches Rocky Clough
Dendrobium Andrée Millar
Dendrobium Charming
Dendrobium Golden Aya
Dendrobium loddigesii
Dendrobium rhodostictum
Dendrochilum filiforme
Dendrochilum glumaceum
Dendrochilum wenzelii
Doritaenopsis Musick Lipstick
Encyclia vitellina var. *majus*
Eria species
Hawkinsara Koolau Sunset 'Hawaii'
    AM/AOS
Iwanagaara Appleblossom 'Fangtastic'
Kefersteinia laminata
Laelia perrinii
Laeliocattleya Angel's Treasure
Laeliocattleya Fire Dance 'Patricia'
Laeliocattleya Green Veil 'Dressy'
Laeliocattleya Irene's Song
Laeliocattleya Mari's Song

Laeliocattleya Rojo
Laeliocattleya Trick or Treat
Lycaste aromatica
Lycaste campbellii
Masdevallia Charisma 'Ingrid'
Masdevallia coccinea
Meiracyllium trinasutum
Mexipedium xerophyticum
Milpasia Leslie Garay
Miltonia Goodale Moir 'Golden Wonder'
    HCC/AOS
Miltonia moreliana
Miltonia spectabilis
Miltoniopsis Golden Butterfly
Miltoniopsis Hajime Ono
Miltoniopsis Maui Pearl
Miltoniopsis phalaenopsis
Miltoniopsis santanaei
Miltoniopsis Venus
Miltoniopsis vexillaria
Miltoniopsis warscewiczii
Odontoglossum crocidipterum
    'Mountainside'
Odontoglossum wyattianum
Odontonia Vesta 'Charm'
Oncidium concolor
Oncidium crispum
Oncidium Tsiku Marguerite
Paphiopedilum Buena Bay 'Golden'
Paphiopedilum Delrosi
Paphiopedilum Gloria Naugle
Paphiopedilum Hsinying Fairbre
Paphiopedilum Langley Pride 'Burlingame'
    HCC/AOS
Paphiopedilum liemianum
Paphiopedilum Maudiae
Paphiopedilum moquettianum
Paphiopedilum Norito Hasegawa
Phalaenopsis bastiani 'Munchkin'
Phalaenopsis borneensis
Phalaenopsis Buena Jewel
Phalaenopsis Ho's Little Caroline

Phalaenopsis Kung's Gelb Lishian
Phalaenopsis Orchid World
Phalaenopsis Penang Girl
Phalaenopsis Perfection Is 'Chen' AM/AOS
Phalaenopsis Samba
Phalaenopsis 'Sweetheart'
Phalaenopsis violacea
Phragmipedium Cape Bonanza
Phragmipedium Carol Kanzer
Phragmipedium Hanne Popow
Phragmipedium hirtzii
Phragmipedium Mountain Maid
Phragmipedium Olaf Gruss
Phragmipedium pearcei
Phragmipedium schlimii
Potinara Burana Beauty 'Burana' HCC/AOS
Potinara Free Spirit
Potinara Hoku Gem 'Freckles' HCC/AOS
Potinara Twentyfour Carat 'Lea' AM/AOS
Renanthera monachica
Rhyncholaelia digbyana
Rhynchostele rossii
Rhynchostylis coelestis
Sophrolaeliocattleya Anzac
Sophrolaeliocattleya Jewel Box 'Dark Waters'
    AM/AOS
Sophrolaeliocattleya Jewel Box
    'Scheherazade' AM/AOS
Sophrolaeliocattleya Orglade's Early Harvest
Sophrolaeliocattleya Paprika 'Black Magic'
    HCC/AOS
Stenoglottis fimbriata
Trichoglottis philippinensis
Trichopilia fragrans
Vanda coerulea
Vanda denisoniana
Vascostylis Tham Yuen Hae 'Blue Queen'
    HCC/RSPC, JC/AOS, HCC/AOS
Woodwardara Beverley Lou
Yonezawaara
Zygoneria Cosmo-Murray

☙ Orchids by Ease of Culture

Easy

Ada aurantiaca 'Cata'
Ada elegantula
Aerangis biloba
Aerangis citrata
Aerangis fastuosa
Aeranthes Grandiose
Angraecum compactum
Angraecum distichum
Angraecum germinyanum
Angraecum leonis
Angraecum White Emblem 'Shooting Stars'
    AM/AOS
Angranthes Grandalena
Anoectochilus regalis
Anoectochilus roxburghii
Anoectochilus sikkimensis
Ascocenda Dong Tarn 'Robert' AM/AOS
Ascocenda Motes Mandarin 'Mary Motes'
    HCC/AOS
Ascocenda Peggy Foo '#1'
Ascocentrum ampullaceum
Ascocentrum ampullaceum var. *aurantiacum*
Ascocentrum ampullaceum 'Crownfox'
Ascocentrum ampullaceum 'Thai Snow'
Ascocentrum garayi
Ascocentrum pumilum
Ascofinetia Cherry Blossom
Barkeria naevosa
Barkeria palmeri
Barkeria shoemakeri
Barkeria skinneri
Barkeria spectabilis
Barkeria strophinx
Beardara Henry Wallbrunn

Bifrenaria harrisoniae
Bothriochilus bellus
Brassavola cordata
Brassavola Little Stars
Brassavola nodosa
Brassavola tuberculata
Brassia gireoudiana
Brassocattleya Binosa 'Kirk' AM/AOS
Brassocattleya Cynthia 'Pink Lady'
Brassolaeliocattleya Keowee
Brassolaeliocattleya Orange Treat
Brassolaeliocattleya Yellow Imp
Broughtonia sanguinea
Bulbophyllum falcatum 'Standing Tall'
    AM/AOS
Bulbophyllum lobbii
Bulbophyllum rothschildianum
Bulbophyllum tingabarinum
Catcylaelia John Davison of Bryn Ingli
Cattleya aurantiaca
Cattleya luteola
Cattleya walkeriana 'Pinkie'
Cattleya walkeriana var. *semi-alba*
Cattleytonia Maui Maid
Cattleytonia Why Not
Cirrhopetalum Daisy Chain
Cischweinfia popowiana
Cischweinfia sheenae
Coelogyne ochracea
Darwinara
Darwinara Charm 'Blue Star'
Dendrobium Andrée Millar
Dendrobium cruentum
Dendrobium Golden Aya
Dendrobium Iki

Dendrobium kingianum
Dendrobium Nalene Bui
Dendrobium unicum
Doritaenopsis Musick Lipstick
Doritaenopsis Musick Surprise
Doritaenopsis Pixie Star 'Norman'
Doritaenopsis Purple Gem
Doritis pulcherrima var. *alba*
Doritis pulcherrima var. *champornensis*
Dyakia hendersoniana
Encyclia polybulbon
Encyclia vitellina var. *majus*
Epidendrum Yoko 'Yokohama'
Hawkinsara Kat Golden Eye
Hawkinsara Koolau Sunset 'Hawaii'
   AM/AOS
Hawkinsara Sogo Doll 'Little Angel'
   HCC/AOS
Holcoglossum kimballianum
Howeara Lava Burst 'Puanani' AM/AOS
Laelia perrinii
Laeliocatonia Sacramento Splash
   'orchidPhile' AM/AOS
Laeliocattleya Angel's Treasure
Laeliocattleya Fire Dance 'Patricia'
Laeliocattleya Green Veil 'Dressy'
Laeliocattleya Hsinying Excell
Laeliocattleya Irene's Song
Laeliocattleya Love Knot var. *coerulea*
Laeliocattleya Mari's Song
Laeliocattleya Mini Purple 'Princess Road'
Laeliocattleya Pixie Gold
Laeliocattleya Rojo
Laeliocattleya Trick or Treat
Laeliocattleya Tsiku Hibiscus
Lycaste aromatica
Masdevallia Pixie Leopard
Maxillaria tenuifolia
Miltoniopsis roezlii
Miltoniopsis santanaei
Neostylis Lou Sneary
Neostylis Lou Sneary 'Blue Moon'
Neostylis Lou Sneary 'Pinky' AM/AOS
Oerstedella endresii
Oncidium cheirophorum

Oncidium longipes
Oncidium ornithorhynchum 'Lilac Blossom'
Oncidium Tsiku Marguerite
Oncidium Twinkle 'Fragrance Fantasy'
Oncidium Twinkle 'Red Fantasy'
Paphiopedilum Angela
Paphiopedilum Armeni White
Paphiopedilum Batalinii
Paphiopedilum Buena Bay 'Golden'
Paphiopedilum callosum
Paphiopedilum charlesworthii
Paphiopedilum Deception II
Paphiopedilum delenatii
Paphiopedilum fairrieanum
Paphiopedilum Fanaticum
Paphiopedilum F. C. Puddle
Paphiopedilum Fumi's Delight
Paphiopedilum Gloria Naugle
Paphiopedilum Hsinying Fairbre
Paphiopedilum Kowloon
Paphiopedilum Langley Pride 'Burlingame'
   HCC/AOS
Paphiopedilum liemianum
Paphiopedilum Magic Lantern
Paphiopedilum Maudiae
Paphiopedilum Mint Chocolate
Paphiopedilum moquettianum
Paphiopedilum Mrs. A W Sutton
Paphiopedilum Norito Hasegawa
Paphiopedilum Pinocchio
Paphiopedilum Pisar
Paphiopedilum primulinum
Paphiopedilum purpuratum
Paphiopedilum Ron Williamson
Paphiopedilum S. Gratix
Paphiopedilum spicerianum
Paphiopedilum sukhakulii
Paphiopedilum Vanda M. Pearman
Paphiopedilum venustum
Paphiopedilum venustum var. *pardinum*
Paphiopedilum Yellow Butterfly
Phalaenopsis Ambo Buddha 'SW'
Phalaenopsis Buena Jewel
Phalaenopsis Caribbean Sunset 'Sweet
   Fragrance'

Phalaenopsis cornu-cervi 'Rhegan'
Phalaenopsis equestris
Phalaenopsis Fantasy Musick
Phalaenopsis Ho's Little Caroline
Phalaenopsis Kung's Gelb Lishian
Phalaenopsis Kuntrarti Rarashati 'Joy'
Phalaenopsis Little Mary 'Cherry Blossom'
Phalaenopsis Mini Mark 'Holm'
Phalaenopsis Nobby's Amy
Phalaenopsis Orchid World
Phalaenopsis Penang Girl
Phalaenopsis Perfection Is 'Chen' AM/AOS
Phalaenopsis Samba
Phalaenopsis Sogo Twinkle
Phalaenopsis 'Sweetheart'
Phalaenopsis Valentinii
Phalaenopsis Yungho Gelb Canary 'GT'
Pleurothallis pterophora
Polystachya bella
Polystachya pubescens
Potinara Free Spirit
Rodriguezia bahiensis
Rodrumnia Orchidom Dancer
Rodrumnia unregistered hybrid
Sigmatostalix radicans 'HMO's Petite
    Prince'
Sophrocattleya Crystelle Smith 'Aileen'
    AM/AOS
Sophrolaelia Psyche 'Prolific' AM/AOS
Sophrolaeliocattleya Jewel Box
    'Scheherazade' AM/AOS
Sophrolaeliocattleya Love Fresh
Sophrolaeliocattleya Memoria Miyo Takeda
Trichopilia suavis
Tuberolabium kotoense
Yonezawaara

Intermediate
Aerangis appendiculata
Aerangis articulata
Aerangis brachycarpa
Aerangis calantha
Aerangis clavigera
Aerangis confusa
Aerangis curnowiana

Aerangis kirkii
Aerangis kotschyana
Aerangis luteo-alba var. *rhodosticta*
Aerangis modesta
Aerangis mooreana
Aerangis mystacidii
Aerangis somalensis
Aerangis Somasticta
Aerangis stylosa
Aeranthes ramosa
Aerides crassifolia
Aerides fieldingii
Aerides flabellata
Aerides maculosa
Agasepalum Blue Butterfly
Amesiella philippinensis
Angraecum aporoides
Angraecum chamaeanthus
Angraecum cultriforme
Angraecum didieri
Angraecum equitans
Angraecum germinyanum
Angraecum humile
Angraecum magdalenae
Angraecum mauritianum
Angraecum pseudofilicornu
Angraecum pusillum
Angraecum rutenbergianum
Angraecum sacciferum
Baptistonia echinata
Barbosella cucullata
Barkeria barkeriola
Barkeria chinensis
Barkeria cyclotella
Barkeria dorotheae
Barkeria elegans
Barkeria halbingeri
Barkeria lindleyana
Barkeria melanocaulon
Bolusiella imbricata
Bolusiella iridifolia
Bolusiella maudiae
Brassia ochroleuca
Brassolaeliocattleya Arthur Bossin
        'Rapture'

Brassolaeliocattleya Haw Yuan Beauty 'Orchis'
Bulbophyllum ambrosia
Bulbophyllum annandalei
Bulbophyllum flammula
Bulbophyllum Jersey
Bulbophyllum medusae
Cadetia chionantha
Cattleya Baby Kay
Cattleya Brabantiae
Cattleya Fascelis
Cattleya forbesii
Cattleya Fort Motte
Cattleya intermedia
Cattleya Landate
Cattleya loddigesii
Cattleya Peckhaviensis
Cattleya Pradit Spot 'Black Prince' AM/AOS
Cattleya schilleriana
Centroglossa macroceras
Cirrhopetalum
Cirrhopetalum robustum
Cirrhopetalum yasnae 'Aussie'
Cochlioda rosea
Cochlioda vulcanica
Coelogyne cristata
Coelogyne fimbriata
Coelogyne lawrenceana
Coelogyne pandurata
Comparettia speciosa
Crepidium mieczyskawi
Cycnoches Rocky Clough
Dendrobium aberrans
Dendrobium aggregatum
Dendrobium bellatulum
Dendrobium Bonnie Riley
Dendrobium Charming
Dendrobium Chinsai
Dendrobium cuthbertsonii pink and white form
Dendrobium cuthbertsonii pink form
Dendrobium cuthbertsonii yellow form
Dendrobium dichaeoides
Dendrobium jenkinsii
Dendrobium kingianum var. *alba*

Dendrobium kingianum 'Baby Blue'
Dendrobium laevifolium
Dendrobium loddigesii
Dendrobium moniliforme
Dendrobium petiolatum
Dendrobium rhodostictum
Dendrobium scabrilingue
Dendrobium violaceum
Dendrobium williamsonii
Dendrochilum cootesii
Dendrochilum filiforme
Dendrochilum formosanum
Dendrochilum glumaceum
Dendrochilum wenzelii
Dipteranthus duchii
Dracula chestertonii
Dracula sodiroi subsp. *erythrocodon*
Dracula venefica
Dracuvallia Blue Boy 'Cow Hollow' AM/AOS
Epidendrum porpax
Eria species
Haraella odorata
Ionopsis paniculata
Isabelia virginalis
Iwanagaara Appleblossom 'Fangtastic'
Jumellea confusa
Kefersteinia laminata
Laelia albida
Laelia dayana
Laelia esalqueana
Laelia lundii
Laelia pumila var. *coerulea*
Laelia pumila 'Snowstorm'
Laelia sincorana
Laeliocattleya Angel Love
Laeliocattleya Carolyn Reid 'Lynchburg'
Lepanthes lucifer
Leptotes bicolor
Leptotes unicolor
Lycaste campbellii
Macodes petola
Masdevallia agaster
Masdevallia Angel Frost
Masdevallia caloptera

Masdevallia calosiphon
Masdevallia Charisma 'Ingrid'
Masdevallia coccinea
Masdevallia Confetti
Masdevallia Copper Angel 'Orange
    Sherbet' HCC/AOS
Masdevallia Copper Cherub
Masdevallia decumana
Masdevallia Elven Magic
Masdevallia erinacea
Masdevallia glandulosa
Masdevallia Golden Monarch
Masdevallia hirtzii
Masdevallia livingstoneana
Masdevallia mendozae
Masdevallia Pat Akehurst
Masdevallia patula
Masdevallia peristeria
Masdevallia pinocchio 'Lucinda'
Masdevallia polysticta
Masdevallia Sunset Jaguar
Masdevallia triangularis
Masdevallia tridens
Masdevallia venezuelana
Maxillaria juergensii
Maxillaria rufescens
Maxillaria sanguinea
Mediocalcar decoratum
Meiracyllium trinasutum
Mexicoa ghiesbreghtiana
Mexipedium xerophyticum
Milpasia Leslie Garay
Miltonia Goodale Moir 'Golden Wonder'
    HCC/AOS
Miltonia moreliana
Miltonia spectabilis
Miltoniopsis Golden Butterfly
Miltoniopsis Hajime Ono
Miltoniopsis Maui Pearl
Miltoniopsis phalaenopsis
Miltoniopsis Venus
Miltoniopsis vexillaria
Miltoniopsis warscewiczii
Mormolyca gracilipes
Nageliella angustifolia

Neofinetia falcata
Octomeria species
Odontoglossum cervantesii
Odontoglossum crocidipterum
    'Mountainside'
Odontoglossum krameri
Odontoglossum wyattianum
Odontonia Vesta 'Charm'
Oncidium concolor
Oncidium crispum
Oncidium cucullatum
Oncidium Kukoo
Oncidium onustum
Ornithocephalus gladiatus
Ornithocephalus manabina
Paphiopedilum ang-thong
Paphiopedilum armeniacum
Paphiopedilum bellatulum
Paphiopedilum concolor
Paphiopedilum Delrosi
Paphiopedilum godefroyae
Paphiopedilum henryanum
Paphiopedilum Joyce Hasegawa
Paphiopedilum Lynleigh Koopowitz
Paphiopedilum malipoense
Paphiopedilum micranthum
Paphiopedilum niveum
Paphiopedilum wilhelminiae
Phalaenopsis amboinensis
Phalaenopsis bastiani 'Munchkin'
Phalaenopsis bellina
Phalaenopsis borneensis
Phalaenopsis fasciata
Phalaenopsis hieroglyphica
Phalaenopsis Kilby Cassviola 'Sweet
    Fragrance'
Phalaenopsis lobbii
Phalaenopsis lueddemanniana
Phalaenopsis mannii
Phalaenopsis mariae 'Chappy'
Phalaenopsis modesta
Phalaenopsis taenialis
Phalaenopsis tetraspis
Phalaenopsis violacea
Phalaenopsis violacea 'Blue Chip'

Phragmipedium Cape Bonanza
Phragmipedium Carol Kanzer
Phragmipedium Hanne Popow
Phragmipedium hirtzii
Phragmipedium Mountain Maid
Phragmipedium Olaf Gruss
Phragmipedium pearcei
Phragmipedium schlimii
Platystele oxyglossa
Pleurothallis cardiothallis
Pleurothallis mystax
Pleurothallis sonderana
Pleurothallis tribuloides
Pleurothallis truncata
Polystachya Darling Star
Ponerorchis graminifolia var. *suzukiana*
Porroglossum eduardii 'Posada'
Porroglossum muscosum
Porroglossum sergioi
Potinara Burana Beauty 'Burana' HCC/AOS
Potinara Heavenly Jewel 'Puanani' AM/AOS
Potinara Hoku Gem 'Freckles' HCC/AOS
Potinara Twentyfour Carat 'Lea' AM/AOS
Propetalum Ayla
Psygmorchis pusilla
Renanthera monachica
Restrepia contorta
Restrepia muscifera
Rhyncholaelia glauca
Rhynchostele rossii
Rhynchostylis coelestis
Sarcochilus Burgundy on Ice
Sarcochilus Cherie
Sarcochilus Fitzhart
Sarcochilus hartmannii
Sarcochilus Sweetheart
Sedirea japonica
Sigmatostalix auriculata
Sigmatostalix graminea
Sophrocattleya Beaufort 'Elizabeth' AM/AOS

Sophrocattleya Royal Beau 'Prince'
Sophrolaeliocattleya Anzac
Sophrolaeliocattleya Jewel Box 'Dark Waters' AM/AOS
Sophrolaeliocattleya Orglade's Early Harvest
Sophrolaeliocattleya Paprika 'Black Magic' HCC/AOS
Sophrolaeliocattleya Sutter Creek
Stelis hallii
Stenocoryne aureo-fulva
Stenoglottis fimbriata
Symphoglossum sanguineum
Tolumnia
Tolumnia Margie Crawford
Tolumnia Potpourri
Tolumnia Savanna La Mar 'Golden Galaxy'
Trichocentrum tigrinum
Trichoglottis philippinensis
Trichoglottis pusilla
Trichopilia fragrans
Trisetella hoeijeri
Vanda coerulea
Vanda denisoniana
Vanda laotica
Vascostylis Tham Yuen Hae 'Blue Queen' HCC/RSPC, JC/AOS, HCC/AOS
Woodwardara Beverley Lou
Zygoneria Cosmo-Murray

Challenging
Cattleya aclandiae
Dendrobium cuthbertsonii orange form
Dendrobium masarangense
Dryadella lilliputana
Encyclia citrina
Lepanthes maduroi
Lepanthes ribes 'Wow'
Masdevallia ignea 'Naranja'
Restrepia iris
Rhyncholaelia digbyana
Sophronitis cernua
Sophronitis coccinea
Sophronitis coccinea subsp. *orgaoensis*

❦ Orchids by Light Requirements

Low

Anoectochilus regalis
Anoectochilus roxburghii
Anoectochilus sikkimensis
Crepidium mieczyskawi
Macodes petola
Paphiopedilum Armeni White
Paphiopedilum delenatii
Paphiopedilum Lynleigh Koopowitz
Phalaenopsis amboinensis
Phalaenopsis Caribbean Sunset 'Sweet Fragrance'
Phalaenopsis Kilby Cassviola 'Sweet Fragrance'
Phalaenopsis lueddemanniana
Phalaenopsis mannii
Phalaenopsis modesta
Phalaenopsis Perfection Is 'Chen' AM/AOS

Low to medium

Angraecum compactum
Ascocentrum pumilum
Barbosella cucullata
Bothriochilus bellus
Bulbophyllum medusae
Doritaenopsis Musick Lipstick
Doritaenopsis Musick Surprise
Doritaenopsis Pixie Star 'Norman'
Doritaenopsis Purple Gem
Doritis pulcherrima var. *champornensis*
Dracula chestertonii
Laeliocattleya Trick or Treat
Masdevallia agaster
Masdevallia Angel Frost
Masdevallia caloptera

Masdevallia calosiphon
Masdevallia Charisma 'Ingrid'
Masdevallia coccinea
Masdevallia Confetti
Masdevallia Copper Angel 'Orange Sherbet' HCC/AOS
Masdevallia Copper Cherub
Masdevallia decumana
Masdevallia Elven Magic
Masdevallia erinacea
Masdevallia glandulosa
Masdevallia Golden Monarch
Masdevallia hirtzii
Masdevallia ignea 'Naranja'
Masdevallia livingstoneana
Masdevallia mendozae
Masdevallia Pat Akehurst
Masdevallia patula
Masdevallia peristeria
Masdevallia pinocchio 'Lucinda'
Masdevallia Pixie Leopard
Masdevallia polysticta
Masdevallia Sunset Jaguar
Masdevallia triangularis
Masdevallia tridens
Masdevallia venezuelana
Mediocalcar decoratum
Miltoniopsis santanaei
Ornithocephalus gladiatus
Ornithocephalus manabina
Paphiopedilum Angela
Paphiopedilum ang-thong
Paphiopedilum armeniacum
Paphiopedilum Batalinii
Paphiopedilum bellatulum

Paphiopedilum Buena Bay 'Golden'
Paphiopedilum callosum
Paphiopedilum charlesworthii
Paphiopedilum concolor
Paphiopedilum Deception II
Paphiopedilum fairrieanum
Paphiopedilum Fanaticum
Paphiopedilum F. C. Puddle
Paphiopedilum Fumi's Delight
Paphiopedilum Gloria Naugle
Paphiopedilum godefroyae
Paphiopedilum henryanum
Paphiopedilum Hsinying Fairbre
Paphiopedilum Joyce Hasegawa
Paphiopedilum Kowloon
Paphiopedilum Langley Pride 'Burlingame'
    HCC/AOS
Paphiopedilum liemianum
Paphiopedilum Magic Lantern
Paphiopedilum malipoense
Paphiopedilum Maudiae
Paphiopedilum micranthum
Paphiopedilum Mint Chocolate
Paphiopedilum moquettianum
Paphiopedilum Mrs. A W Sutton
Paphiopedilum niveum
Paphiopedilum Pinocchio
Paphiopedilum Pisar
Paphiopedilum primulinum
Paphiopedilum purpuratum
Paphiopedilum Ron Williamson
Paphiopedilum S. Gratix
Paphiopedilum spicerianum
Paphiopedilum sukhakulii
Paphiopedilum Vanda M. Pearman
Paphiopedilum venustum
Paphiopedilum venustum var. *pardinum*
Paphiopedilum wilhelminiae
Paphiopedilum Yellow Butterfly
Phalaenopsis Ambo Buddha 'SW'
Phalaenopsis bastiani 'Munchkin'
Phalaenopsis bellina
Phalaenopsis cornu-cervi 'Rhegan'
Phalaenopsis equestris
Phalaenopsis Fantasy Musick

Phalaenopsis fasciata
Phalaenopsis hieroglyphica
Phalaenopsis Ho's Little Caroline
Phalaenopsis Kuntrarti Rarashati 'Joy'
Phalaenopsis Little Mary 'Cherry Blossom'
Phalaenopsis lobbii
Phalaenopsis mariae 'Chappy'
Phalaenopsis Mini Mark 'Holm'
Phalaenopsis Nobby's Amy
Phalaenopsis Orchid World
Phalaenopsis Penang Girl
Phalaenopsis Samba
Phalaenopsis 'Sweetheart'
Phalaenopsis tetraspis
Phalaenopsis Valentinii
Phalaenopsis violacea
Phalaenopsis violacea 'Blue Chip'
Phalaenopsis Yungho Gelb Canary 'GT'
Phragmipedium schlimii
Pleurothallis tribuloides

Medium

Ada aurantiaca 'Cata'
Ada elegantula
Aerangis appendiculata
Aerangis articulata
Aerangis biloba
Aerangis brachycarpa
Aerangis calantha
Aerangis citrata
Aerangis clavigera
Aerangis confusa
Aerangis curnowiana
Aerangis fastuosa
Aerangis kirkii
Aerangis kotschyana
Aerangis luteo-alba var. *rhodosticta*
Aerangis modesta
Aerangis mooreana
Aerangis mystacidii
Aerangis somalensis
Aerangis Somasticta
Aerangis stylosa
Aeranthes Grandiose
Aerides fieldingii

Agasepalum Blue Butterfly
Amesiella philippinensis
Angraecum chamaeanthus
Angraecum cultriforme
Angraecum didieri
Angraecum distichum
Angraecum equitans
Angraecum germinyanum
Angraecum humile
Angraecum leonis
Angraecum magdalenae
Angraecum mauritianum
Angraecum pseudofilicornu
Angraecum pusillum
Angraecum rutenbergianum
Angraecum sacciferum
Angranthes Grandalena
Ascocentrum ampullaceum var. *aurantiacum*
Ascocentrum ampullaceum 'Crownfox'
Ascocentrum ampullaceum 'Thai Snow'
Ascocentrum garayi
Ascofinetia Cherry Blossom
Baptistonia echinata
Barkeria barkeriola
Barkeria chinensis
Barkeria cyclotella
Barkeria dorotheae
Barkeria elegans
Barkeria halbingeri
Barkeria melanocaulon
Barkeria naevosa
Barkeria palmeri
Barkeria shoemakeri
Barkeria skinneri
Barkeria spectabilis
Barkeria strophinx
Beardara Henry Wallbrunn
Bifrenaria harrisoniae
Bolusiella imbricata
Bolusiella iridifolia
Bolusiella maudiae
Brassavola cordata
Brassolaeliocattleya Arthur Bossin 'Rapture'
Brassolaeliocattleya Keowee

Brassolaeliocattleya Orange Treat
Brassolaeliocattleya Yellow Imp
Bulbophyllum ambrosia
Bulbophyllum annandalei
Bulbophyllum falcatum 'Standing Tall' AM/AOS
Bulbophyllum flammula
Bulbophyllum Jersey
Bulbophyllum lobbii
Bulbophyllum rothschildianum
Cadetia chionantha
Catcylaelia John Davison of Bryn Ingli
Cattleya aurantiaca
Cattleya Baby Kay
Cattleya loddigesii
Cattleya Peckhaviensis
Cattleya Pradit Spot 'Black Prince' AM/AOS
Cattleya walkeriana 'Pinkie'
Centroglossa macroceras
Cirrhopetalum
Cirrhopetalum Daisy Chain
Cirrhopetalum robustum
Cirrhopetalum yasnae 'Aussie'
Cischweinfia popowiana
Cischweinfia sheenae
Cochlioda rosea
Cochlioda vulcanica
Coelogyne fimbriata
Coelogyne lawrenceana
Coelogyne ochracea
Comparettia speciosa
Cycnoches Rocky Clough
Darwinara
Darwinara Charm 'Blue Star'
Dendrobium aberrans
Dendrobium aggregatum
Dendrobium Andrée Millar
Dendrobium Charming
Dendrobium Chinsai
Dendrobium cruentum
Dendrobium cuthbertsonii orange form
Dendrobium cuthbertsonii pink and white form
Dendrobium cuthbertsonii pink form
Dendrobium cuthbertsonii yellow form

Dendrobium dichaeoides
Dendrobium Golden Aya
Dendrobium Iki
Dendrobium kingianum var. *alba*
Dendrobium kingianum 'Baby Blue'
Dendrobium laevifolium
Dendrobium masarangense
Dendrobium Nalene Bui
Dendrobium rhodostictum
Dendrobium scabrilingue
Dendrobium unicum
Dendrobium violaceum
Dendrochilum cootesii
Dendrochilum filiforme
Dendrochilum formosanum
Dendrochilum glumaceum
Dendrochilum wenzelii
Dipteranthus duchii
Doritis pulcherrima var. *alba*
Dracula sodiroi subsp. *erythrocodon*
Dracula venefica
Dracuvallia Blue Boy 'Cow Hollow'
    AM/AOS
Dryadella lilliputana
Dyakia hendersoniana
Encyclia citrina
Epidendrum porpax
Eria species
Haraella odorata
Hawkinsara Kat Golden Eye
Hawkinsara Koolau Sunset 'Hawaii'
    AM/AOS
Hawkinsara Sogo Doll 'Little Angel'
    HCC/AOS
Howeara Lava Burst 'Puanani' AM/AOS
Ionopsis paniculata
Isabelia virginalis
Jumellea confusa
Kefersteinia laminata
Laelia dayana
Laeliocatonia Sacramento Splash
    'orchidPhile' AM/AOS
Laeliocattleya Angel Love
Laeliocattleya Angel's Treasure
Laeliocattleya Carolyn Reid 'Lynchburg'

Laeliocattleya Fire Dance 'Patricia'
Laeliocattleya Green Veil 'Dressy'
Laeliocattleya Irene's Song
Laeliocattleya Love Knot var. coerulea
Laeliocattleya Mini Purple 'Princess Road'
Laeliocattleya Pixie Gold
Laeliocattleya Rojo
Laeliocattleya Tsiku Hibiscus
Lepanthes lucifer
Lepanthes maduroi
Lepanthes ribes 'Wow'
Leptotes bicolor
Leptotes unicolor
Lycaste aromatica
Lycaste campbellii
Maxillaria juergensii
Maxillaria rufescens
Maxillaria sanguinea
Maxillaria tenuifolia
Meiracyllium trinasutum
Mexicoa ghiesbreghtiana
Mexipedium xerophyticum
Milpasia Leslie Garay
Miltonia Goodale Moir 'Golden Wonder'
    HCC/AOS
Miltonia moreliana
Miltonia spectabilis
Miltoniopsis Golden Butterfly
Miltoniopsis Hajime Ono
Miltoniopsis Maui Pearl
Miltoniopsis phalaenopsis
Miltoniopsis roezlii
Miltoniopsis Venus
Miltoniopsis vexillaria
Miltoniopsis warscewiczii
Mormolyca gracilipes
Nageliella angustifolia
Neofinetia falcata
Neostylis Lou Sneary
Neostylis Lou Sneary 'Blue Moon'
Neostylis Lou Sneary 'Pinky' AM/AOS
Octomeria species
Odontoglossum cervantesii
Odontonia Vesta 'Charm'
Oerstedella endresii

Oncidium cheirophorum
Oncidium concolor
Oncidium cucullatum
Oncidium Kukoo
Oncidium longipes
Oncidium ornithorhynchum 'Lilac Blossom'
Oncidium Tsiku Marguerite
Oncidium Twinkle 'Fragrance Fantasy'
Oncidium Twinkle 'Red Fantasy'
Paphiopedilum Delrosi
Paphiopedilum Norito Hasegawa
Phalaenopsis borneensis
Phalaenopsis Buena Jewel
Phalaenopsis Kung's Gelb Lishian
Phalaenopsis Sogo Twinkle
Phalaenopsis taenialis
Phragmipedium Cape Bonanza
Phragmipedium Carol Kanzer
Phragmipedium Hanne Popow
Phragmipedium hirtzii
Phragmipedium Mountain Maid
Phragmipedium Olaf Gruss
Phragmipedium pearcei
Platystele oxyglossa
Pleurothallis cardiothallis
Pleurothallis mystax
Pleurothallis pterophora
Pleurothallis sonderana
Pleurothallis truncata
Polystachya bella
Polystachya Darling Star
Polystachya pubescens
Ponerorchis graminifolia var. *suzukiana*
Porroglossum eduardii 'Posada'
Porroglossum muscosum
Porroglossum sergioi
Potinara Burana Beauty 'Burana' HCC/AOS
Potinara Free Spirit
Potinara Heavenly Jewel 'Puanani'
    AM/AOS
Potinara Hoku Gem 'Freckles' HCC/AOS
Potinara Twentyfour Carat 'Lea' AM/AOS
Propetalum Ayla
Psygmorchis pusilla
Restrepia contorta

Restrepia iris
Restrepia muscifera
Rhyncholaelia glauca
Rhynchostele rossii
Rhynchostylis coelestis
Rodrumnia unregistered hybrid
Sarcochilus Burgundy on Ice
Sarcochilus Cherie
Sarcochilus Fitzhart
Sarcochilus hartmannii
Sarcochilus Sweetheart
Sedirea japonica
Sigmatostalix auriculata
Sigmatostalix graminea
Sigmatostalix radicans 'HMO's Petite
    Prince'
Sophrocattleya Beaufort 'Elizabeth'
    AM/AOS
Sophrocattleya Crystelle Smith 'Aileen'
    AM/AOS
Sophrocattleya Royal Beau 'Prince'
Sophrolaelia Psyche 'Prolific' AM/AOS
Sophrolaeliocattleya Anzac
Sophrolaeliocattleya Jewel Box 'Dark Waters'
    AM/AOS
Sophrolaeliocattleya Jewel Box
    'Scheherazade' AM/AOS
Sophrolaeliocattleya Love Fresh
Sophrolaeliocattleya Memoria Miyo Takeda
Sophrolaeliocattleya Orglade's Early Harvest
Sophrolaeliocattleya Paprika 'Black Magic'
    HCC/AOS
Sophrolaeliocattleya Sutter Creek
Sophronitis coccinea
Sophronitis coccinea subsp. *orgaoensis*
Stelis hallii
Stenocoryne aureo-fulva
Stenoglottis fimbriata
Symphoglossum sanguineum
Tolumnia
Tolumnia Potpourri
Tolumnia Savanna La Mar 'Golden Galaxy'
Trichoglottis philippinensis
Trichoglottis pusilla
Trichopilia fragrans

Trichopilia suavis
Trisetella hoeijeri
Tuberolabium kotoense
Vascostylis Tham Yuen Hae 'Blue Queen'
    HCC/RSPC, JC/AOS, HCC/AOS

Medium to high
Aeranthes ramosa
Aerides crassifolia
Aerides flabellata
Aerides maculosa
Angraecum aporoides
Angraecum White Emblem 'Shooting Stars'
    AM/AOS
Ascocenda Dong Tarn 'Robert' AM/AOS
Ascocenda Motes Mandarin 'Mary Motes'
    HCC/AOS
Ascocenda Peggy Foo '#1'
Barkeria lindleyana
Brassavola Little Stars
Brassavola nodosa
Brassavola tuberculata
Brassia gireoudiana
Brassia ochroleuca
Brassocattleya Binosa 'Kirk' AM/AOS
Brassocattleya Cynthia 'Pink Lady'
Brassolaeliocattleya Haw Yuan Beauty
    'Orchis'
Broughtonia sanguinea
Bulbophyllum tingabarinum
Cattleya Brabantiae
Cattleya Fascelis
Cattleya forbesii
Cattleya Fort Motte
Cattleya intermedia
Cattleya Landate
Cattleya luteola
Cattleya schilleriana
Cattleya walkeriana var. *semi-alba*
Cattleytonia Maui Maid
Cattleytonia Why Not
Coelogyne cristata
Coelogyne pandurata
Dendrobium bellatulum

Dendrobium Bonnie Riley
Dendrobium jenkinsii
Dendrobium kingianum
Dendrobium loddigesii
Dendrobium moniliforme
Dendrobium petiolatum
Dendrobium williamsonii
Encyclia polybulbon
Encyclia vitellina var. *majus*
Epidendrum Yoko 'Yokohama'
Holcoglossum kimballianum
Iwanagaara Appleblossom 'Fangtastic'
Laelia albida
Laelia esalqueana
Laelia lundii
Laelia perrinii
Laelia pumila var. *coerulea*
Laelia pumila 'Snowstorm'
Laelia sincorana
Laeliocattleya Hsinying Excell
Laeliocattleya Mari's Song
Odontoglossum crocidipterum
    'Mountainside'
Odontoglossum krameri
Odontoglossum wyattianum
Oncidium crispum
Oncidium onustum
Rhyncholaelia digbyana
Rodriguezia bahiensis
Rodrumnia Orchidom Dancer
Sophronitis cernua
Tolumnia Margie Crawford
Trichocentrum tigrinum
Woodwardara Beverley Lou
Yonezawaara
Zygoneria Cosmo-Murray

High
Cattleya aclandiae
Renanthera monachica
Vanda coerulea
Vanda denisoniana
Vanda laotica

❦ Orchids by Temperature Preferences

Cool
Coelogyne ochracea
Masdevallia calosiphon
Masdevallia coccinea
Masdevallia ignea 'Naranja'
Masdevallia peristeria
Trisetella hoeijeri

Cool to intermediate
Ada aurantiaca 'Cata'
Ada elegantula
Aerangis luteo-alba var. *rhodosticta*
Aerangis Somasticta
Agasepalum Blue Butterfly
Angraecum chamaeanthus
Angraecum pusillum
Angraecum rutenbergianum
Barbosella cucullata
Bifrenaria harrisoniae
Cadetia chionantha
Cochlioda rosea
Dendrobium aberrans
Dendrobium bellatulum
Dendrobium Bonnie Riley
Dendrobium cuthbertsonii orange form
Dendrobium cuthbertsonii pink and white form
Dendrobium cuthbertsonii pink form
Dendrobium cuthbertsonii yellow form
Dendrobium dichaeoides
Dendrobium laevifolium
Dendrobium petiolatum
Dendrobium violaceum
Dracula sodiroi subsp. *erythrocodon*
Dracula venefica

Dracuvallia Blue Boy 'Cow Hollow' AM/AOS
Dryadella lilliputana
Encyclia polybulbon
Holcoglossum kimballianum
Laelia esalqueana
Lepanthes lucifer
Lepanthes maduroi
Lepanthes ribes 'Wow'
Masdevallia Angel Frost
Masdevallia caloptera
Masdevallia Charisma 'Ingrid'
Masdevallia Confetti
Masdevallia Copper Angel 'Orange Sherbet' HCC/AOS
Masdevallia Copper Cherub
Masdevallia decumana
Masdevallia Elven Magic
Masdevallia Golden Monarch
Masdevallia hirtzii
Masdevallia mendozae
Masdevallia Pat Akehurst
Masdevallia patula
Masdevallia pinocchio 'Lucinda'
Masdevallia Pixie Leopard
Masdevallia polysticta
Masdevallia Sunset Jaguar
Masdevallia triangularis
Masdevallia tridens
Miltoniopsis phalaenopsis
Miltoniopsis Venus
Odontoglossum cervantesii
Odontoglossum crocidipterum 'Mountainside'
Odontoglossum krameri

Odontoglossum wyattianum
Oerstedella endresii
Paphiopedilum fairrieanum
Pleurothallis mystax
Pleurothallis truncata
Polystachya bella
Porroglossum muscosum
Propetalum Ayla
Rhynchostele rossii
Sarcochilus Burgundy on Ice
Sarcochilus Cherie
Sarcochilus Fitzhart
Sarcochilus hartmannii
Sarcochilus Sweetheart
Sigmatostalix auriculata
Sophronitis coccinea subsp. *orgaoensis*
Symphoglossum sanguineum
Woodwardara Beverley Lou

Intermediate
Aerangis calantha
Aerangis clavigera
Aerangis confusa
Aerangis fastuosa
Aerangis kirkii
Aerangis kotschyana
Aerangis mystacidii
Aerangis somalensis
Aerangis stylosa
Aeranthes ramosa
Aerides flabellata
Aerides maculosa
Angraecum germinyanum
Angraecum humile
Angraecum mauritianum
Angraecum pseudofilicornu
Angraecum sacciferum
Angranthes Grandalena
Anoectochilus regalis
Ascocentrum pumilum
Baptistonia echinata
Barkeria barkeriola
Barkeria chinensis
Barkeria cyclotella
Barkeria dorotheae

Barkeria elegans
Barkeria halbingeri
Barkeria lindleyana
Barkeria naevosa
Barkeria palmeri
Barkeria shoemakeri
Barkeria skinneri
Barkeria spectabilis
Barkeria strophinx
Bolusiella imbricata
Bolusiella iridifolia
Bolusiella maudiae
Brassia ochroleuca
Brassocattleya Cynthia 'Pink Lady'
Brassolaeliocattleya Arthur Bossin 'Rapture'
Brassolaeliocattleya Haw Yuan Beauty
   'Orchis'
Brassolaeliocattleya Keowee
Brassolaeliocattleya Orange Treat
Brassolaeliocattleya Yellow Imp
Broughtonia sanguinea
Bulbophyllum ambrosia
Bulbophyllum annandalei
Bulbophyllum falcatum 'Standing Tall'
   AM/AOS
Bulbophyllum flammula
Bulbophyllum Jersey
Bulbophyllum medusae
Catcylaelia John Davison of Bryn Ingli
Cattleya aclandiae
Cattleya aurantiaca
Cattleya Baby Kay
Cattleya Brabantiae
Cattleya Fascelis
Cattleya Fort Motte
Cattleya intermedia
Cattleya Landate
Cattleya loddigesii
Cattleya Peckhaviensis
Cattleya Pradit Spot 'Black Prince' AM/AOS
Cattleya schilleriana
Cattleya walkeriana 'Pinkie'
Cattleya walkeriana var. *semi-alba*
Cattleytonia Maui Maid
Cattleytonia Why Not

Centroglossa macroceras
Cirrhopetalum
Cirrhopetalum Daisy Chain
Cirrhopetalum robustum
Cischweinfia popowiana
Cischweinfia sheenae
Cochlioda vulcanica
Coelogyne fimbriata
Coelogyne pandurata
Comparettia speciosa
Cycnoches Rocky Clough
Darwinara
Darwinara Charm 'Blue Star'
Dendrobium aggregatum
Dendrobium Andrée Millar
Dendrobium Charming
Dendrobium Chinsai
Dendrobium Golden Aya
Dendrobium Iki
Dendrobium jenkinsii
Dendrobium kingianum
Dendrobium kingianum var. *alba*
Dendrobium kingianum 'Baby Blue'
Dendrobium masarangense
Dendrobium moniliforme
Dendrobium Nalene Bui
Dendrobium rhodostictum
Dendrobium scabrilingue
Dendrobium unicum
Dendrobium williamsonii
Dendrochilum cootesii
Dendrochilum filiforme
Dendrochilum formosanum
Dendrochilum glumaceum
Dendrochilum wenzelii
Dracula chestertonii
Encyclia citrina
Encyclia vitellina var. *majus*
Epidendrum porpax
Epidendrum Yoko 'Yokohama'
Eria species
Haraella odorata
Hawkinsara Kat Golden Eye
Hawkinsara Koolau Sunset 'Hawaii'
    AM/AOS

Hawkinsara Sogo Doll 'Little Angel'
    HCC/AOS
Howeara Lava Burst 'Puanani' AM/AOS
Isabelia virginalis
Iwanagaara Appleblossom 'Fangtastic'
Jumellea confusa
Kefersteinia laminata
Laelia albida
Laelia dayana
Laelia lundii
Laelia perrinii
Laelia pumila var. *coerulea*
Laelia pumila 'Snowstorm'
Laelia sincorana
Laeliocatonia Sacramento Splash
    'orchidPhile' AM/AOS
Laeliocattleya Angel Love
Laeliocattleya Angel's Treasure
Laeliocattleya Carolyn Reid 'Lynchburg'
Laeliocattleya Fire Dance 'Patricia'
Laeliocattleya Green Veil 'Dressy'
Laeliocattleya Hsinying Excell
Laeliocattleya Irene's Song
Laeliocattleya Love Knot var. *coerulea*
Laeliocattleya Mari's Song
Laeliocattleya Mini Purple 'Princess Road'
Laeliocattleya Pixie Gold
Laeliocattleya Rojo
Laeliocattleya Trick or Treat
Laeliocattleya Tsiku Hibiscus
Leptotes bicolor
Lycaste aromatica
Masdevallia agaster
Masdevallia glandulosa
Masdevallia venezuelana
Maxillaria juergensii
Maxillaria tenuifolia
Mediocalcar decoratum
Meiracyllium trinasutum
Mexicoa ghiesbreghtiana
Mexipedium xerophyticum
Milpasia Leslie Garay
Miltonia Goodale Moir 'Golden Wonder'
    HCC/AOS
Miltonia moreliana

Miltonia spectabilis
Miltoniopsis Golden Butterfly
Miltoniopsis Hajime Ono
Miltoniopsis Maui Pearl
Miltoniopsis roezlii
Miltoniopsis santanaei
Miltoniopsis vexillaria
Miltoniopsis warscewiczii
Mormolyca gracilipes
Nageliella angustifolia
Octomeria species
Odontonia Vesta 'Charm'
Oncidium cheirophorum
Oncidium concolor
Oncidium cucullatum
Oncidium Kukoo
Oncidium longipes
Oncidium onustum
Oncidium ornithorhynchum 'Lilac Blossom'
Paphiopedilum Angela
Paphiopedilum ang-thong
Paphiopedilum armeniacum
Paphiopedilum Armeni White
Paphiopedilum Batalinii
Paphiopedilum bellatulum
Paphiopedilum Buena Bay 'Golden'
Paphiopedilum callosum
Paphiopedilum charlesworthii
Paphiopedilum concolor
Paphiopedilum Deception II
Paphiopedilum delenatii
Paphiopedilum Delrosi
Paphiopedilum Fanaticum
Paphiopedilum F. C. Puddle
Paphiopedilum Fumi's Delight
Paphiopedilum Gloria Naugle
Paphiopedilum godefroyae
Paphiopedilum henryanum
Paphiopedilum Hsinying Fairbre
Paphiopedilum Joyce Hasegawa
Paphiopedilum Langley Pride 'Burlingame'
    HCC/AOS
Paphiopedilum Lynleigh Koopowitz
Paphiopedilum Magic Lantern
Paphiopedilum malipoense

Paphiopedilum Maudiae
Paphiopedilum micranthum
Paphiopedilum Mint Chocolate
Paphiopedilum moquettianum
Paphiopedilum Mrs. A W Sutton
Paphiopedilum niveum
Paphiopedilum Pinocchio
Paphiopedilum Pisar
Paphiopedilum primulinum
Paphiopedilum purpuratum
Paphiopedilum S. Gratix
Paphiopedilum spicerianum
Paphiopedilum sukhakulii
Paphiopedilum Vanda M. Pearman
Paphiopedilum venustum
Paphiopedilum venustum var. *pardinum*
Paphiopedilum wilhelminiae
Paphiopedilum Yellow Butterfly
Phalaenopsis taenialis
Phragmipedium Cape Bonanza
Phragmipedium Carol Kanzer
Phragmipedium Hanne Popow
Phragmipedium hirtzii
Phragmipedium Mountain Maid
Phragmipedium Olaf Gruss
Phragmipedium pearcei
Phragmipedium schlimii
Platystele oxyglossa
Pleurothallis cardiothallis
Pleurothallis pterophora
Pleurothallis sonderana
Pleurothallis tribuloides
Polystachya Darling Star
Polystachya pubescens
Ponerorchis graminifolia var. *suzukiana*
Porroglossum eduardii 'Posada'
Porroglossum sergioi
Potinara Burana Beauty 'Burana' HCC/AOS
Potinara Free Spirit
Potinara Heavenly Jewel 'Puanani'
    AM/AOS
Potinara Hoku Gem 'Freckles' HCC/AOS
Potinara Twentyfour Carat 'Lea' AM/AOS
Psygmorchis pusilla
Restrepia contorta

Restrepia iris
Restrepia muscifera
Rhyncholaelia digbyana
Rodriguezia bahiensis
Rodrumnia Orchidom Dancer
Rodrumnia unregistered hybrid
Sigmatostalix graminea
Sigmatostalix radicans 'HMO's Petite
    Prince'
Sophrocattleya Beaufort 'Elizabeth'
    AM/AOS
Sophrocattleya Crystelle Smith 'Aileen'
    AM/AOS
Sophrocattleya Royal Beau 'Prince'
Sophrolaelia Psyche 'Prolific' AM/AOS
Sophrolaeliocattleya Anzac
Sophrolaeliocattleya Jewel Box 'Dark
    Waters' AM/AOS
Sophrolaeliocattleya Jewel Box
    'Scheherazade' AM/AOS
Sophrolaeliocattleya Love Fresh
Sophrolaeliocattleya Memoria Miyo Takeda
Sophrolaeliocattleya Orglade's Early Harvest
Sophrolaeliocattleya Paprika 'Black Magic'
    HCC/AOS
Sophrolaeliocattleya Sutter Creek
Sophronitis coccinea
Stelis hallii
Stenoglottis fimbriata
Tolumnia
Tolumnia Potpourri
Tolumnia Savanna La Mar 'Golden Galaxy'
Trichocentrum tigrinum
Trichoglottis philippinensis
Trichoglottis pusilla
Trichopilia fragrans
Trichopilia suavis
Zygoneria Cosmo-Murray

Intermediate to warm
Aerangis appendiculata
Aerangis articulata
Aerangis biloba
Aerangis brachycarpa
Aerangis citrata

Aerangis modesta
Aerangis mooreana
Aerangis mystacidii
Aeranthes Grandiose
Aerides crassifolia
Aerides fieldingii
Amesiella philippinensis
Angraecum cultriforme
Angraecum equitans
Angraecum leonis
Ascocenda Dong Tarn 'Robert' AM/AOS
Ascocenda Motes Mandarin 'Mary Motes'
    HCC/AOS
Ascocenda Peggy Foo '#1'
Ascocentrum ampullaceum var. aurantiacum
Ascocentrum ampullaceum 'Crownfox'
Ascocentrum ampullaceum 'Thai Snow'
Ascocentrum garayi
Ascofinetia Cherry Blossom
Barkeria melanocaulon
Beardara Henry Wallbrunn
Bothriochilus bellus
Brassavola cordata
Brassavola Little Stars
Brassavola nodosa
Brassavola tuberculata
Brassocattleya Binosa 'Kirk' AM/AOS
Bulbophyllum rothschildianum
Cattleya forbesii
Cattleya luteola
Cirrhopetalum yasnae 'Aussie'
Coelogyne cristata
Crepidium mieczyskawi
Dendrobium cruentum
Dendrobium loddigesii
Dipteranthus duchii
Doritaenopsis Pixie Star 'Norman'
Doritis pulcherrima var. alba
Doritis pulcherrima var. champornensis
Dyakia hendersoniana
Ionopsis paniculata
Leptotes unicolor
Lycaste campbellii
Masdevallia erinacea
Masdevallia livingstoneana

Maxillaria rufescens
Maxillaria sanguinea
Neofinetia falcata
Neostylis Lou Sneary
Neostylis Lou Sneary 'Blue Moon'
Neostylis Lou Sneary 'Pinky' AM/AOS
Oncidium crispum
Oncidium Tsiku Marguerite
Oncidium Twinkle 'Fragrance Fantasy'
Oncidium Twinkle 'Red Fantasy'
Ornithocephalus gladiatus
Ornithocephalus manabina
Paphiopedilum Kowloon
Paphiopedilum liemianum
Paphiopedilum Norito Hasegawa
Paphiopedilum Ron Williamson
Renanthera monachica
Sophronitis cernua
Stenocoryne aureo-fulva
Tolumnia Margie Crawford
Tuberolabium kotoense
Vascostylis Tham Yuen Hae 'Blue Queen'
   HCC/AOS, JC/AOS, HCC/AOS
Yonezawara

Warm
Aeranthes arnowiana
Angraecum aporoides
Angraecum compactum
Angraecum didieri
Angraecum distichum
Angraecum germinyanum
Angraecum magdalenae
Angraecum White Emblem 'Shooting Stars'
   AM/AOS
Anoectochilus roxburghii
Anoectochilus sikkimensis
Brassia gireoudiana
Bulbophyllum lobbii
Bulbophyllum tingabarinum
Coelogyne lawrenceana
Doritaenopsis Musick Lipstick
Doritaenopsis Musick Surprise
Doritaenopsis Purple Gem

Macodes petola
Phalaenopsis Ambo Buddha 'SW'
Phalaenopsis amboinensis
Phalaenopsis bastiani 'Munchkin'
Phalaenopsis bellina
Phalaenopsis borneensis
Phalaenopsis Buena Jewel
Phalaenopsis Caribbean Sunset 'Sweet Fragrance'
Phalaenopsis cornu-cervi 'Rhegan'
Phalaenopsis equestris
Phalaenopsis Fantasy Musick
Phalaenopsis fasciata
Phalaenopsis hieroglyphica
Phalaenopsis Ho's Little Caroline
Phalaenopsis Kilby Cassviola 'Sweet Fragrance'
Phalaenopsis Kung's Gelb Lishian
Phalaenopsis Kuntrarti Rarashati 'Joy'
Phalaenopsis Little Mary 'Cherry Blossom'
Phalaenopsis lobbii
Phalaenopsis lueddemanniana
Phalaenopsis mannii
Phalaenopsis mariae 'Chappy'
Phalaenopsis Mini Mark 'Holm'
Phalaenopsis modesta
Phalaenopsis Nobby's Amy
Phalaenopsis Orchid World
Phalaenopsis Penang Girl
Phalaenopsis Perfection Is 'Chen' AM/AOS
Phalaenopsis Samba
Phalaenopsis Sogo Twinkle
Phalaenopsis 'Sweetheart'
Phalaenopsis tetraspis
Phalaenopsis Valentinii
Phalaenopsis violacea
Phalaenopsis violacea 'Blue Chip'
Phalaenopsis Yungho Gelb Canary 'GT'
Rhyncholaelia glauca
Rhynchostylis coelestis
Sedirea japonica
Vanda coerulea
Vanda denisoniana
Vanda laotica

❦ Orchids by Season of Bloom

Spring

Aerangis calantha
Aerangis citrata
Aerangis curnowiana
Aerangis fastuosa
Aerangis modesta
Angraecum chamaeanthus
Angraecum germinyanum
Angraecum White Emblem 'Shooting Stars'
    AM/AOS
Anoectochilus regalis
Anoectochilus roxburghii
Barkeria halbingeri
Bifrenaria harrisoniae
Brassia gireoudiana
Brassia ochroleuca
Cattleya loddigesii
Cattleya luteola
Cattleya Pradit Spot 'Black Prince' AM/AOS
Coelogyne ochracea
Dendrobium Bonnie Riley
Dendrobium kingianum
Dendrobium loddigesii
Dendrobium moniliforme
Dendrochilum filiforme
Dendrochilum glumaceum
Dracula chestertonii
Holcoglossum kimballianum
Iwanagaara Appleblossom 'Fangtastic'
Laelia lundii
Masdevallia agaster
Masdevallia Confetti
Meiracyllium trinasutum
Odontoglossum crocidipterum 'Mountainside'
Oncidium concolor

Paphiopedilum Hsinying Fairbre
Paphiopedilum moquettianum
Paphiopedilum venustum var. *pardinum*
Phalaenopsis amboinensis
Phalaenopsis lueddemanniana
Phalaenopsis modesta
Phragmipedium schlimii
Polystachya Darling Star
Rhyncholaelia glauca
Rhynchostele rossii
Trichopilia suavis
Woodwardara Beverley Lou

Spring to summer

Aerangis appendiculata
Aerangis brachycarpa
Aerangis confusa
Aerangis kirkii
Aerangis kotschyana
Aerangis mooreana
Aerangis somalensis
Aerangis stylosa
Angraecum compactum
Angraecum cultriforme
Angraecum didieri
Angraecum equitans
Angraecum germinyanum
Angraecum humile
Angraecum magdalenae
Brassolaeliocattleya Keowee
Bulbophyllum annandalei
Bulbophyllum falcatum 'Standing Tall'
    AM/AOS
Bulbophyllum flammula
Cattleya forbesii

Cattleya Fort Motte
Cattleya Peckhaviensis
Cattleya schilleriana
Cattleytonia Maui Maid
Cattleytonia Why Not
Cirrhopetalum
Cirrhopetalum Daisy Chain
Cirrhopetalum yasnae 'Aussie'
Cischweinfia popowiana
Cischweinfia sheenae
Crepidium mieczyskawi
Darwinara
Darwinara Charm 'Blue Star'
Dendrobium Golden Aya
Dendrobium petiolatum
Dendrobium scabrilingue
Dendrobium williamsonii
Dendrochilum cootesii
Dendrochilum wenzelii
Doritaenopsis Musick Surprise
Doritaenopsis Pixie Star 'Norman'
Doritaenopsis Purple Gem
Doritis pulcherrima var. *alba*
Doritis pulcherrima var. *champornensis*
Dracuvallia Blue Boy 'Cow Hollow' AM/AOS
Dyakia hendersoniana
Encyclia polybulbon
Encyclia vitellina var. *majus*
Epidendrum porpax
Epidendrum Yoko 'Yokohama'
Eria species
Howeara Lava Burst 'Puanani' AM/AOS
Ionopsis paniculata
Isabelia virginalis
Laelia dayana
Laelia esalqueana
Lepanthes maduroi
Macodes petola
Masdevallia caloptera
Masdevallia coccinea
Masdevallia decumana
Masdevallia hirtzii
Masdevallia ignea 'Naranja'
Masdevallia mendozae
Masdevallia peristeria

Masdevallia pinocchio 'Lucinda'
Masdevallia polysticta
Mexicoa ghiesbreghtiana
Miltonia moreliana
Miltoniopsis vexillaria
Miltoniopsis warscewiczii
Mormolyca gracilipes
Nageliella angustifolia
Odontoglossum cervantesii
Oncidium crispum
Oncidium Kukoo
Oncidium ornithorhynchum 'Lilac Blossom'
Paphiopedilum Angela
Paphiopedilum ang-thong
Paphiopedilum Armeni White
Paphiopedilum bellatulum
Paphiopedilum concolor
Paphiopedilum Kowloon
Paphiopedilum liemianum
Paphiopedilum Magic Lantern
Paphiopedilum malipoense
Paphiopedilum Pinocchio
Paphiopedilum primulinum
Paphiopedilum purpuratum
Paphiopedilum sukhakulii
Phalaenopsis hieroglyphica
Phalaenopsis lobbii
Phragmipedium hirtzii
Platystele oxyglossa
Pleurothallis pterophora
Pleurothallis truncata
Polystachya bella
Ponerorchis graminifolia var. *suzukiana*
Porroglossum eduardii 'Posada'
Porroglossum muscosum
Porroglossum sergioi
Psygmorchis pusilla
Renanthera monachica
Restrepia contorta
Rhyncholaelia digbyana
Rhynchostylis coelestis
Rodriguezia bahiensis
Rodrumnia Orchidom Dancer
Rodrumnia unregistered hybrid
Sarcochilus Cherie

Sarcochilus Fitzhart
Sarcochilus Sweetheart
Sedirea japonica
Sophrocattleya Beaufort 'Elizabeth' AM/AOS
Sophrolaelia Psyche 'Prolific' AM/AOS
Sophrolaeliocattleya Jewel Box
    'Scheherazade' AM/AOS
Sophrolaeliocattleya Love Fresh
Tolumnia
Tolumnia Potpourri
Tolumnia Savanna La Mar 'Golden Galaxy'
Trichocentrum tigrinum
Vanda coerulea
Vanda denisoniana
Vanda laotica

Summer
Aerangis mystacidii
Angraecum pseudofilicornu
Angraecum rutenbergianum
Bolusiella imbricata
Bolusiella maudiae
Bothriochilus bellus
Brassolaeliocattleya Arthur Bossin 'Rapture'
Bulbophyllum medusae
Dendrobium bellatulum
Masdevallia erinacea
Masdevallia triangularis
Maxillaria rufescens
Maxillaria tenuifolia
Oncidium cucullatum
Phalaenopsis cornu-cervi 'Rhegan'
Stenocoryne aureo-fulva

Summer to fall
Aerangis mystacidii
Aeranthes ramosa
Aerides crassifolia
Aerides fieldingii
Aerides flabellata
Aerides maculosa
Angraecum mauritianum
Barkeria barkeriola
Barkeria spectabilis
Barkeria strophinx

Brassocattleya Cynthia 'Pink Lady'
Bulbophyllum Jersey
Bulbophyllum lobbii
Bulbophyllum rothschildianum
Cattleya aclandiae
Cirrhopetalum robustum
Cochlioda vulcanica
Coelogyne fimbriata
Comparettia speciosa
Haraella odorata
Miltonia spectabilis
Miltoniopsis roezlii
Miltoniopsis Venus
Neofinetia falcata
Pleurothallis cardiothallis
Pleurothallis mystax
Yonezawaara

Fall
Aerangis articulata
Aerangis kirkii
Aerangis luteo-alba var. *rhodosticta*
Aerangis Somasticta
Angraecum pusillum
Angraecum sacciferum
Anoectochilus sikkimensis
Barkeria lindleyana
Laelia perrinii
Oncidium longipes
Paphiopedilum charlesworthii
Paphiopedilum wilhelminiae
Sigmatostalix radicans 'HMO's Petite Prince'

Fall to winter
Agasepalum Blue Butterfly
Amesiella philippinensis
Angraecum aporoides
Barbosella cucullata
Barkeria elegans
Barkeria melanocaulon
Barkeria naevosa
Barkeria palmeri
Barkeria shoemakeri
Barkeria skinneri
Brassavola Little Stars

Brassolaeliocattleya Haw Yuan Beauty
　'Orchis'
Broughtonia sanguinea
Bulbophyllum ambrosia
Bulbophyllum tingabarinum
Dendrobium cuthbertsonii orange form
Dendrobium dichaeoides
Masdevallia glandulosa
Mediocalcar decoratum
Oncidium onustum
Pleurothallis sonderana
Polystachya pubescens
Symphoglossum sanguineum
Trichopilia fragrans
Tuberolabium kotoense

Winter to spring
Ada aurantiaca 'Cata'
Ada elegantula
Aerangis biloba
Aerangis clavigera
Angraecum leonis
Barkeria chinensis
Barkeria cyclotella
Barkeria dorotheae
Beardara Henry Wallbrunn
Brassolaeliocattleya Orange Treat
Brassolaeliocattleya Yellow Imp
Catcylaelia John Davison of Bryn Ingli
Cattleya aurantiaca
Cattleya Baby Kay
Cattleya Landate
Centroglossa macroceras
Cochlioda rosea
Coelogyne cristata
Coelogyne lawrenceana
Cycnoches Rocky Clough
Dendrobium aberrans
Dendrobium aggregatum
Dendrobium Andrée Millar
Dendrobium Charming
Dendrobium Chinsai
Dendrobium cruentum
Dendrobium cuthbertsonii pink and white
　form
Dendrobium cuthbertsonii pink form

Dendrobium cuthbertsonii yellow form
Dendrobium Iki
Dendrobium jenkinsii
Dendrobium kingianum var. *alba*
Dendrobium kingianum 'Baby Blue'
Dendrobium laevifolium
Dendrobium masarangense
Dendrobium Nalene Bui
Dendrobium rhodostictum
Dendrobium unicum
Dendrobium violaceum
Dendrochilum formosanum
Dipteranthus duchii
Doritaenopsis Musick Lipstick
Dryadella lilliputana
Hawkinsara Koolau Sunset 'Hawaii'
　AM/AOS
Hawkinsara Sogo Doll 'Little Angel'
　HCC/AOS
Kefersteinia laminata
Laelia albida
Laelia sincorana
Laeliocatonia Sacramento Splash
　'orchidPhile' AM/AOS
Laeliocattleya Angel's Treasure
Laeliocattleya Carolyn Reid 'Lynchburg'
Laeliocattleya Fire Dance 'Patricia'
Laeliocattleya Green Veil 'Dressy'
Laeliocattleya Hsinying Excell
Laeliocattleya Love Knot var. *coerulea*
Laeliocattleya Pixie Gold
Laeliocattleya Rojo
Laeliocattleya Trick or Treat
Laeliocattleya Tsiku Hibiscus
Lepanthes lucifer
Leptotes bicolor
Leptotes unicolor
Lycaste aromatica
Lycaste campbellii
Masdevallia calosiphon
Masdevallia Charisma 'Ingrid'
Masdevallia Copper Angel 'Orange
　Sherbet' HCC/AOS
Masdevallia Copper Cherub
Masdevallia Elven Magic
Masdevallia Golden Monarch

Masdevallia livingstoneana
Masdevallia Pat Akehurst
Masdevallia patula
Masdevallia Pixie Leopard
Masdevallia Sunset Jaguar
Masdevallia tridens
Masdevallia venezuelana
Maxillaria juergensii
Maxillaria sanguinea
Mexipedium xerophyticum
Milpasia Leslie Garay
Miltonia Goodale Moir 'Golden Wonder'
    HCC/AOS
Miltoniopsis Golden Butterfly
Miltoniopsis Hajime Ono
Miltoniopsis Maui Pearl
Miltoniopsis phalaenopsis
Octomeria species
Odontoglossum krameri
Odontoglossum wyattianum
Odontonia Vesta 'Charm'
Oncidium cheirophorum
Paphiopedilum armeniacum
Paphiopedilum Batalinii
Paphiopedilum Buena Bay 'Golden'
Paphiopedilum callosum
Paphiopedilum Delrosi
Paphiopedilum fairrieanum
Paphiopedilum Fanaticum
Paphiopedilum F. C. Puddle
Paphiopedilum Fumi's Delight
Paphiopedilum Gloria Naugle
Paphiopedilum godefroyae
Paphiopedilum henryanum
Paphiopedilum Langley Pride 'Burlingame'
    HCC/AOS
Paphiopedilum Maudiae
Paphiopedilum micranthum
Paphiopedilum Mint Chocolate
Paphiopedilum Mrs. A W Sutton
Paphiopedilum niveum
Paphiopedilum Norito Hasegawa
Paphiopedilum Pisar
Paphiopedilum S. Gratix
Paphiopedilum spicerianum
Paphiopedilum Vanda M. Pearman

Paphiopedilum venustum
Paphiopedilum Yellow Butterfly
Phalaenopsis Ambo Buddha 'SW'
Phalaenopsis bastiani 'Munchkin'
Phalaenopsis borneensis
Phalaenopsis Buena Jewel
Phalaenopsis equestris
Phalaenopsis Fantasy Musick
Phalaenopsis fasciata
Phalaenopsis Ho's Little Caroline
Phalaenopsis Kung's Gelb Lishian
Phalaenopsis Little Mary 'Cherry Blossom'
Phalaenopsis mannii
Phalaenopsis mariae 'Chappy'
Phalaenopsis Nobby's Amy
Phalaenopsis Orchid World
Phalaenopsis Penang Girl
Phalaenopsis Samba
Phalaenopsis Sogo Twinkle
Phalaenopsis tetraspis
Phalaenopsis Valentinii
Phalaenopsis violacea 'Blue Chip'
Phalaenopsis Yungho Gelb Canary 'GT'
Phragmipedium Cape Bonanza
Phragmipedium Carol Kanzer
Phragmipedium Hanne Popow
Phragmipedium Mountain Maid
Phragmipedium Olaf Gruss
Phragmipedium pearcei
Pleurothallis tribuloides
Potinara Burana Beauty 'Burana' HCC/AOS
Potinara Free Spirit
Potinara Heavenly Jewel 'Puanani' AM/AOS
Potinara Hoku Gem 'Freckles' HCC/AOS
Potinara Twentyfour Carat 'Lea' AM/AOS
Restrepia iris
Restrepia muscifera
Sarcochilus Burgundy on Ice
Sarcochilus hartmannii
Sigmatostalix graminea
Sophrocattleya Crystelle Smith 'Aileen'
    AM/AOS
Sophrocattleya Royal Beau 'Prince'
Sophrolaeliocattleya Anzac
Sophrolaeliocattleya Jewel Box 'Dark Waters'
    AM/AOS

Sophrolaeliocattleya Memoria Miyo Takeda
Sophrolaeliocattleya Orglade's Early Harvest
Sophrolaeliocattleya Paprika 'Black Magic'
    HCC/AOS
Sophrolaeliocattleya Sutter Creek
Sophronitis cernua
Sophronitis coccinea subsp. *orgaoensis*
Stelis hallii
Stenoglottis fimbriata
Trichoglottis philippinensis
Trichoglottis pusilla
Zygoneria Cosmo-Murray

Variable

Aeranthes Grandiose
Angraecum distichum
Angranthes Grandalena
Ascocenda Dong Tarn 'Robert' AM/AOS
Ascocenda Motes Mandarin 'Mary Motes'
    HCC/AOS
Ascocenda Peggy Foo '#1'
Ascocentrum ampullaceum var. *aurantiacum*
Ascocentrum ampullaceum 'Crownfox'
Ascocentrum ampullaceum 'Thai Snow'
Ascocentrum garayi
Ascocentrum pumilum
Ascofinetia Cherry Blossom
Baptistonia echinata
Bolusiella iridifolia
Brassavola cordata
Brassavola nodosa
Brassavola tuberculata
Brassocattleya Binosa 'Kirk' AM/AOS
Cadetia chionantha
Cattleya Brabantiae
Cattleya Fascelis
Cattleya intermedia
Cattleya walkeriana 'Pinkie'
Cattleya walkeriana var. *semi-alba*
Coelogyne pandurata
Dracula sodiroi subsp. *erythrocodon*
Dracula venefica
Encyclia citrina

Hawkinsara Kat Golden Eye
Jumellea confusa
Laelia pumila var. *coerulea*
Laelia pumila 'Snowstorm'
Laeliocattleya Angel Love
Laeliocattleya Irene's Song
Laeliocattleya Mari's Song
Laeliocattleya Mini Purple 'Princess Road'
Lepanthes ribes 'Wow'
Masdevallia Angel Frost
Miltoniopsis santanaei
Neostylis Lou Sneary
Neostylis Lou Sneary 'Blue Moon'
Neostylis Lou Sneary 'Pinky' AM/AOS
Oerstedella endresii
Oncidium Tsiku Marguerite
Oncidium Twinkle 'Fragrance Fantasy'
Oncidium Twinkle 'Red Fantasy'
Ornithocephalus gladiatus
Ornithocephalus manabina
Paphiopedilum Deception II
Paphiopedilum delenatii
Paphiopedilum Joyce Hasegawa
Paphiopedilum Lynleigh Koopowitz
Paphiopedilum Ron Williamson
Phalaenopsis bellina
Phalaenopsis Caribbean Sunset 'Sweet
    Fragrance'
Phalaenopsis Kilby Cassviola 'Sweet
    Fragrance'
Phalaenopsis Kuntrarti Rarashati 'Joy'
Phalaenopsis Mini Mark 'Holm'
Phalaenopsis Perfection Is 'Chen' AM/AOS
Phalaenopsis 'Sweetheart'
Phalaenopsis taenialis
Phalaenopsis violacea
Propetalum Ayla
Sigmatostalix auriculata
Sophronitis coccinea
Tolumnia Margie Crawford
Trisetella hoeijeri
Vascostylis Tham Yuen Hae 'Blue Queen'
    HCC/RSPC, JC/AOS, HCC/AOS

❦ Fragrant Orchids

Aerangis appendiculata—gardenia
Aerangis articulata—jasmine
Aerangis brachycarpa—vanilla, jasmine
Aerangis citrata—lemon
Aerangis confusa—tuberose, gardenia
Aerangis curnowiana—jasmine
Aerangis fastuosa—tuberose, lily
Aerangis kirkii—tuberose, gardenia
Aerangis kotschyana—gardenia
Aerangis modesta—minty spice
Aerangis mooreana—jasmine
Aerangis mystacidii—lily-of-the-valley
Aerangis somalensis—gardenia
Aeranthes Grandiose—jasmine
Aerides crassifolia—lily-of-the-valley
Aerides fieldingii—lily-of-the-valley
Aerides flabellata—lily-of-the-valley
Aerides maculosa—lily-of-the-valley
Amesiella philippinensis—mint
Angraecum aporoides—gardenia
Angraecum compactum—spicy, citrus
Angraecum didieri—sweet, spicy
Angraecum distichum—jasmine
Angraecum equitans—jasmine
Angraecum germinyanum—jasmine
Angraecum leonis—jasmine
Angraecum magdalenae—jasmine
Angraecum rutenbergianum—jasmine
Angraecum White Emblem 'Shooting Stars' AM/AOS—jasmine
Angranthes Grandalena—jasmine
Ascofinetia Cherry Blossom—sweet floral
Bifrenaria harrisoniae—fruity
Bothriochilus bellus—almond/poppy pastry filling

Brassavola cordata—soapy-sweet
Brassavola Little Stars—soapy-sweet
Brassavola nodosa—freesia, lily-of-the-valley
Brassavola tuberculata—nicotiana, gardenia
Brassia gireoudiana—musky
Brassia ochroleuca—spicy, spiced apple pie
Brassocattleya Binosa 'Kirk' AM/AOS—spicy
Brassocattleya Cynthia 'Pink Lady'—citrus
Brassolaeliocattleya Arthur Bossin 'Rapture'—sweet floral
Brassolaeliocattleya Haw Yuan Beauty 'Orchis'—vanilla
Brassolaeliocattleya Keowee—light floral at night
Brassolaeliocattleya Yellow Imp—light floral
Bulbophyllum ambrosia—honey, bitter almonds
Bulbophyllum lobbii—jasmine, orange blossoms
Bulbophyllum rothschildianum—peach, fruity
Cadetia chionantha—sweet floral
Cattleya aclandiae—spicy
Cattleya Brabantiae—spicy
Cattleya Fascelis—spicy
Cattleya forbesii—bubble gum
Cattleya Fort Motte—spicy
Cattleya intermedia—sweet floral
Cattleya Landate—spicy
Cattleya loddigesii—baked milk chocolate
Cattleya luteola—fresh floral
Cattleya Peckhaviensis—honey

R. F. Orchids, Inc.
28100 SW 182nd Avenue,
Homestead, FL 33030-1804
Phone: (305) 245-4570
Fax: (305) 247-6568
One of the world leaders in the breeding and growing of vandas, ascocendas, and their relatives. Some of their plants will not be suitable for small spaces and for parts of the country with low light, but others, such select forms of *Ascocentrum* species and compact ascocendas, are.

Robert Bedard Horticulture
475 Blair Ranch Road,
Scotts Valley, CA 95066
Phone: (831) 439-9484
E-mail: rbedard@robert-bedard.com
Web site: www.robert-bedard.com
Specializes in miniature and multifloral phalaenopsis. Free catalog.

Santa Barbara Orchid Estate
1250 Orchid Drive,
Santa Barbara, CA 93111
Phone: (805) 967-1284
E-mail: sboe@sborchid.com
Web site: www.sborchid.com
This long respected company focuses on orchids that will grow well outdoors in mild climates. Also offers a broad selections of miniature to compact growing species and hybrids.

Seal Rock Orchids
1825 Brindle Lane, Eureka, CA 95501
Phone: (707) 845-6858
E-mail: bill@sealrockorchids.com

Web site: www.sealrockorchids.com
Small orchid nursery specializes in growing and breeding species and miniatures including mini-catts, masdevallias, and pleurothallids. Web catalog. Sells on e-Bay.

SLO Gardens
955 Branch Mill Road,
Arroya Grande, CA 93420
Phone: (805) 489-3319
E-mail: slogardens@thegrid.net
Web site: www.slogardens.com
Carries a broad range of species and hybrids including compact cattleya intergenerics, masdevallias, and draculas. Free catalog.

Whimsey Orchids, Inc.
18755 SW 248th Street,
Homestead, FL 33092-1333
Phone: (305) 242-1333
Fax: (305) 247-9888
E-mail: whimsy@bellsouth.net
Specializes in miniature oncidiums.

Woodstream Orchids
5810 Huntington Road,
Huntington, MD 20639
Phone and fax: (410) 286-2664
E-mail: woodstream@chesapeake.net
Web site: www.woodstreamorchids.com/miniature.html
Probably best known for its fine selection of paphiopedilums and phragmipediums, but also offers a broad range of orchids including an entire section of miniatures. Web catalog. Open by appointment.

☙ Bibliography

Adams, Peter B., and Sheryl D. Lawson. 1995. *Dendrobium kingianum: A Unique Australian Orchid*. Rockhampton, Queensland: Central Queensland University Press.

Atwood, John T. 1994. Maxillarias. American Orchid Society Bulletin 63(4) 372–383.

Averyanov, Leonid, Phillip Cribb, Phan Ke Loc, and Nguyen Tien Hiep. 2003. *Slipper Orchids of Vietnam*. Portland, Oregon: Timber Press.

Baker, Margaret L., and Charles O. Baker. 1991. *Orchid Species Culture, Pescatorea, Phaius, Pholidota, Phragmipedium, Pleione*. Portland, Oregon: Timber Press.

———. 1996. *Orchid Species Culture, Dendrobium*. Portland, Oregon: Timber Press.

Bechtel, Helmut, Phillip Cribb, and Edmund Launert. 1986. *The Manual of Cultivated Orchid Species*. Revised edition. Cambridge, Massachusetts: The MIT Press.

Bennett, Keith S. 1986. *The Tropical Asiatic Slipper Orchids*. North Ryde, Australia: Angus & Robertson Publishers.

Birk, Lance A. 2004. *The Paphiopedilum Grower's Manual*, Second Edition. Santa Barbara, California: Pisang Press.

Bray, Helga and Joseph. 2005. Wildcatt Orchids. Ames, Iowa: Wildcatt Database Co.

Cash, Catherine. 1991. *The Slipper Orchids*. Portland, Oregon: Timber Press.

Christenson, Eric A. 2001. *Phalaenopsis: A Monograph*. Portland, Oregon: Timber Press.

Cootes, Jim. 2001. *The Orchids of the Philippines*. Singapore: Times Editions.

Cribb, Phillip. 1987. *The Genus Paphiopedilum*. Portland, Oregon: Timber Press.

Dressler, Robert L. 1993. *Field Guide to the Orchids of Costa Rica and Panama*. Ithaca, New York: Comstock Publishing Associates.

Dressler, Robert L., and Glenn E. Pollard. 1976. *The Genus Encyclia in Mexico*. Mexico: Asociacion Mexicana de Orquideologia, A. C.

Dunmire, John R., and editors of Sunset Books. *Orchids*. Menlo Park, California: Sunset Books.

Fitch, Charles Marden. 2002. *Growing Orchids Under Lights*. Delray Beach, Florida: American Orchid Society.

———. 2004a. *The Best of Orchids for Indoors*. Brooklyn Botanic Garden All Region Guides. Brooklyn, New York: Brooklyn Botanic Garden.

———. 2004b. *The Gardener's Guide to Growing Orchids*. Brooklyn Botanic Garden All Region Guides. Brooklyn, New York: Brooklyn Botanic Garden.

Fowlie, J. A. 1970. *The Genus Lycaste: Its Speciation, Distribution, Literature, and Cultivation—A Monographic Revision*. Pomona, California: Day Printing Corp.

Frowine, Steven A. 2005a. *Fragrant Orchids*. Portland, Oregon: Timber Press.

———. 2005b. *Orchids for Dummies*. Hoboken, New Jersey: Wiley Publishing.

Gerritsen, Mary E., and Ron Parsons. 2005. *Masdevallias: Gems of the Orchid World*. Portland, Oregon: Timber Press.

Gordon, Bob. 1985. *Culture of the Phalaenopsis Orchid*. Rialto, California: Laid Back Publications.

Grove, David L. 1995. *Vandas and Ascocendas and their Combination with Other Genera*. Portland, Oregon: Timber Press.

Hamilton, Robert M. 1977. *When Does It Flower?* British Colombia, Canada: Robert M. Hamilton.

Hennessy, Esmé F., and Tessa A. Hedge. 1989. *The Slipper Orchids*. Randburg, Republic of South Africa: Acorn Books.

Hetherington, Ernest. 1985. *Cattleya* Hybrids and Hybridizers: Yellow Cattleyas 1. *American Orchid Society Bulletin* 54(2) 149–159.

———. 1986. *Cattleya* Hybrids and Hybridizers: Prospects for the Future. *American Orchid Society Bulletin* 55(5) 452–461.

Hillerman, Fred E. 1992. *A Culture Manual for Angraecoid Orchid Growers*. Grass Valley, California: Fred Hillerman.

Hillerman, Fred E., and Arthur W. Horst. 1986. *An Introduction to Cultivated Angraecoid Orchids of Madagascar*. Portland, Oregon: Timber Press.

Kamemoto, Haruyuki, and Rapee Sagaraik. 1975. *Beautiful Thai Orchid Species*. Bangkok, Thailand: The Orchid Society of Thailand.

Kelleher, Jo. 1984. *Intriguing Masdevallias*. Berkshire, England: H G H Publications.

Koopowitz, Harold, and Norito Hasagawa. 1989. *Novelty Slipper Orchids: Breeding and Cultivation Paphiopedilum Hybrids*. London: Angus & Robertson Publishers.

Kramer, Jack, and Roy L. Crafton. 1982. *Miniature Orchids to Grow and Show*. New York: W. W. Norton & Company.

Kranz, Frederick H. and Jacqueline L. 1971. *Gardening Indoors Under Lights: A Complete Guide*. New York: The Viking Press.

La Croix, Isobyl and Eric. 1997. *African Orchids in the Wild and in Cultivation*. Portland, Oregon: Timber Press.

Lavarack, Bill, Wayne Harris, and Geoff Stocker. 2002. *Dendrobium and Its Relatives*. Reprint. Portland, Oregon: Timber Press.

Logan, Harry B., and Lloyd C. Cosper. 1949. *Orchids Are Easy To Grow*. Englewood Cliffs, New Jersey: Prentice-Hall Inc.

McQueen, Jim and Barbara. 1992. *Miniature Orchids: The World of Orchids*. Portland, Oregon: Timber Press.

———. 1993. *Orchids of Brazil*. East Melbourne, Victoria, Australia: The Text Company Pty Ltd.

Millar, Andrée. 1990. *Orchids of Papua New Guinea*. Portland, Oregon: Timber Press.

Miranda, Francisco E. 1990. Brazilian Laelias—Part I: Section Cattleyodes. *American Orchid Society Bulletin* 59(3) 234–245.

Motes, Martin R. 1997. *Vanda: Their Botany, History and Culture*. Portland, Oregon: Timber Press.

Noble, Mary. 1994. *You Can Grow Phalaenopsis Orchids* Revised edition II. Jacksonville, Florida: Mary Noble McQuerry.

Northen, Rebecca Tyson. 1970. *Home Orchid Growing* Third ed. New York: Van Nostrand Reinhold Co.

————. 1996. *Miniature Orchids and How to Grow Them*. New York: Dover Publications, Inc.

Rentoul, J. N. 1982. *Growing Orchids. Book Three: Vandas, Dendrobiums and Others*. Portland, Oregon: Timber Press.

Ritterhausen, Brian and Wilma. 2002. *The Practical Encyclopedia of Orchids*. London: Lorenz Books.

Rose, James. 1994. *Neofinetia falcata* Hybrids. *American Orchid Society Bulletin* 63(4) 384–391.

Schelpe, Sybella, and Joyce Stewart. 1990. *Dendrobiums: An Introduction to the Species in Cultivation*. Gillingham, Dorset: Orchid Sundries Ltd.

Sessler, Gloria Jean. 1978. *Orchids and How To Grow Them*. Englewood Cliffs, New Jersey: Prentice-Hall, Inc.

Sheehan, Tom and Marion. 1994. *An Illustrated Survey of Orchid Genera*. Portland, Oregon: Timber Press.

Siegerist, Emily S. 2001. *Bulbophyllums and Their Allies: A Grower's Guide*. Portland, Oregon: Timber Press.

Stewart, Joyce. 1996. *Orchids of Kenya*. Portland, Oregon: Timber Press.

Sweet, Herman R. 1980. *The Genus Phalaenopsis*. Pomona, California: The Orchid Digest Inc.

Szyren, Jan. 2003. Without High Phosphorous: A New Fertilizer Proves Itself With Orchids. *Orchids* (June) 454–459.

Teo, Chris K. H. 1985. *Native Orchids of Peninsular Malaysia*. Singapore: Times Book International.

Watson, James B., ed. 2002. *Orchid Pests and Diseases*. Delray Beach, Florida: American Orchid Society.

White, Judy. 1994. The Nose Knows. *American Orchid Society Bulletin* 63(2): 118–124.

————. 1996. *Taylor's Guide to Orchids*. Boston: Houghton Mifflin Co.

Williams, Louis O., and Paul H. Allen. 1980. *Orchids of Panama: Monographs in Systematic Botany*. St. Louis: Missouri Botanical Garden.

Withner, Carl L. 1988. *The Cattleyas and Their Relatives. Volume I: The Cattleyas*. Portland, Oregon: Timber Press.

————. 1990. *The Cattleyas and Their Relatives. Volume III:* Schomburgkia, Sophronitis, *and Other South American Genera*. Portland, Oregon: Timber Press.

————. 1996. *The Cattleyas and Their Relatives. Volume IV: The Bahamian and Caribbean Species*. Portland, Oregon: Timber Press.

————. 1998a. *The Cattleyas and Their Relatives. Volume II: The Laelias*. Portland, Oregon: Timber Press.

————. 1998b. *The Cattleyas and Their Relatives. Volume V:* Brassavola, Encyclia, *and Other Genera of Mexico and Central America*. Portland, Oregon: Timber Press.

————. 2000. *The Cattleyas and Their Relatives. Volume VI: The South American* Encyclia *Species*. Portland, Oregon: Timber Press.

Withner, Carl L., and Patricia A. Harding. 2004. *The Cattleyas and Their Relatives: The Debatable Epidendrums*. Portland, Oregon: Timber Press.

Zelenko, Harry, and Mark W. Chase. 2002. *Orchids: The Pictorial Encyclopedia of Oncidium*. Stamford, Connecticut: ZAI Publications.

ꙮ Index of Plant Names